ENVIRONMENTAL LIFE CYCLE ASSESSMENT OF GOODS AND SERVICES

An Input-Output Approach

CHRIS T. HENDRICKSON
LESTER B. LAVE
H. SCOTT MATTHEWS

With

ARPAD HORVATH
SATISH JOSHI
FRANCIS C. MCMICHAEL
HEATHER L. MACLEAN
GYORGYI CICAS
DEANNA MATTHEWS
JOULE BERGERSON

RESOURCES FOR THE FUTURE
WASHINGTON, DC, USA

Printed in the United States of America

No part of this publication may be reproduced by any means, whether electronic or mechanical, without written permission. Requests to photocopy items for classroom or other educational use should be sent to the Copyright Clearance Center, Inc., Suite 910, 222 Rosewood Drive, Danvers, MA 01923, USA (fax +1 978 646 8600; www.copyright.com). All other permissions requests should be sent directly to the publisher at the address below.

An RFF Press book
Published by Resources for the Future
1616 P Street NW
Washington, DC 20036–1400
USA
www.rffpress.org

Library of Congress Cataloging-in-Publication Data

Environmental life cycle assessment of goods and services: An input-output approach / Chris T. Hendrickson ... [et al.].
   p. cm.
   Includes bibliographical references and index.
   ISBN 1-933115-23-8 (hardcover : alk. paper) — ISBN 1-933115-24-6 (pbk. : alk. paper)
   1. Industrial ecology. 2. Product life cycle—Environmental aspects.
   3. Input-output analysis.   I. Hendrickson, Chris T.
TS161.E625 2006
658.5'752--dc22   2005020489

The paper in this book meets the guidelines for permanence and durability of the Committee on Production Guidelines for Book Longevity of the Council on Library Resources. This book was typeset by Peter Lindeman. It was copyedited by Steven Jent. The cover was designed by Maggie Powell.

ISBN 1-933115-23-8 (cloth)   ISBN 1-933115-24-6 (paper)

About Resources for the Future *and* RFF Press

RESOURCES FOR THE FUTURE (RFF) improves environmental and natural resource policymaking worldwide through independent social science research of the highest caliber. Founded in 1952, RFF pioneered the application of economics as a tool for developing more effective policy about the use and conservation of natural resources. Its scholars continue to employ social science methods to analyze critical issues concerning pollution control, energy policy, land and water use, hazardous waste, climate change, biodiversity, and the environmental challenges of developing countries.

RFF PRESS supports the mission of RFF by publishing book-length works that present a broad range of approaches to the study of natural resources and the environment. Its authors and editors include RFF staff, researchers from the larger academic and policy communities, and journalists. Audiences for publications by RFF Press include all of the participants in the policymaking process—scholars, the media, advocacy groups, NGOs, professionals in business and government, and the public.

Contents

Part III: Further Developments in the EIO-LCA Method

Preface

This book had its inception over a decade ago. A group of researchers from Carnegie Mellon's Green Design Initiative (now the Green Design Institute) became interested in the topic of environmental life cycle assessment as a tool to improve the design of products, processes, and policies. We wished to find cost-effective ways to reduce pollution and move toward a more sustainable economy. We were convinced that a system-wide view was essential for success in green design, including studying the entire life cycle of products from a variety of disciplinary perspectives.

Unfortunately, the existing tools for environmental life cycle assessment had numerous problems. Data were difficult to assemble. Life cycle studies took months of effort. Comprehensive analysis was prohibitive, so analysts simply ignored many facets of life cycle impacts. Numerous references describe existing tools (Curran 1996).

While sitting around a table, a group of us realized that economic input–output models could offer an alternative or complementary approach. We proceeded to elaborate on this idea, culminating in numerous application studies and a widely used website providing a series of economic input–output life cycle assessment (EIO-LCA) models: www.eiolca.net. The www.eiolca.net/book portion of the website is a companion to this text.

We cannot claim to be the originators of the idea of using economic input–output models for environmental analysis. The father of input–output models, Wassily Leontief, also recognized their usefulness for assessing environmental impacts. However, we have been fortunate to be able to exploit modern information technology (to make computations and communications relatively easy) and a variety of new information (such as the Toxics Releases Inventory first released in 1989) for our models.

This book summarizes the EIO-LCA method, provides example applications, and illustrates some model extensions. Green design should be a widely shared activity. We have provided free access to our models and written this book to help you.

The EIO-LCA method has proven to be useful for a number of student projects. The Green Design Institute has been fortunate in having a talented group of student researchers. It is they who have done the detailed work of assembling appropriate data and linking it together. It is they who have worked to extend the models and apply them to new topics. We are indebted to their work. Some of the students worked specifically on this book and appear as co-authors, but many others added to the EIO-LCA models in their research. In particular, we should thank Luis Aguirre, Chantal Brandon, Rebecca Cassler, Silvia Chacon-Comparini, Rosy Chen, Gwen Christini, Elisa Cobas-Flores, Troy Hawkins, Cortney Higgins, Cheryl Horney, Antje Januschkowetz, Octavio Juarez, Markus Klausner, Mark Krofchik, Ajay Labshmanan, Rebecca Lankey, Garrick Louis, Joe Marriott, Bill Morrow, Alex Muller, Luis Ochoa, Ruth Reyna-Caamano, Robert Ries, Jeff Rosenblum, Aurora Sharrard, Chris Weber, and Tse-Sung Wu. We are also grateful to students enrolled in our courses and workshops, including professionals in continuing education, undergraduate students, secondary students, and graduate students. We have learned much from you.

Finally, we thank the various colleagues who have provided suggestions and sponsors for providing research support. Linda Argote, Larry Biegler, Jon Cagan, Noellette Conway-Schempf, Cliff Davidson, Paul Fischbeck, Jim Garrett, Mike Griffin, Granger Morgan, Indira Nair, Ed Rubin, Sangwon Suh, Joel Tarr, and Eric Williams have been valuable colleagues here at Carnegie Mellon. We also thank other external collaborators, including David Allen, Brad Allenby, John Crittenden, Faye Duchin, Harald Florin, Greg Keoleian, and Karen Polenske. Colleagues elsewhere who have been helpful are too numerous to list, including anonymous reviewers of our peer-reviewed publications. We thank the production editors and staff at Resources for the Future. We are grateful to our sponsors at the Bureau of Economic Analysis, Department of Energy, Environmental Protection Agency, and the National Science Foundation. We thank sponsors at the W. Alton Jones, AT&T, Heinz Endowments, Sloan, and Surdna Foundations. We are grateful to companies in the Green Design Initiative Industrial Consortium (Alcoa, American Iron and Steel Institute, AT&T, Bosch, GE Plastics, IBM, Hughes, Lucent Technologies, Monsanto, NCR, Quantum, Texaco, Union Camp, Union Carbide, Vehicle Recycling Partnership—Daimler-Chrysler, Ford, and General Motors—and XEROX). We particularly wish to thank William Recker for his support.

PART I

Introduction to the EIO-LCA Method

Part I introduces economic input–output environmental life cycle assessment (EIO-LCA). Chapter 1 describes the method and explains why it may be useful in informing decisions about activities, products, processes, and policies. Chapter 2 sets the EIO-LCA method in the context of other approaches to life cycle assessment; in many cases EIO-LCA can complement other methods. Chapter 3 discusses how monetary costs may be balanced against improved environmental impacts. Of course, we all wish to find new designs or technologies that are less expensive and more capable, and have lesser environmental impacts. However, sometimes we have to consider the tradeoffs between costs and environmental impact. Chapter 4 discusses uncertainty in the EIO-LCA results and suggests some ways to improve confidence in them. Finally, Chapter 5 provides a nuts-and-bolts overview of the method and some example problems for readers wishing to use the EIO-LCA software (www.eiolca.net) directly. This chapter is self-contained and may be safely skipped by readers who do not yet need to use the software.

1

Exploring Environmental Impacts and Sustainability through Life Cycle Assessment

Paper or plastic? This simple question at the grocery store checkout counter might seem to sort those who care about the quality of the environment and the sustainability of our economy from ignorant or apathetic shoppers. We know that the correct answer is "paper," because it is a "natural" product rather than some chemical. We can feel self-satisfied, even if the bag gets wet and tears, spilling our purchases on the ground.

Consumers are confronted with other questions: Paper or foam cups? Cloth or paper (disposable) diapers? The last question causes a particular stir, as disposable diapers are more convenient and less time-consuming than cloth diapers.

A few scientists have seen that these questions can, and should, be answered by data and analysis, rather than a feeling that the natural product is better. The ensuing analysis has ignited a major controversy over how to decide which product is better for the environment, beginning with an analysis of paper versus polystyrene cups (Hocking 1991). The controversy and scientific analysis have created the field of life cycle assessment, or LCA (Matthews et al. 2002).

This book is about life cycle thinking and getting the information to make sound decisions to improve environmental quality and sustainability. How can we design products, choose materials and processes, and decide what to do at the end of a product's life in ways that produce less environmental discharges and use less material and energy?

Defining Life Cycle Assessment

Life cycle assessment "studies the environmental aspects and potential impacts throughout a product's life (i.e. cradle-to-grave) from raw material acquisition

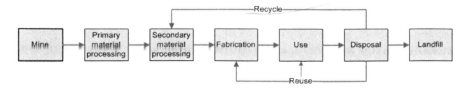

FIGURE 1-1. A Generic Supply Chain Life Cycle Model

through production, use, and disposal" (ISO 1997). Figure 1-1 summarizes the components of a life cycle. The life cycle assessment consists of three complementary components—inventory, impact, and improvement—and an integrative procedure known as "scoping." The LCA "process analysis" developed by the Society of Environmental Toxicology and Chemistry (SETAC) and the U.S. Environmental Protection Agency (EPA) uses engineering to create energy and materials balances for each relevant process: mining ore, making materials and subcomponents, making the product, and the end of product life. Each material and energy balance tabulates the energy and material inputs, the desired outputs, and the undesired outputs that become environmental discharges.

LCA requires careful energy and materials balances for all the stages of the life cycle (for example, the production of a car):

1. the facilities extracting the ores, coal, and other energy sources;
2. the vehicles, ships, pipelines, and other infrastructure that transport the raw materials, processed materials, and subcomponents along the supply chain to manufacture the consumer product, and transport the products to the consumer: iron ore ships, trucks carrying steel, engines going to an automobile assembly plant, trucks carrying the cars to dealers, trucks transporting gasoline, lubricating oil, and tires to service stations;
3. the factories that make each of the components that go into a car, including replacement parts, and the car itself;
4. the refineries and electricity generation facilities that provide energy for making and using the car; and
5. the factories that handle the vehicle at the end of its life: battery recycling, shredding, landfills for shredder waste.

Each of these tasks requires energy and materials. Reducing requirements saves energy, as well as reducing the environmental discharges, along the entire supply chain. Often a new material requires more energy to produce, but promises energy savings or easier recycling later. Evaluating whether a new material helps improve environmental quality and sustainability requires an examination of the entire life cycle of the alternatives. To make informed decisions, consumers, companies, and government agencies must know the implications of their choices for environmental quality and sustainability. Having good intentions is not sufficient when a seemingly attractive choice, such as a battery-powered car, can wind up harming what the manufacturer and regulator were trying to protect. This book provides some of the tools that allow manufacturers and consumers to make the right choices.

Life Cycle Controversies

The initial life cycle assessments surprised many people, since they found that paper bags, paper cups (or even ceramic cups), and cloth diapers were not obviously superior in terms of using less energy and materials, producing less waste, or even disposal at the end of life. Paper requires cutting trees and transporting them to a paper mill, both of which use a good deal of energy. Paper-making results in air emissions (the sulfite process) and water discharges of chlorine and biological waste (UNEP 1996). After use, the bag goes to a landfill where it gradually decays, releasing methane. A paper hot-drink cup generally has a plastic coating to keep the hot liquid from dissolving the cup. The plastic coating introduces the same problems as the foam plastic cup. The plastic is made from petroleum with relatively small environmental discharges. Perhaps most surprising, washing a ceramic cup by hand uses a good deal of hot water and soap, resulting in discharges of waste water that has to be treated and the expenditure of a substantial amount of fuel to heat the water, although washing the cup in a fully loaded dish washer uses less soap and hot water per cup. In short, it is not obvious which product is more environmentally benign and more sustainable.

The amount of hot water and electricity required to wash and dry the cloth diapers is substantial. If water is scarce or sewage is not treated, washing cloth diapers is likely to cause more pollution than depositing disposable diapers in a landfill. The best option turns on the issue of water availability (washing uses much more water) and heating the water.

The analyses found that the environmental implications of choosing paper versus plastic were closer than people initially thought. Which is better depends on how bad one thinks water pollution is compared to air pollution compared to using a nonrenewable resource. Perhaps most revealing was the contrast between plants and processes to make paper versus plastic. The best plant-process for making paper cups was much better than the worst plant-process; the same was true for plastic cups. Similarly, the way in which the cups were disposed of made a great deal of difference. Perhaps the most important lesson for consumers was not whether to choose one material over another, but rather to insist that the material chosen be made in an environmentally friendly plant.

The original analyses showed that myriad processes are used to produce a material or product, and so the analyst has to specify the materials, design, and processes in great detail. This led to another problem: in a dynamic economy,

materials, designs, and processes are continually changing in response to factor prices, innovation, regulations, and consumer preferences. For example, in
a life cycle assessment of a U.S.-manufactured automobile, the design and
materials had changed significantly by the time the analysis was completed.
Still another problem is that performing a careful material and energy balance
for a process is time-consuming and expensive. The number of processes that
are practical to analyze is limited. Indeed, the rapid change in designs, materials, and processes together with the expense of analyzing each one means that
it is impractical and inadvisable to attempt to characterize a product in great
detail.

The use phase of a product raises still more controversy. For example, foam
plastic cups are good insulators while paper cups are not. Thus it is common
to use two paper cups instead of one foam plastic cup. If this is the assumed
comparison, paper cups are worse for the environment. A highway paved with
concrete lasts longer than one paved with asphalt, but making the steel reinforced concrete requires more energy and results in more discharges than
making asphalt. How much longer must a concrete highway last than an asphalt
roadway in order to pay back the additional energy and environmental discharges (see Chapter 10)?

Still another issue is the end of life of a product (Lave et al. 1999). Is the
product reused, recycled, put into a modern landfill, burned to generate electricity, or discarded into the environment? Some products contain toxic
materials, such as lead-acid automobile batteries. If the batteries are not recycled, a great deal of lead goes into the environment. Indeed, many small
consumer batteries are thrown into the trash and some times burned in a
municipal waste incinerator, putting appreciable quantities of toxins into the
air. If aluminum is recycled, the energy premium declines each time the material is recycled. Thus recycled aluminum represents a much smaller energy use
than does virgin aluminum.

Another lesson from the early comparisons is that the scope of the analysis
has to be appropriately broad. For example, California environmental regulations required that 3% of the new cars sold in 1998 had to be "zero emissions"
vehicles. From a life cycle perspective, there are no zero emissions vehicles,
since all vehicles are made with energy and materials, all require energy for
propulsion, and all involve some disposal at the end of their lives. That perspective encourages an analyst to consider the difference between vehicles in terms
of the full life cycle, not just the use of the vehicle. The only technology that produced no emissions directly from the vehicle was a battery-powered car. The
first commercial model, General Motors EV-1, had 1,100 pounds of lead-acid
batteries. One study estimated that generating the electricity to charge the batteries would result in greater emissions of NO_x than gasoline-powered cars
(Lave et al. 1995a). Another study focused on the amount of lead being discharged to the environment from mining and smelting the lead, as well as

making and recycling the batteries (Lave et al. 1996). The lead discharges are substantial, with potentially much greater health effects than the emissions of gasoline-powered vehicles. The lesson again is that life cycle thinking is needed to make informed decisions about environmental quality and sustainability.

Deciding whether to make a car out of aluminum or steel involves a complicated series of analyses:

- Would the two materials provide the same level of functionality? Would structural strength or safety be a problem for either material? Lighter vehicles have been found to be less safe in crashes, although improved design might remove this difference (NRC 2002). A significant drop in safety for the lighter vehicles would outweigh the energy savings.
- Are there any implications for disposal and reuse of the materials? At present, about 60% of the mass of old cars is recycled or reused. Moreover, motor vehicles are among the most frequently recycled of all products since recycling is usually profitable; both aluminum and steel are recycled and reused from automobiles (Boon et al. 2000). It takes much less energy to recycle aluminum than to refine it from ore. The advantage for recycling steel is smaller.
- What is the relative cost of the two materials, both for production and over the lifetime of the vehicle? An aluminum vehicle would cost more to build, but be lighter than a comparable steel vehicle, saving some gasoline expenses over the lifetime of the vehicle. Do the gasoline savings exceed the greater cost of manufacturing? Of energy? Of environmental quality?

In this example, steel, aluminum, copper, glass, rubber, and plastics are the materials, while electricity, natural gas, and petroleum are the energy that go into making, using, and disposing of a car. The vehicle runs on gasoline, but also needs lubricating oil and replacement parts such as tires, filters, and brake linings. At the end of its life, the typical American car is shredded; the metals are recycled, and the shredder waste (plastic, glass, and rubber) goes to a landfill.

The SETAC-EPA Approach to Life Cycle Assessment

In the United States, SETAC and EPA have played the leading roles in standardizing LCA. Numerous individuals and organizations have worked to develop the process model approach for LCA (Curran 1996; Keoleian and Menerey 1993; Vigon et al. 1993). Numerous commercial software products are offered for this purpose (e.g. GaBi, Ecobalance, Franklin Associates). The ISO 14040 series formalizes the process model approach (ISO 1997). In the ISO standard, a variety of process steps are required, including:

- Define the goal of the LCA study—ISO 14041 (ISO 1998)
  - intended applications

- reasons for carrying out the study
- intended audience
• Define the scope of the study—ISO 14041
  - function of the system
  - functional unit
  - description of the system
  - system boundaries
  - allocation procedures
  - impact categories and the impact model
  - requirements for data
  - data assumptions
  - limitations
  - data quality requirements
  - peer review
  - type of reporting
• Conduct a Life Cycle Inventory (LCI)—ISO 14041
  - data collection
  - description of the inventory
• Conduct a Life Cycle Impact Assessment (LCIA)—ISO 14042 (ISO 2000a)
  - classification
  - characterization
  - normalization
• Perform the interpretation—ISO 14043 (ISO 2000b)
  - evaluation and discussion
• Report

We illustrate these steps in an analysis of the life cycle of reinforced concrete pavement, as shown in Figure 1-2. Each of the boxes and transportation links is a separate process model, with resource requirements and environmental impacts. In this case, there are up to 25 separate process models required, including all the transport links. The process model assessment typically consists of a detailed inventory of resource inputs and environmental outputs for the analysis period and processes considered. These outputs can then be evaluated for environmental harm or possible design changes. As production technologies change, process models require updating.

Doing a complete SETAC-EPA life cycle assessment of a complicated product is impossible. An automobile has roughly 30,000 components. Tens of thousands of processes are involved in mining the ores, making the ships, trucks, and railcars used to transport the materials, refining the materials, making the components, and assembling the vehicle. A SETAC-EPA life cycle analysis requires materials and energy balances for each of these processes. Compiling and updating all the materials and energy balances is all but impossible. Furthermore, each of the processes directly involved in producing the

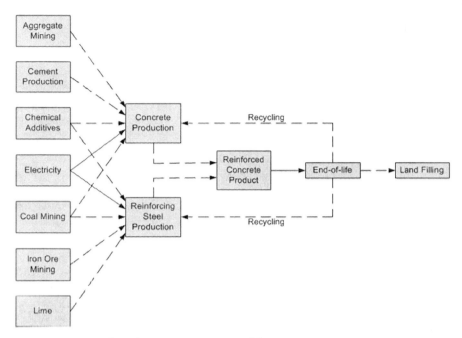

FIGURE 1-2. Reinforced Concrete Process Model

components requires inputs from other processes. For example, steel making requires coke and oxygen directly, but also electricity, environmental consulting, natural gas exploration, production, and pipelines, real estate services, and lawyers. Directly or indirectly, making cars involves the entire economy, and getting detailed mass and energy balances for the entire economy is impossible.

Since conducting a complete LCA is impossible, what can we do? Focusing on the product itself while ignoring all other parts of the life cycle would lead to inaccurate and biased results, as shown in the example of the battery-powered car. The SETAC-EPA approach draws a tight boundary around the processes to be investigated. For example, a major LCA of a generic American automobile looked carefully at the processes for extracting ore and petroleum and making steel, aluminum, and plastic. It also looked carefully at making the major components of a car and assembling the vehicle. The study was forced to compromise by selecting a few steel mills and plastics plants as "representative" of all plants. Similarly, only a few components and assembly plants were analyzed. Whether the selected facilities were really representative of all plants cannot be known. A further criticism of the study is that many aspects of the process were not studied, such as much of the transportation of materials and fuels and the "minor" components. Nonetheless, the study took two years and is estimated to have cost almost $8 million.

The Input–Output Approach to Life Cycle Assessment

A second approach, the economic input–output life cycle assessment approach (EIO-LCA), takes a more aggregate view of the sectors producing all of the goods and services in the U.S. economy. It uses two major simplifications. First, if 10% more output from a particular factory is needed, each of the inputs will have to increase 10%. Second, all production facilities that make products and provide services can be aggregated into approximately 500 sectors. Thus, the average sector in this model represents $27 billion of output. Some sectors, like electricity generation, are much larger ($213 billion), and others, such as tree nut farming, are much smaller ($2 billion).

The two simplifications enable the Department of Commerce to produce an "input–output" (I-O) table for an economy. To this I-O table, we have appended data on resources extracted and environmental discharges to create the EIO-LCA tool (available on the Internet at http://www.eiolca.net).

The advantage of the SETAC-EPA approach is that it can answer as detailed a question as desired concerning the materials and energy balances of each facility studied. In practice, getting these balances is sufficiently difficult that they rarely are designed to answer detailed questions. The disadvantage is that the expense and time means that a tight boundary must be drawn that excludes almost all the facilities involved in making a product or process. The advantage of the EIO-LCA approach is that it does not need to draw any boundary and so covers the entire economy, including all the material and energy inputs. The disadvantage is that it is at an aggregate level, such as the sector "steel and iron mills," rather than the particular steels and iron that go into making an automobile. This approach has a second major advantage: it is quick and cheap. An LCA can be done in a few hours at no cost other than the time involved.

This book is focused on the EIO-LCA approach, although we explore an amalgam of the two approaches in Chapter 2 and in several application chapters.

What Environmental Impacts Are of Interest?

In 1945, coal mines and steel mills discharged enormous amounts of air, water, and solid pollution into the Pittsburgh environment. In 1948, an atmospheric thermal inversion just outside Pittsburgh caused pollution that killed 20 people and incapacitated most of the small population of Donora (Snyder 2003). Although the rivers and ground were highly polluted, reducing air pollution became the first priority. In the 1950s, the high levels of acidity from acid mine drainage and untreated sewage shifted much of the attention to reducing water pollution. In the 1980s, pollutants leaking out of the Love Canal hazardous waste dump shifted attention to solid waste. In the 1980s, acid rain was harming many lakes in the United States, Canada, and Scandinavia, as well as killing forests and causing other problems. About the same time, chemicals like CFCs were shown to destroy stratospheric ozone, allowing destructive amounts of ultraviolet radiation to reach the Earth's surface. More recently, the public became aware of global warming due to the emissions of carbon dioxide and other greenhouse gases. In all of these cases, problems built up over time with relatively little attention until a special event prompted government intervention.

Since the time of acrid smoke and rivers without fish, our recognition of environmental problems has become more sophisticated. No lives are immediately threatened by the thinning of the stratospheric ozone layer or global warming, although left unchecked these conditions could kill more people and have a more profound effect on the environment.

One measure of the success of our environmental efforts is that the problems have become less of an immediate threat. But as one crisis recedes, we are left with more difficult problems in discovering the implications of less toxic pollutants or the implications of small discharges of highly toxic materials. Environmental decisionmaking has always had to set priorities among discharges. Setting priorities is now more difficult. We consider prioritization among environmental discharges in chapter 3.

Depletion of nonrenewable resources is also a concern. For the past century, there have been regular predictions of the exhaustion of one natural resource or another. Despite these concerns, the prices of nearly all natural resources have been dropping over time while their use has been increasing (Simon 1996). Technological progress has increased the efficiency of exploration, extraction, and processing the ore. However, a century of good fortune might not continue forever. Petroleum production may peak soon. More subtle nonrenewable resources may also be under siege, such as biodiversity in selected ecosystems.

One recommended set of impacts to include in life cycle assessments includes (Reijnders 1996):

- Impact on resources: use of nonrenewable resources, use of renewable resources, pollution of resources.
- Direct impact on nature and landscape: loss of nature, undesirable change in landscape.
- Air pollution: contribution to global warming, contribution to deterioration of the ozone layer, toxics in ambient air, contribution to smog, contribution to acid deposition, smells.
- Soil pollution: solid waste added to soil, eutrophication, toxins added to soil, contributions to groundwater pollution.
- Surface water: biological or chemical discharges with oxygen demand, toxins discharged, warming of surface water, contribution to eutrophication.
- Noise.
- Electromagnetic radiation or fields.
- Ionizing radiation.

The International Organization for Standardization (ISO) also defines impact factors for life cycle assessments (ISO 1997, 1998, 2000a, 2000b). In this standard, impact categories, indicators, and characterization models are defined as an initial step within an LCA. For example, an impact category might be climate change as indicated by greenhouse gas emissions weighted by potency for climate change (often called global warming potential, GWP).

In this book, we estimate a broad range of environmental impact indicators, although this range may not include all factors of interest. Our factors are chosen to ensure feasibility of calculation rather than comprehensive coverage. The factors include:

- Conventional pollutants discharged into the environment, as well as pollutants capable of causing global warming. Conventional pollutants are often the target of regulatory emissions control from industrial plants and mobile sources such as automobiles.
- Hazardous and toxic wastes discharged to air, land, water, or recycling facilities.
- Energy inputs, including electricity and various fuels.
- Resources such as ores, fertilizers, and water.

We shall also discuss some approaches that set priorities or apply weighting schemes for these various environmental indicators in Chapter 3. For example, one possible weighting scheme would estimate the social or "external" costs associated with various environmental impacts in dollar amounts. External costs are real costs to society but are not costs to the producer. Thus, the producer seeks to minimize cost and pours discharges into the environment, causing social suffering. Conventional air pollution emissions may cause public health problems including illnesses and fatalities. These are real costs to society, but they are not paid by the polluting plants nor included in the prices that consumers pay for the goods that the plant produces. If all the impacts were expressed in dollar terms, then the life cycle cost of a product or process could be obtained by summing all the relevant private and external costs over the life cycle. Unfortunately, valuing these amounts in dollar terms is not easy, as we discuss in Chapter 3. Perhaps the best way of managing the externalities is to "internalize" them so that the producer faces the full social cost of its actions.

Economic Input–Output Life Cycle Assessment

The basic steps of EIO-LCA are shown in Figure 1-3. First, a purchase associated with a product or process is identified. This purchase might be a manufactured item such as a motor vehicle or a use item such as the petroleum to fuel the motor vehicle. This purchase is used as the desired output for the economic input–output model. Once this purchase is specified, all the supply

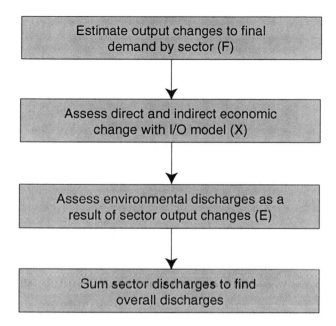

FIGURE 1-3. Steps in the EIO-LCA Process

chain requirements are estimated, from extracting the raw materials to producing high-grade materials to components. The software simultaneously computes the environmental discharges resulting from the initial purchase and the entire supply chain. The process of identifying purchases continues until all the initial manufacture, use, and disposal stages of the product are represented.

Working in the 1930s, Harvard University economist Wassily Leontief developed input–output models of the United States economy (Leontief 1986). His models represented the various inputs required to produce a unit of output in each economic sector. By assembling all the sectors, he was able to trace all the direct and indirect inputs to produce outputs in each sector. The result was a comprehensive model of the U.S. economy. For this work, Leontief received the Nobel Prize in economics in 1973.

The input–output model divides an entire economy into distinct sectors. The model we will use in this book can be visualized as a set of large tables (or matrices) with 480 rows and 480 columns. Each sector of the economy is represented by one row and one column. The tables can represent total sales from one sector to others, purchases from one sector, or the amount of purchases from one sector to produce a dollar of output for the sector. Most nations routinely develop such input–output models, although none publishes as detailed a table as the 480-sector model of the United States used here. The economic input–output model is linear, so that the effects of a $1,000 purchase from a sector will be ten times greater than the effects of a $100 purchase from the same sector.

TABLE 1-1. Example Structure of an Economic Input–Output Table

					Intermediate output O	*Final demand Y*	*Total output X*
		Input to sectors (j)					
Output from sectors (*i*) 1	2	3	*n*				
1	X_{11}	X_{12}	X_{13}	X_{1n}	O_1	Y_1	X_1
2	X_{21}	X_{22}	X_{23}	X_{2n}	O_2	Y_2	X_2
3	X_{31}	X_{32}	X_{33}	X_{3n}	O_3	Y_3	X_3
n	X_{n1}	X_{n2}	X_{n3}	X_{nn}	O_n	Y_n	X_n
Intermediate input *I*	I_1	I_2	I_3	I_n			
Value added *V*	V_1	V_2	V_3	V_n		GDP	
Total input *X*	X_1	X_2	X_3	X_n			

Notes: Matrix entries X_{ij} are the input to sector *j* from sector *i*. Total output for each sector *i*, X_i, is the sum of intermediate outputs used by other sectors, O_i, and final demand by consumers. Gross domestic product (GDP) is the sum of all final demands, Y_i. Value added for each sector V_j is the difference between total output (equal to total input for each sector) X_j, and intermediate input I_j.

In the remainder of this section, we will describe the mathematical structure of the EIO-LCA model. Readers without an interest in linear algebra equations can skip ahead. A "nuts-and-bolts" discussion of the EIO-LCA software follows in Chapter 5.

Table 1-1 shows the structure of an input–output model. Each entry X_{ij} represents the input to sector *j* from sector *i* in the production process. The total output of each sector (X_i) is the sum across the rows of the inputs from the other sectors (or the intermediate output O_i) plus the output supplied to final demand by consumers. The gross domestic product (GDP) is the sum of all the final demands. Within the input–output table, the column sum represents the total amount of inputs to each sector from other sectors.

For calculation purposes, it is helpful to define a different table, which represents the proportional input from each sector for a single dollar of output. This table is calculated by dividing each X_{ij} entry by the total output of the sector, X_{ij}/X_i. We shall denote the result table with entries between zero and one as a matrix *A* showing the requirements of other sectors required to produce a dollar of output for each sector.

Algebraically, the required economic purchases in all 500 sectors of the U.S. economy required to make a vector of desired output *y* (which is simply a list of the 480 sector final demands) can be calculated as:

$$x = (I + A + A \times A + A \times A \times A + ...)y = (I - A)^{-1} y \qquad (1-1)$$

where *x* is the vector (or list) of required inputs, *I* is the identity matrix (a table of all zeros except for the diagonal entries containing a one), *A* is the input–output direct requirements matrix (with rows representing the required inputs from all other sectors to make a unit of output for that row's sector), and *y* is the vector of desired output. For example, the model might be applied to represent the various supply chain requirements for producing electricity or natural gas purchased by residences. In Equation 1-1, the terms represent the production of the desired output itself $(I \times y)$, contributions from the direct or first level suppliers $(A \times y)$, the second level indirect supplies $(A \times A \times y)$, etc. The infinite series of the supply chain can be replaced by $(I–A)^{-1}$ (where the -1 indicates multiplicative inverse). In the EIO-LCA model, the vector of required outputs is multiplied by the average environmental impact or resource requirement for each sector, and the aggregation of these individual impacts represents the total supply chain impact of a purchase. Appendix II provides more derivation details.

Using the model in Equation 1-1, we can estimate the outputs required throughout the economy to produce a specified set of products or services. The total of these outputs is often called the "supply chain" for the product or service, where the "chain" is the sequence of suppliers. For example, an iron ore mine supplies a blast furnace to make steel, a steel mill supplies a fabricator that in turn ships their product to a motor vehicle assembly plant. The fabricator is a direct supplier, while the steel mill is indirect. To make an automobile with its 20,000–30,000 components, numerous chains of this sort are required. The input–output model includes all such chains within the linear model in Equation 1-1.

Once the economic output for each sector is calculated, then a vector of direct environmental outputs can be obtained by multiplying the output at each stage by the environmental impact per dollar of output:

$$b_i = R_i x = R_i(I - A)^{-1} y \qquad (1\text{-}2)$$

where b_i is the vector of environmental burdens (such as toxic emissions or electricity use for each production sector), and R_i is a matrix with diagonal elements representing the impact per dollar of output for each stage (Lave et al. 1995b, Hendrickson et al. 1998, Leontief 1970). A large variety of environmental burdens may be included in this calculation. For example, we can estimate resource inputs (electricity, fuels, ores, and fertilizers) and environmental outputs (toxic emissions by media, hazardous waste generation and management, conventional air pollutant emissions, global warming potential, and ozone depleting substances).

This is a relatively simple model, but it can have a multitude of uses. The calculations required for Equations 1-1 and 1-2 are well within the capabilities of personal computers. The result is a quick and inexpensive way to trace out the supply chain impacts of any purchase, such as the $1 million purchase of computer peripherals described below. In this book, we will use the 1997 U.S. economy model to explore a variety of design and purchase decisions.

Complementary Approaches to Life Cycle Assessment

In this book, we will focus upon the economic input–output LCA approach. This approach has several advantages:

- *Faster:* EIO-LCA studies can be conducted in a few hours or days, rather than the months required for conventional process model developments.
- *Cheaper:* EIO-LCA software is available free-of-charge on the Internet. Process model software sold by consulting companies can be quite expensive, ranging from hundreds to thousands of dollars. Also, the labor in EIO-LCA studies is much less.
- *Better:* The EIO-LCA model includes the entire national economy, whereas process model LCA studies must draw arbitrary analysis boundaries to make the studies tractable. As a result, the EIO-LCA approach is more comprehensive.

The EIO-LCA approach has a major disadvantage: It uses aggregate data for a sector rather than detailed data for a process. The U.S. input–output table does not distinguish between generating electricity using a 50-year-old coal plant and using a new combined-cycle gas turbine. The former puts perhaps ten times as much pollution per kilowatt-hours (kWh) into the environment as the latter. A process model could compare the different processes to the degree desired. The process models can be specific to particular materials or processes, rather than the output from a sector of the economy. Even with 500 sectors available, analysts would often like to disaggregate the EIO-LCA, such as dividing the plastics sector into production of different types of plastic. Process models can also handle nonlinear effects.

While we focus on the use of EIO-LCA in this book, we also describe "hybrid" models in which EIO-LCA and process models are combined to give the advantages of both (see Chapter 2). For example, the production of a chemical might be a process model, while the effects of the inputs to the process might be assessed with EIO-LCA. With the hybrid model, the reliance on process models can vary from slight (such as one model) to very extensive (EIO-LCA might be used only for a single input such as electricity).

An Example of Supply Chain Impacts: Computer Peripherals

This section examines the manufacture of computer peripherals. A supply chain consists of all the firms and procedures that are required as inputs to a delivered product or service. Automobile assembly plants require a large number of component suppliers as well as ancillary services such as trucking. In turn, the component suppliers themselves require parts and materials from other firms. The entire set of these different inputs constitutes the supply chain for motor vehicles. The supply chain is only one portion of a life cycle assessment, but it includes the important stage of manufacturing.

As defined by the U.S. Department of Commerce, the computer peripherals sector is composed of three major types of manufacturers:

- Computer storage devices, such as disk drives;
- Computer terminals, such as cathode ray tubes; and
- Other computer peripherals, such as plotters, printers, and scanners.

In this example, we trace through the supply chain for the production of $1 million of these peripherals in 1992. This production would represent the peripherals for roughly 2,000 to 5,000 computers.

Table 1-2 shows the economic contributions of the largest 25 suppliers, direct and indirect, within the supply chain for computer peripherals. The table has been calculated using the EIO-LCA model.

According to our estimates, production of $1 million in computer peripherals requires economic activity in the supply chain of $2,985,000. The largest activity occurs in the computer peripheral equipment sector itself: $1,080,000. The additional $83,000 of production indicates that computer peripherals are used in the production of computer peripherals themselves or by firms within the supply chain. Note that the change in gross domestic product as a result would be only $1 million, since GDP measures only changes in final output, and not all purchases of intermediate goods (i.e. not the $2,985,000 value).

Many of the top 25 sectors are direct suppliers solely to the computer peripheral industry, such as semiconductors and other electronic components. Others also supply the other suppliers. Electric services (utilities) and chemicals are good examples, along with a number of service sectors such as advertising or legal services. A few sectors in the top 25 are primarily indirect suppliers, such as blast furnaces and steel mills.

As a general indicator of environmental impact, the energy and electricity supply chain requirements for our example are shown in Table 1-3, sorted by total energy. We estimate a total of 6.7 terajoules (TJ) and 410,000 kilowatt-hours of electricity are required throughout the supply chain for this production. Not surprising, electric services is the largest energy consumer to produce and supply electricity throughout the supply chain. The 2.5 TJ represents the coal, oil, and gas used to generate and distribute this electricity. It is interesting that trucking and air transportation show up among the top 10 energy users. Air freight is commonly used in the computer peripherals industry because of tight production schedules, rapid obsolescence, and high product value per pound. Transportation is an energy-intensive sector of the supply chain.

Tracing the supply chain requirements for production has yielded surprises.

TABLE 1-2. Supply Chain Economic Transaction for Production of $1 Million of Computer Peripherals Equipment in 1992$

Sector	Output ($)
Total for all supply sectors	2,985,000
Computer peripheral equipment	1,080,000
Semiconductors and related devices	347,000
Wholesale trade	241,000
Other electronic components	211,000
Noncomparable imports	73,000
Motors and generators	60,000
Miscellaneous plastics products	48,000
Real estate	45,000
Advertising	43,000
Electronic computers	40,000
Other repair and maintenance construction	36,000
Industrial inorganic and organic chemicals	30,000
Computer and data processing services	27,000
Electric services (utilities)	27,000
Banking	25,000
Legal services	24,000
Telephone and communications	23,000
Trucking and courier services, except air	21,000
Blast furnaces and steel mills	20,000
Nonferrous wiredrawing and insulating	17,000
Air transportation	17,000
Management and public relations services	16,000
Crude petroleum and natural gas	16,000
Personnel supply services	16,000
Metal stampings	15,000

The most important suppliers in one dimension often are not the most important in another. For example, some of the largest energy users in the supply chain do not even show up among the top 25 economic supply sectors. A system-wide view is critical in assessing life cycle effects.

Approximating Life Cycle Discharges and Energy Use

Is it really necessary to go through an elaborate life cycle analysis? Could a decisionmaker get a good approximation of the life cycle environmental discharges and energy use by some simple metric? For example, one might hypothesize that each dollar of GDP uses about the same amount of resources and energy and discharges about the same amount of pollutants into the environment.

TABLE 1-3. Supply Chain Energy and Electricity Requirements for Production of $1 Million in Computer Peripherals in 1992

Energy and electricity	Energy (terajoules)	Electricity (kWh)
Total for all sectors	6.7	410,000
Electric services (utilities)	2.5	34
Wholesale trade	0.5	19,000
Industrial inorganic and organic chemicals	0.4	14,000
Trucking	0.4	1,000
Blast furnaces and steel mills	0.3	14,000
Computer peripherals	0.3	74,000
Air transportation	0.3	460
Paper and paperboard mills	0.2	9,000
Semiconductors and related devices	0.2	60,000
Petroleum refining	0.1	2,000

(handwritten annotations: "fuel to generate electricity" next to 2.5; "use air freight b/c of deadlines" next to 0.3 Air transportation; "not in Table 1-2" pointing to Paper and paperboard mills and Petroleum refining rows)

Alternatively, one might hypothesize that each pound of product uses the same amount of energy and resources and results in the same pollution discharge. Finally, if the concern is oil use, one might hypothesize that each gallon of petroleum used is a good surrogate for total resource use and total pollutant discharges.

We have tested these hypotheses with EIO-LCA; the results are shown in Table 1-4. The sectors we examine are electronic computers, automobile manufacturing, banking, air transportation, electricity production, and shoe manufacturing. For each of the six sectors we have computed the conventional air pollutants emitted per million dollars of output, the air pollutants per pound of output, and the air pollutants per terajoule of petroleum used. Pollutant emissions per million dollars of output range from 3.7 for banking to 110 metric tons for electricity. Pollution emissions per pound are undefined for the three service sectors and range from 4.9 kg for automobiles to 620 for computers. Pollution emissions per TJ of petroleum range from 0.62 metric tons for air travel to 16 for electricity. The table reveals large ranges across the six sectors for the other six measures: toxic discharges per dollar (0.09 to 32), toxic discharges per pound (670 to 3,200), toxic discharges per TJ of petroleum (0.59 to 18), total energy used per dollar (3.6 to 130), total energy used per pound (0.004 to 11), and total energy used per TJ of petroleum (1.1 to 18).

Thus, none of the three approximations is a good surrogate for a life cycle analysis. The weight approximation fails completely for the service sectors and covers a wide range for the product sectors. The dollar and petroleum use approximations vary widely for the three environmental and sustainability measures across the six sectors. Thus, we conclude that none of these approximations are accurate. However, EIO-LCA is sufficiently quick and easy that little is lost in trying a full life cycle analysis.

TABLE 1-4. Approximating Life Cycle Analysis

Sector	Computers	Automobiles	Banking	Air travel	Electricity	Shoes
Air pollutants per $1M (metric tons)	6.2	15	3.7	17	110	13
Air pollutants per lb of production (kg)	620	4.9	NA	NA	NA	13
Air pollutants per TJ of petroleum (metric tons)	4.0	4.3	3.2	0.62	16	4.0
Toxic discharges per $1M (metric tons)	32	2.0	0.09	0.16	0.17	1.1
Toxic discharges per lb (kg)	3,200	670	NA	NA	NA	1,100
Toxic discharges per TJ of petroleum (kg)	2.1	0.59	3.2	1.2	18	3.5
Energy used per $1M (TJ)	6.0	13	3.6	31	130	11
Energy used per lb (TJ)	0.6	0.004	NA	NA	NA	11
Energy used per TJ of petroleum (TJ)	4.0	1.8	3.2	1.1	18	3.5

NA = not applicable.

Summary

Almost all people in the developed nations share the goals of improving environmental quality and making sure that future generations have sufficient resources. Accomplishing these goals requires life cycle analysis. Unfortunately consumers, business leaders, and government officials do not have the information required to make informed decisions. We need to develop tools that tell these decisionmakers the life cycle implications of each of their choices in selecting a material, product, or energy source. These decisions are complicated: they depend on the environmental and sustainability aspects of all products and services that contribute to making, operating, and disposing of the material, product, or energy source. This means that a life cycle assessment is required.

We have shown several examples of a life cycle assessment and the complications of exploring the entire supply chain. We introduced two models for conducting this life cycle assessment. One computes mass and energy balances for each aspect of production and use. This approach is highly detailed, but is so expensive and time-consuming that it cannot be implemented fully; instead, tight boundaries are drawn around the problem and most aspects of the supply chain are ignored. The other model is more aggregate, but encompasses all of the supply chain. This book will explore the latter model in many applications.

2

Hybrid LCA Analysis

Combining the EIO-LCA Approach with Other Models

In Chapter 1 we pointed out that EIO-LCA is only one approach to performing life cycle assessment. While it has many advantages, it operates at an aggregate level and does not give the detailed information required for some analyses. The other common approach is to model the materials and energy balances for each important process involved in manufacturing, running, servicing, and retiring the item of interest. The advantage of the process model is its ability to examine in whatever detail is desired the inputs and discharges for a particular process or product. The disadvantage is that constructing each unit process model is time consuming and expensive.

In this chapter, we present a hybrid model that combines the scope of the economy-wide EIO-LCA model with the detail of process analysis. Process models improve and extend the possibilities for analysis, but we don't want to rely wholly on process models. EIO-LCA simplifies the modeling effort and avoids errors arising from the necessary truncation or boundary definition for the network of process models. We wish to use the best features of both approaches.

In this chapter, we consider alternative approaches for hybrid methods. In the same way that others have estimated environmental impacts from input–output models, hybrid LCA models have also received considerable attention in the literature. Several approaches to hybrid LCA modeling have been suggested. The common thread is combining LCA models to yield improved results. The approaches vary in their theoretical basis, the ways in which the submodels are combined, and how they have been used and tested. Below we explore several kinds of hybrid process and input–output models; other methods also exist. Suh et al. (2004) examine boundary problems and integrated input–output models. Florin and Horvath (2004) define potential data interactions. Joshi (1998) has developed disaggregation schemes for input–output models. Cano-Ruiz (2000) provides an input–output process model framework. Lin and Polenske (1998) develop enterprise input–output models.

Process Models

The LCA standard of the International Organization for Standardization (ISO 1997) defines a unit process as the "smallest portion of a product system for which data are collected when performing a Life Cycle Assessment." Unit processes have a series of associated inputs and outputs, such as the following ISO 14040 categories:

Elementary flow:
  • "material or energy entering the system being studied, which has been drawn from the environment without previous human transformation
  • material or energy leaving the system being studied, which is discarded into the environment without subsequent human transformation"

Input:
  • "material or energy which enters a unit process; NOTE: materials may include raw materials and products"

Output:
  • "material or energy which leaves a unit process; NOTE: materials may include raw materials, intermediate products, products, emissions, and waste"

Raw material:
  • "primary or secondary material that is used to produce a product"

Waste:
  • "any output from the product system which is disposed of"

Figure 2-1 illustrates a unit process model for a coke oven. Coke is an essential ingredient in the production of steel. The process model in Figure 2-1 includes only the different materials flows associated with coke production. In this case, coke is the primary product. Coal and water are material inputs. Coke oven gas, ammonia liquor, tar, evaporated water, and purge wastewater are byproduct emissions. A more detailed analysis would include energy inputs and the composition of gas emissions.

An important feature of a unit process model is a mass balance in which the mass of inputs equals the mass of outputs over a period of time. In the case of Figure 2-1, the balance is achieved since the input mass equals the output mass:

$$\text{Input Mass} = \text{Output Mass} \qquad (2\text{-}1)$$
$$1.378 + 1.150 = 2.528 = 0.134 + 0.222 + 0.022 + 0.450 + 0.700 + 1$$

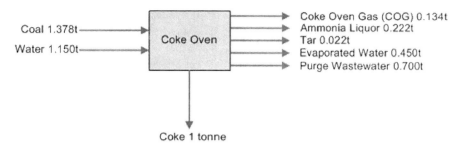

FIGURE 2-1. Coke Oven Mass Balance
Source: Lupis and McMichael 1999.

Mass balance calculations provide a means of validating the unit process flows or estimating a single unobserved emission.

Numerous unit process models are usually required to model environmental life cycle impacts. For example, the ancillary processes for the coke oven would include coal washing, tar and byproduct chemical recovery, and external quench of hot coke. These processes are shown in Figure 2-2 with major inputs and outputs. A process-based LCA would sum up the impacts from each unit process model to obtain a total impact. Of course, additional process models would be required for factors such as coal mining and transport.

A difficulty in summing up impacts arises when process models incorporate loops, as with the recovery of coke oven gas for further combustion in the coke oven shown in Figure 2-2. In essence, the recovered coke-oven gas input is not known until the raw coke oven gas output is known, but the raw coke oven gas depends upon the flow of recovered gas. This is the same problem of indirect suppliers noted in developing the EIO-LCA model in Chapter 1. Representing the process models in matrix form and using the EIO-LCA calculations can solve this problem, as illustrated in Chapter 18. Alternatively, analysts often choose to approximate the correct results or ignore loops of processes altogether.

Comparing EIO-LCA with Process Models

Both EIO-LCA and process modeling have their advantages and drawbacks. In principle, they could give quite different results. If so, the analyst would need to make a closer examination to determine the reason for the differences and which one or combination of the two gives the best estimate. Table 2-1 compares the strengths and weaknesses of the two types of LCA models.

In Chapter 8 we report parallel analyses, one using EIO-LCA, the other using GaBi, a commercial LCA software package. The results are similar. The comparison is also useful in revealing areas in which diverging results may create

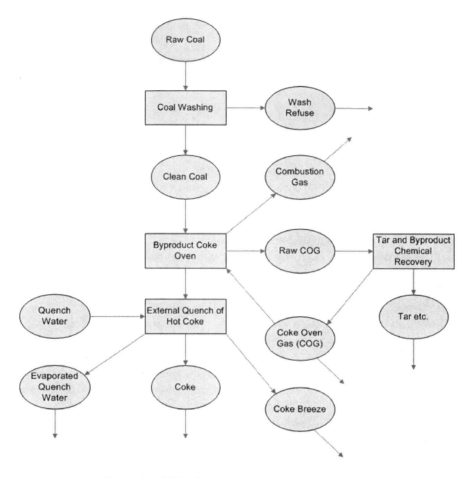

FIGURE 2-2. An Example of Coke Oven Processes
Source: Polenske and McMichael 2002.

problems in one of the systems. This would be an example of parallel application of the two modeling approaches.

Sequential uses may also be of interest. For example, an EIO-LCA sector analysis may be used initially to suggest which sectors are critical in the supply chain for particular environmental impacts. This might be followed up by a process model analysis in which the critical sectors are included and noncritical sectors ignored. This approach could improve the accuracy of a process model analysis. It would be appropriate for cases in which the underlying EIO-LCA is too aggregate to provide the necessary detail. For example, the analysis might be focused on the effects of substituting one non-ferrous metal for another. In EIO-LCA, production of all non-ferrous metals except aluminum is aggregated into a single sector.

TABLE 2-1. Advantages and Disadvantages of Two Life Cycle Assessment Approaches

	Process models	*EIO-LCA*
Advantages	• Detailed process-specific analyses • Specific product comparisons • Process improvements, weak point analyses • Future product development assessments	• Economy-wide, comprehensive assessments (all direct and indirect environmental effects included) • System LCA: industries, products, services, national economy • Sensitivity analyses, scenario planning • Publicly available data, reproducible results • Future product development assessments • Information on every commodity in the economy
Disadvantages	• System boundary setting subjective • Tend to be time intensive and costly • New process design difficult • Use of proprietary data • Cannot be replicated if confidential data are used • Uncertainty in data	• Some product assessments contain aggregate data • Process assessments difficult • Difficulty in linking dollar values to physical units • Economic and environmental data may reflect past practices • Imports treated as U.S. products • Difficult to apply to an open economy (with substantial non-comparable imports) • Non-U.S. data availability a problem • Uncertainty in data

EIO-LCA Results as Input to Processes

For relatively standard services, the EIO-LCA model can be used to estimate the inputs and outputs of particular products or processes. This is illustrated in Figure 2-3, where the outputs from the EIO-LCA model for particular commodity purchases are used directly as the input and output estimates for unit process models. On the right side of Figure 2-3 is a set of process models to be used for an LCA. Figure 2-2 illustrated a possible set of such process models. The EIO-LCA model might be used to estimate the environmental impacts associated with a particular input such as power or petroleum.

An example of this use is the analysis of e-commerce impacts. As described in Chapter 9, the e-commerce logistics chain consists of production, trucking to a warehouse, air freight, and then local delivery to a home via truck. For each of these logistics processes, a sector in the EIO-LCA model is identified and used to estimate the environmental impacts. Side calculations are performed to

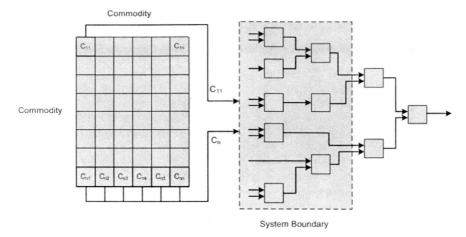

FIGURE 2-3. Use of EIO-LCA Results to Estimate Impacts of a Process

estimate the dollar cost of each logistic purchase and to sum the resulting impact estimates for each process.

In other cases, the EIO-LCA model is used for some of the process steps. In our analysis of a mid-sized automobile (Chapter 6) the EIO-LCA model does not give emissions during driving. Thus the analysis requires a process analysis to supply the missing data. Similarly, in our analysis of coal transport versus electricity transmission (Chapter 13), we employ special models to estimate the parameters of the generating station, and then use EIO-LCA for the expected inputs.

The advantage of the EIO-LCA model is its comprehensiveness; its disadvantage is its aggregate nature. The advantage of the process model is its disaggregate nature while its disadvantage is the need to draw a tight boundary so that only a few process models are required. A hybrid system uses the two models together to get the best of each. For example, the process analysis can give the detailed inputs, outputs, and discharges for manufacturing a gas tank for a van (see Chapter 7). The analysis then approximates each of these detailed inputs by one of the input–output sectors in order to give a comprehensive LCA of the gas tank. The analysis uses the detail of the process analysis to define precisely the gas tank to be considered, then uses EIO-LCA to trace out the economy-wide implications of buying the desired quantity of each material.

The interaction of EIO-LCA with process models by data exchange, called a tiered hybrid approach by Suh (2004), has a number of advantages. A user need not alter the input–output matrix or coefficients at all, and thus can use a standard model such as EIO-LCA. Analysis can be performed rapidly, allowing integration with design procedures and consideration of a wide range of alternatives. The use of EIO-LCA for standard inputs can avert truncation

TABLE 2-2. Use of Local Environmental Impact Estimates for $1M Power Generation

Emission	EIO-LCA	Local estimate	Ratio multiplier (local estimate/EIO-LCA)
Global warming potential (metric ton CO_2 equiv.)	10,000	8,000	0.80
Sulfur dioxide (metric ton SO_2)	54	50	0.93

errors. Process models can be introduced whenever greater detail is needed or the EIO-LCA is inadequate. For example, process models may be used to estimate environmental impacts from imported goods or specialized chemical production.

Modifications or Extensions of the EIO-LCA Model

A second approach to developing hybrid LCA models is to alter the EIO-LCA model itself. In this case, process models (or other information) are used to change the coefficients or the underlying structure of the model.

Using Process Analysis to Supplement EIO-LCA

Some parts of the EIO-LCA model in Chapter 1 were developed in just this fashion. The estimates of emissions in EIO-LCA for some sectors rely on process models of combustion or other phenomena. Thus the environmental impact vectors (denoted R_i in Equation 1-2) could be modified to represent changes in the industry or special production characteristics. For example, selected air emissions for the power generation sector are shown in Table 2-2 as developed by EIO-LCA from the national average. To estimate emissions based on a change in abatement standards for the power generation industry, one can use a series of process models to develop a local set of emission factors per dollar of electricity. To modify the results of the EIO-LCA model, one multiplies the estimated emissions by the ratio of the two estimates as shown in Table 2-2.

Using Process Estimates to Disaggregate or Modify the I-O Matrix

More generally, the coefficients of the input–output model itself may be modified. One option is to subdivide or disaggregate a particular sector into multiple sectors. This allows greater specificity of production processes. For

Society of Env.
Toxicology + Chemistry

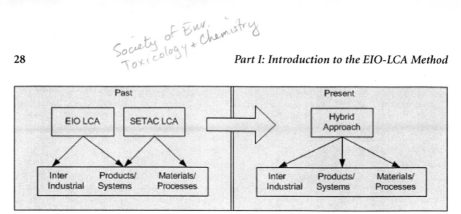

FIGURE 2-4. Application Areas of EIO-LCA, Process LCA, and Hybrid Approaches

example, the non-ferrous metal production sector might be subdivided into lead and other non-ferrous metals to allow more detailed analysis for products incorporating lead. This type of disaggregation requires estimation of the full row and column associated with the new sector, or 480 x 2 = 960 coefficients for the EIO-LCA model. Mathematical details of this disaggregation are discussed in Appendix III.

Another approach is to develop an alternative to the economic input–output table altogether. For example, Chapter 18 illustrates the use of enterprise input–output models in which the coefficients are developed for a particular facility or firm. The enterprise input–output models could be integrated with the national tables as long as consistency was maintained (Suh 2004; Joshi 1998).

Conclusions

The two approaches to LCA are not rivals, but rather have comparative advantages. A hybrid analysis enhances the value of each approach to give better, more confident answers. We have shown combinations that:

- Perform the analyses in parallel to check one against the other.
- Use the detailed answers from process analysis to get more detailed answers from the EIO-LCA model.
- Use the comprehensive scope of EIO-LCA to overcome the boundary limitations of process analysis.
- Use process analysis to get data with which to modify coefficients or disaggregate a sector.

Figure 2-4 illustrates the advantages of the hybrid LCA approach.

3

Environmental Valuation for Life Cycle Assessment

Environmental scientists and engineers have made notable progress in assessing the consequences of environmental discharges and in advancing technologies for the prevention or abatement of emissions. Estimating the costs of abatement programs is somewhat problematic, but environmental engineers and economists have developed acceptable methods. The largest difficulty for federal, state, and local regulators and for companies has been finding ways to value the physical consequences of abating discharges to satisfy congressional requirements and to set abatement priorities.

As pointed out in Chapter 1, there is a substantial need to translate the kinds and types of data generated in Life Cycle Inventory (LCI) work into a more straightforward form for comparison of alternatives and impacts. As an example, a typical LCI of air pollution results in estimates of conventional, hazardous, toxic, and greenhouse gas emissions to the air. Even focused on this small subset of environmental effects, it is unclear how to make sense of the multiple outputs and further how to make a judgment as to tradeoffs or substitutions of pollutants among alternative designs. What is needed is a way of collapsing these multiple impacts (vectors) into single value (scalar) metrics.

Without a means of setting priorities among discharges, inefficient or even counterproductive decisions will be made. For example, the uncontrolled emissions of a coal-burning power plant contain huge quantities of fly ash, tiny amounts of small particles ($PM_{2.5}$), and even smaller amounts of toxic metals such as lead and mercury. Despite its dominant mass, fly ash poses little or no threat to health, in contrast to $PM_{2.5}$ or the toxic metals. Are additional controls required for a modern plant with a precipitator and flue gas desulfurization? If so, is the priority additional removal of particles, of NO_x and SO_x, or of heavy metals?

The increasing controversy over new regulations reflects the increased costs and growing uncertainty about benefits from further abatement, e.g. the $PM_{2.5}$

and ozone rules. Congress required the Environmental Protection Agency (EPA) to examine the costs and benefits of the Clean Air Act retrospectively from 1970 to 1990 and then prospectively from 1990 to 2010. Congress has also required EPA to assess the social benefits and costs of every major new regulation.

Environmental economists have performed a great deal of research associating the release of pollutants with the resulting economic damage (Matthews and Lave 2000; Matthews 2001). This chapter collects many of these estimates and uses them to show how they can be applied to life cycle inventory data, e.g. as estimated with EIO-LCA, to make useful comparisons. Finally, the existing economic literature on environmental damage is compared to some national-level studies for validation.

While much work has been devoted to the topic of valuing environmental impacts, we should emphasize that the results are both controversial and uncertain. No consensus on comprehensive valuations yet exists. In this chapter we merely describe the typical approaches to developing relative valuations. Many schemes exist, but none can claim widespread acceptance or comprehensive coverage for all environmental impacts of interest. As a result, life cycle environmental impacts are typically reported as a series of estimated impacts for different dimensions, rather than a simple dollar amount of benefits and costs.

A Primer on Valuation

For goods and services purchased in a competitive market (a market in which both buyers and sellers are "price takers" who have no long term influence on price), the market price represents the economy's best valuation of an additional unit of that good or service. Under some assumptions, this price is also society's best estimate of value. These statements are not correct for markets where a few buyers or sellers have monopoly power, or where people don't have "reasonable" information or expectations about future supplies and future technologies. Most economists view the U.S. economy as "reasonably" competitive and accept market prices as a measure of social value, except in cases with important externalities.

External effects or externalities are spillovers (positive or negative) from the production of a good or service. For example, air pollution from a coal-fired power plant can present a health hazard to the neighboring community. The market provides no signal that too much coal is being burned or that the plant ought to control its air emissions. The problem might be solved by centralized command-and-control regulation: EPA could require the plant to add precipitators and flue gas desulfurization to reduce emissions. Alternatively, the incentives to the plant could be changed so that it had to pay the social costs of its emissions. A third alternative would let consumers pay the social costs of emissions when they purchased each kilowatt-hour, leading them to buy less electricity. All three approaches would lower pollutant emissions, although the party bearing the initial costs and the efficiency of the solutions would likely differ.

Determining a social value for a good or service is difficult in the absence of a competitive market. One approach is to search for "similar" goods and services that are sold in the market, for example, valuing camping in public campgrounds by the amount people pay to camp in a private campground, valuing freeway services by willingness to pay for toll roads, and valuing a particular aluminum alloy sold only to the Department of Defense by looking at a "similar" alloy that has a more competitive market.

For goods and services (such as emissions) not valued in the market, economists have developed a number of tools to help estimate their social values: damage functions, willingness to pay, measures of damage (lost wages, medical expenditures, jury awards for wrongful injury), and travel cost. We briefly explore the advantages and disadvantages of the most relevant approaches. We use as examples the EPA's retrospective study of the benefits and costs of the Clean Air Act (U.S. EPA 1997a) and a series of studies on the siting of electricity generation plants. These are well documented examples of life cycle assessments for particular regulatory approaches.

Damage Functions

The first step in evaluating the benefits of pollution abatement is to estimate the effect of pollution emissions on things we care about, like health, visibility, materials deterioration, and damage to the natural environment. The next step is monetizing these estimated damages, such as the costs of preventing or repairing materials deterioration. Suppose an additional 100,000 tons of SO_2 emissions might be estimated to increase the deterioration of steel structures in the region by 1% per year. Furthermore, the cost of earlier replacement, repair, or preventing corrosion might be $1 million. If so, the value of abating SO_2 emissions is $10/ton in preventing materials corrosion.

Damage functions must be estimated for the most important effects of environmental pollution. In particular, human health effects from air pollution include restricted activity days, more cases of asthma and bronchitis, and even premature deaths. Additional effects include ecological damage and reduced visibility.

Each of these physical effects is modeled to determine the quantitative effects of changes in ambient levels of pollution. For example, how does the incidence of asthma or bronchitis change as air pollution levels change? The next step is to ascribe a monetary value to each change in the physical damages, for instance the costs of replacing a steel structure earlier, repairing corrosion, or preventing corrosion by painting. These steps estimate the type and extent of physical damage that results from increased air pollution as well as a dollar measure of this damage.

Despite decades of research, both the qualitative and quantitative effects of environmental pollution are uncertain. For example, EPA's retrospective benefit–cost analysis ascribed most premature mortality associated with air pollution to particulate matter, assuming the contribution of other pollutants was negligible. Estimating damage functions is complicated by interactions with other factors and the changing nature of air pollution across areas and over time. Uncertainties in the damage functions are more important than uncertainties in monetizing and estimating the benefits of abatement.

Willingness to Pay

Estimating the cost of painting or replacing a steel structure is straightforward. The materials and labor are valued in reasonably competitive markets and so the bill for replacement or repair is a good estimate of the monetary damage. In contrast, it is more difficult to monetize the value of fewer asthma attacks or being able to see a landmark 30 miles away rather than 10 miles. A prospective buyer scrutinizes the attributes of available products and their prices before making a choice. Products that are less desirable or more expensive than their competitors suffer in markets, eventually being eliminated. Thus, market prices reflect consumer evaluations. But there are no markets for asthma attacks or visibility.

Economists construct a surrogate market by asking people what they would be willing to pay for these improvements. Many questions have been raised about whether people can give accurate answers, and whether they are motivated to answer honestly. Some studies indicate that there is a reasonable level of validity for these responses. However, the answers are controversial and uncertain, particularly where the good or service is outside the experience of the people doing the evaluation, e.g. willingness to pay to protect sea otters in Prince William Sound. Such methods are called contingent valuation.

In EPA's analysis of the Clean Air Act, the category responsible for more than 90% of the benefits was premature mortality. We will focus on this category.

Economists confuse readers, and even themselves, by using the term "value of life." This term calls to mind the value of a person's birthright or perhaps the deliberate sacrifice of an individual. Neither interpretation is relevant here. What is being monetized is a small change in the likelihood that individuals at risk will experience a premature death. What is being valued is, for example, an increased chance of 1 in 10,000 that an individual will die prematurely this year. Economists ask for the social willingness to pay to lower this chance of dying from, for example, 1 in 10,000 to 1 in 20,000. Realistically a "statistical life" rather than a specific life is being valued.

Initial attempts at monetizing this small chance of premature death examined the earnings that that individual would have received over the rest of his life. Earnings are not a socially acceptable measure of the social willingness to pay to prevent premature death. In accordance with society's practices, an earn-ing measure values women less than men and blacks less than whites. It values retired persons at zero.

A second valuation was the amounts that juries awarded plaintiffs in suits for wrongful death. Juries awarded a wide range of amounts and many people were given no award at all. In addition, a premature death due to air pollution does not have the same emotional connotation as a death due to a drunk driver or other negligent action.

There is now a substantial base of literature related to the social willingness to pay (WTP) to avert statistical premature mortality. EPA's retrospective analy-sis used 26 individual WTP studies as the basis of its distribution on health effects from premature mortality.

The literature on medical procedures and devices uses a different metric. Here analysts estimate the number of "quality-adjusted life-years" that a patient would be expected to gain by a medical procedure. If the cost of a quality-adjusted life-year is less than $30,000, there is general consensus that society benefits from going ahead. If the cost is greater than $50,000 or $100,000 the general recommendation is that society does not benefit.

In the end, the EPA analysis used a distribution for WTP estimates, with a median estimate of $4.8 million per life (and a standard deviation of $3.2 mil-lion). Although not used explicitly in the analysis, the estimated value of a life-year was approximately $300,000. Of course, the uncertainty associated with using either of these estimates is significant.

Externality Adders

In the 1990s several U.S. states—California, Massachusetts, Nevada, and New York—conducted "externality adder" studies to select new electricity generation capacity. They expressly sought estimates of the social damage from different types of power generation plants. They recognized that utilities based invest-ment decisions on cost per kilowatt-hour. The state regulatory commissions saw that a utility might choose a polluting plant because it was cheaper to the utility, even though emissions would impose large social costs; they sought externality adders that would recognize the social costs of these emissions. They would then order the utilities to select the technology that had the low-est costs, including both the utility's private costs and these externality adders. Thus, when building a new coal-fired power plant, the company would need to consider not only the stream of discounted net benefits, including construction and maintenance costs offset by revenues, but also the sulfur dioxide and other conventional pollutants released by the facility over its lifetime.

If the plant was expected to produce 100,000 tons per year of SO_2, and the externality adder set by the state was $2,000 per ton, then $20 million per year of "environmental externality costs" had to be included in the investment

TABLE 3-1. Unit Social Damage Estimates (1997$) from Air Emissions of Environmental Externalities

Species	Number of studies	Estimated external costs ($ per metric ton of air emissions)			
		Min	*Median*	*Mean*	*Max*
Carbon monoxide (CO)	2	1	580	580	1,200
Nitrogen oxides (NO_x)	9	230	1,200	3,100	11,000
Sulfur dioxide (SO_2)	10	850	1,900	2,200	5,200
Particulate matter (PM_{10})	12	1,000	3,100	4,700	18,000
Volatile organic compounds (VOCs)	5	200	1,500	1,800	4,900
Global warming potential (CO_2 equivalents)	4	2	15	15	25

analysis to determine which technology was most desirable. The adders were to be used to decide, for example, among coal, oil, natural gas turbines, windmills, and other technologies. One immediate difficulty was that these externality adders were not to be used in the dispatch decisions. Thus, new plants would have the lowest social costs; however the day-to-day management of generation sources would depend on private costs, so that the new plants might not be used.

A Statistical Look at Existing Damage Valuation Studies

Table 3-1 summarizes the existing literature, which presents a wide range of estimates of the damage resulting from an additional ton of pollution (see Matthews and Lave 2000 for the underlying sources). Uncertainty is conspicuous, as the maximum estimates are 5 to 1,000 times greater than the minimum estimates.

Sources of Uncertainty

The wide range in values comes from several sources. The principal source is variation in the underlying damage function. A second is the air chemistry and diffusion modeling, transforming point emissions to ambient concentrations at the receptor. Third, some studies considered only health effects while others accounted for visibility and other effects. While monetization is responsible for some of the variation, it is not the principal source.

In addition, the analysts did not specify a uniform basis for their damage functions and valuations. However, the values emerged in a political process through hearings and public comment. Thus these figures have a reasonable claim to be the social valuations that should be used in making social decisions.

Despite their shortcomings, economic valuations of environmental releases can assist in estimating environmental benefits. Many different classes of policies and projects can be studied, but we focus on a few for illustration. First, policies that attempt to adjust aggregate governmental accounting measures; second, policies that attempt to bring product and process prices in line with the social costs of production; and finally, benefit–cost analysis of environmental regulations.

Other adjustments, for example, to governmental aggregate measures are also possible. Matthews (1999) shows that green price indices could be calculated using the estimates in Table 3-1, and that the necessary Consumer Price Index (CPI) adjustment in 1992 would be about 3%, and Producer Price Indices would range between 9% (for crude materials) and 5% (for finished goods). In particular, if industrial emissions of the air pollutants in Table 3-1 are considered and multiplied by the valuation range, the annual external cost ranges from $40 to $615 billion, with a median estimate of $178 billion per year in 1992 dollars—about 5% of 1992 gross domestic product (GDP). This is a significant adjustment despite almost 30 years of clean air legislation. The estimate includes only air pollution externalities of conventional and global warming pollutants. It could be seen as a minimum or lower bound estimate of the air pollution externality, as it does not include airborne toxic substances, or discharges to land and water. However, even this limited measure can be useful in adjusting national environmental performance.

Full Cost Pricing of Products and Processes

One way to support improved corporate environmental accounting systems is to make product- or process-level social costs more widely available. This would entail estimating the external costs of environmental releases associated with a firm's production technologies. Ideally, these external cost estimates would be based on product or process life cycles, including emissions from extraction of raw materials, component fabrication, manufacture, use, and disposal.

The EIO-LCA model shows the economic and environmental effects of mining, producing, and transporting coal to a power plant in addition to the actual effects of burning the coal to make electricity. Table 3-2 shows the total economic supply chain requirements for producing $1 million worth of electricity in the United States in 1997.

The values in Table 3-2 indicate that to make the average $1 million of electricity, there is about $98,000 of oil and gas, $78,000 of coal, etc. Note that the 1997 U.S. input–output table used as the basis of the model does not disaggregate electricity production into coal-fired, hydroelectric, nuclear, etc. Thus the supply chain above represents the average purchases at the national level to make $1 million of average national generation source electricity.

Table 3-3 shows the top 10 contributing sectors in terms of conventional pol-

TABLE 3-2. EIO-LCA Supply Chain Effects of Producing $1 Million of Electricity in the United States, 1997

Sector	Economic ($)
Total for all sectors	1,700,000
Power generation and supply	1,000,000
Oil and gas extraction	98,000
Coal mining	78,000
Pipeline transportation	34,000
Rail transportation	30,000
Wholesale trade	25,000
Lessors of nonfinancial intangible assets	23,000
Petroleum refineries	22,000
Legal services	20,000
Real estate	19,000
All other sectors	37,000

lutant and global warming potential (GWP) releases for producing $1 million of electricity from EIO-LCA.

As stated above, such information is not very useful in determining environmental strategies since 1 ton of sulfur dioxide is not worth the same as 1 ton of suspended particles. Using the minimum, median, and maximum external cost valuation statistics in Table 3-1, the emissions in Table 3-3 were dollar-weighted, and are summarized in Table 3-4.

As Table 3-4 shows, the total supply chain external costs for producing $1 million of electricity range from $75,000 to $860,000, with a median estimate of $300,000. This estimates a median external cost of 30% of the price of elec-

TABLE 3-3. Top Ten Contributing Sectors to Conventional Pollutant and Global Warming Releases Associated with Producing $1 Million of Electricity in the United States

| Sector | Metric tons of releases | | | | | |
	SO_2	CO	NO_2	VOC	PM_{10}	GWP
Total for all sectors	54	5.5	26	0.89	1.3	11,000
Power generation and supply	54	2.7	24	0.24	1.1	10,000
Rail transportation	0.04	0.09	0.79	0.04	0.02	86
Oil and gas extraction	0.10	0.16	0.07	0.11	0.00	100
Petroleum refineries	0.02	0.01	0.01	0.02	0.00	30
Water transportation	0.02	0.02	0.12	0.11	0.01	2
Cement manufacturing	0.03	0.02	0.04	0.03	0.00	9
Stone mining and quarrying	0.05	0.09	0.03	0.02	0.01	1
Support activities for oil and gas operations	0.04	0.03	0.02	0.01	0.01	1
Iron and steel mills	0.01	0.07	0.01	0.00	0.01	4
Primary smelting and refining of copper	0.01	0.00	0.00	0.00	0.00	0
All other sectors	0.06	2.4	0.26	0.31	0.14	410

TABLE 3-4. Top Ten External Cost-generating Sectors in the Supply Chain Associated with Producing $1 Million of Electricity in the United States

Sector	External cost ($)		
	Low	Median	High
Total for all sectors	75,000	300,000	860,000
Power generation and supply	72,000	290,000	820,000
Rail transportation	420	2,400	12,000
Oil and gas extraction	330	2,100	4,700
Petroleum refineries	89	550	1,100
Water transportation	84	430	2,300
Cement manufacturing	66	320	1,100
Stone mining and quarrying	63	250	1,000
Support activities for oil and gas operations	47	160	660
Iron and steel mills	25	160	450
Primary smelting and refining of copper	13	31	97
All other sectors	1,100	8,900	20,000

Notes: Conventional pollutants and GWP only, using Min, Median, and Max externality costs from Table 3-1; totals do not sum because of rounding.

tricity. Of this, the majority of the externality ($290,000 out of $300,000, or 95%) comes directly from the production of electricity, and the remainder of the supply chain is not so important.

This analysis can be done for all of the sectors in the U.S. economy to yield an assessment of the air pollution damage from industrial production. In a similar fashion, Matthews (1999) shows that there were many obvious heavy industry sectors with high external cost percentages (energy, metals, and construction materials production all above 15%). In addition, the average total external air pollution cost across all sectors is about 3%.

However, percentages only tell half of the story. To find the total external costs of production in a sector, one would multiply the total output of the sector by its external cost percentage. As the power generation and supply sector had output of $226 billion in 1997, the total external costs of electricity are $226 million × 30% or about $68 billion per year. Since the total external costs are highly dependent on output, some surprising sectors rise to the top when listing the largest overall external costs—service sectors such as retail and wholesale trade and restaurants. Matthews (1999) shows that these service sectors had annual external air pollution costs of $5–10 billion, while the average sector generated only about $0.6 billion in external costs.

Firms can use these numbers to assess the relative merits of various materials, product, and process design choices. For example, a process designer could see that the price of electricity was 30% higher than the price quoted by the firm's electricity provider, and choose a design that required less electricity to produce (though the estimates above provide no insight as to which available local electricity generation types would be better or worse). Making such decisions would lower the social costs of a product or process. This could be implemented as an information system presenting the true private costs of the two materials, along with additional information on the external costs of each. If implemented, results of such a system could be inputs to broader national environmental accounting efforts, and could support more advanced measures of GDP and national welfare.

Regulatory Analysis

A final example of the use of economic valuation is illustrated by examining the overall net benefits of regulation. A recent example of valuation-based regulatory analysis is the EPA's retrospective study of the net benefits of the Clean Air Act as required by Section 812 (U.S. EPA 1997b). The study suggests that the benefits of cleaner air have far exceeded the costs.

The report relied on extensive modeling to estimate both the emissions that have occurred since passage of the Clean Air Act and the emissions that would have occurred had the Act never been passed. For each year since 1970, the difference between the two estimates is assumed to be the "emissions avoided" as a result of the regulation. Separately, the health effect benefits from the reduced emissions (including lead) are estimated using the damage function methods discussed above. The health benefits and calculated net benefits (including control costs) totaled more than $22 trillion (in 1990 dollars) from 1970 to 1990.

More than 80% of the health effect benefits came from all avoided mortality (using the WTP valuations above); 75% came from reducing mortality just from suspended particles. EPA's judgment as to which pollutant caused premature mortality did not reflect the full range of available epidemiological studies. Using EPA's assumptions, not a single American died in the last 25 years as a result of sulfur dioxide emissions. Also note that the report estimated total suspended particulate (TSP) emissions, not PM_{10} (particulates less than 10 microns in diameter). TSPs were the more commonly measured emissions early in the Clean Air Act history; more recently we have become concerned with PM_{10}.

While the 812 report does not explicitly publish estimated dollar-per-ton costs for the various air pollutants measured, it provides overall estimates of the benefits of pollution abatement. For example, the report gives an estimate of $16.7 trillion (1990 dollars) from avoided mortality due to particulate exposure. As noted above, all premature mortality was associated with particulates. Similarly the report estimates $13 billion from coronary heart disease due to lead. Since the report also estimates the differential with and without the Clean Air Act, the effective dollar per ton can be estimated.

We then can consider the 1990 valuation of fine particulate mortality in dollars per ton by dividing the total emissions of particulates avoided (214 mil-

TABLE 3-5. Categories of Damages in EPA Retrospective Report (1990$, short tons)

Source	Abated (million tons)	Billions 1990$			
		Mortality benefits	*Other benefits*	*Total benefits*	*Implied $/ton*
Total suspended particulates (TSP)	210	20,000	200	20,000	94,000
Lead	2.5	1,300	540	1,900	740,000
Carbon monoxide (CO)	760	0	3	3	3
Nitrogen oxides (NO_x)	72	0	2	2	28
Sulfur dioxide (SO_2)	190	0	0	0	0

lion tons) by the total benefit of $16.7 trillion. This result alone is over $78,000 per short ton (or $86,000 per metric ton). Note, though, that mortality from particulate emissions was assumed to result from emissions of fine particulates (e.g. PM_{10} or $PM_{2.5}$), not total particulates. Assuming a ratio of PM_{10} to TSP of 0.5, reduced emissions of PM_{10} would be only 107 million tons, increasing the valuation to $172,000 per metric ton.

Table 3-5 shows the breakdown of total damages ($22 trillion) across the studied pollutants. Generally, each line in this table has health effects attributed to a particular species of pollutant in the 812 study.

The results show that the vast majority (99%) of all benefits cited are attributable to prevented deaths. This also sheds light on several of the assumptions used to create the report. Most of the benefit comes from avoided deaths from exposure to particulate emissions (91%). In effect, EPA has put most of its eggs in the particulate mortality basket. As a result, the implication from the report is that future regulation should only target reduced emissions of particulate matter, and would achieve 90% of the benefit by regulating all conventional pollutants at a much lower cost. This result is unfortunate, but not surprising because of the classification done by EPA.

The only sources of mortality in the retrospective study were lead and long-term exposure to particulates. Although few would question the independence of lead in the environment as a cause of death, it is difficult to attach the cause of mortality from breathing dirty air to a specific pollutant source. The various pollutants are often released together, and several studies have failed to show statistical differences in the causation of death from a particular emission. This being determined, EPA attributed all mortality from non-lead sources to particulate matter, a highly controversial assumption. To be fair, one of the reasons behind this assumption is that studies have inconsistently attributed the cause of health effects to particular pollutants. In other words, it is unclear whether PM or SO_2 or NO_x is the culprit, but it is known that in the presence of these pollutants, adverse health effects occur.

As shown in Table 3-5, the retrospective analysis implies that the benefit per ton of reduced particulates is on the order of $100,000, and nearly $750,000 per ton of lead. The benefits from reduced carbon monoxide, sulfur dioxide, and

TABLE 3-6. Emission-fraction Adjustments to $/Ton Values (1990$, short tons)

Source	Abated (million tons)	Distributed across all non-lead sources (billions 1990$)				Distributed across non-lead sources (not CO) (billions 1990$)			
		Mortality benefits	Other benefits	Total benefits	Implied $/ton	Mortality benefits	Other benefits	Total benefits	Implied $/ton
PM	210	3,400	260	3,700	17,000	9,000	260	9,200	43,000
Lead	2.5	1,300	590	1,900	750,000	1,300	590	1,900	750,000
CO	760	12,000	2	12,000	16,000	0	2	2	3
NO$_x$	72	1,200	2	1,200	16,000	3,000	2	3,000	42,000
SO$_2$	190	3,100	0	3,100	16,000	7,900	0	7,900	42,000

nitrogen oxides are basically negligible. As compared with the values in Table 3-1, these values are all significantly different from what is found in the literature. Particulates are more than an order of magnitude higher as implied by the 812 report, while the conventional pollutants are several orders of magnitude lower.

To bound the dollar-per-ton estimates in Table 3-5, an allocation mechanism was used to "spread out" the mortality from non-lead sources among the other pollutants. This was done by taking the simplified results above, aggregating the emissions of non-lead sources, and then distributing the monetary values for particulate mortality across the non-lead sources. For example, particulates are only 17% of total non-lead emissions (214 million out of a total of 1.2 billion tons) so only 17% of the original particulate mortality value was distributed to particulate matter. This assumption is not based on any health science, and is just used for illustration. The result of the proportionally adjusted process is shown in Table 3-6. One further adjustment was considered in Table 3-6, given the lack of literature on serious health damages resulting from carbon monoxide emissions. In this final adjustment, only PM, NO$_x$, and SO$_2$ received distributions of the original particulate mortality value. Even when these distributions are made, the values implicitly used by EPA do not agree with the literature for the conventional pollutants.

Conclusions

As future accounting, management, and policy tools are developed to consider the effectiveness of environmental programs, significant improvements will need to be made in the models used to value environmental damage. Such models will need to encompass geographic differences and rely less on mortality and willingness-to-pay estimates. As atmospheric concentrations decrease and the population ages, the morbidity effects may become increasingly important. In addition, more local, state, and federal studies on externality costs will help guide corporate and governmental decisionmakers to develop environmental strategies that are socially accepted and less costly.

Consensus-based movements continue to embrace public perceptions of environmental effects. Some of these consensus-based programs work toward general principles of agreement that are then translated into consensus valuations to be considered for public policy purposes. In this way, they are similar to the externality adders mentioned above. Europe has led the way in these consensus-based programs. If done appropriately, these would make a valuable addition to external cost models to aid decisionmakers.

Future work in this area should be expected to consider the entire life cycle of products and processes, not just the direct emissions easily seen and reported. Improved data can focus regulatory and industry efforts toward meeting national emissions reduction goals. If there is social consensus on the goals, and firms use common reference measures, then companies that meet the goals can be rewarded—and vice versa. A large improvement will result from linking the enterprise resource planning systems of firms with the tracking and monitoring databases of government environmental protection agencies.

Armed with better valuations and more reliable emissions data by source, future policies could make much more cost-effective improvements in the quality of the energy we produce, the products we buy, and the air we breathe.

4

Uncertainty in Estimating Impacts

Every number we measure or estimate is uncertain. In this chapter, we describe various sources of uncertainty and the implications for a life cycle assessment (LCA). We also suggest means by which users of the EIO-LCA model can reduce errors. Appendix IV contains examples and additional information on formal uncertainty analysis.

There are numerous sources of uncertainty in the EIO-LCA model. Some of the more important include:

1. *Survey errors*: Uncertainties of basic source data can result from sampling and reporting errors. For example, particular manufacturing plants may produce products for more than one sector. In this case, an allocation must be made of input and outputs associated with the different products, and the allocation method may introduce errors. Minimizing survey errors depends upon the actions of the firms surveyed and the data compilers in the federal government, so users of the EIO-LCA model cannot reduce this uncertainty.

2. *Old data*: The latest economic input–output table developed by the Department of Commerce may be up to seven years old. Similarly, there is a lag in receiving environmental data. The lag matters little for some data, such as the economic input–output coefficients for existing industries, but will be more important for other data, such as air emissions from vehicles. Fortunately, modern information technology is speeding up the process of compiling input–output tables so the lag in data is getting shorter, particularly for annual models, which are based upon aggregate updates to the benchmark models estimated every five years.

3. *Incomplete data*: The EIO-LCA software relies on public databases and so is limited by their accuracy and completeness. For example, the toxic release inventory is not collected for some industrial sectors or for plants below a specified size. As a result, toxic emissions are likely to be underestimated.

4. *Missing data*: The EIO-LCA software does not include all environmental effects, generally because of the absence of comprehensive data. For example, habitat destruction for manufacturing plants is not included. Similarly, the external costs of production are limited to health effects of conventional air emissions because of lack of data on the valuation of other effects.

5. *Aggregation*: Even the nearly 500 sectors do not give us detailed information on particular products or processes. For example, we might like data on lead-acid or nickel-metal hydride batteries, but have to be content with a single rechargeable battery sector.

6. *Imports*: The eiolca.net software represents typical U.S. production within each sector, even though some products and services might be produced outside the United States and imported.

Unfortunately, many of these types of errors are inherent in any LCA study, including the process-oriented approach described in Chapters 1 and 2. The process model approach is particularly vulnerable to missing data resulting from choices of analytical boundaries, sometimes called the truncation error. Lenzen (2000) reports that truncation errors on the boundaries will vary with the type of product or process considered, but can be on the order of 50%. To make process-oriented LCA possible at all, truncation of some sort is essential.

Errors Due to Changes Over Time

It takes considerable time to assemble the data required for national input–output tables and the various environmental impacts. During this time, many elements of the economy may change. There may be technological change in some sectors, as new techniques of production are introduced; replacing human labor with robotics is a typical example. There may be changes in the demand for certain sectors, resulting in capacity constraints and changes in the production mix. New products may be invented and introduced. Relative price changes may occur which lead manufacturers to change their production process.

LCA analysts compound the problems of change over time by extrapolating into the future. LCA users are usually more interested in impacts in the future, after the introduction of new designs and products.

While the national economy is dynamic, there is considerable consistency over time. For example, an electricity generation plant lasts 30 to 50 years and variations from year to year are small. Input–output coefficients are relatively stable over time. Carter (1970) calculated the total intermediate output in the economy to satisfy 1961 final demand using five different U.S. national input–output tables. The results varied by only 3.8% over the preceding 22 years:

TABLE 4-1. Effects of the Generation of $1 Million of Electricity in 1992 and 1997 from the EIO-LCA Benchmark Models

Impact	1992	1997	Percent difference
Economic transactions ($ million)	1.7	1.7	+3
Energy use (terajoules)	130	100	−29
Greenhouse gas emissions (metric tons CO_2 equiv.)	14,000	11,000	−31
RCRA hazardous waste generated (metric tons)	15	20	+25
Toxic emissions (metric tons)	0.2	2.9	+93

- Using 1939 coefficients: $324, 288
- Using 1947 coefficients: $336,296
- Using 1958 coefficients: $336,941
- Actual 1961 output: $334,160

Environmental discharges change more rapidly. Table 4-1 shows several impacts for the generation of $1 million of electricity as calculated by EIO-LCA using the 1992 and 1997 benchmark models. The economic transactions expected in the supply chain are comparable for the two periods, with only a 3% difference, even though the sector definitions changed over time. The 1997 benchmark separated out corporate headquarters operations into its own economic sector; energy use and greenhouse gas emissions each declined from 1992 to 1997 by about 30%, suggesting that the sector and its supply chain became somewhat more efficient and cleaner over time. However, the generation of hazardous wastes and the emission of toxic materials increased. Both of these effects may be due to changes in reporting requirements rather than changes in the performance of different sectors. In particular, the electric utility industry was not required to report toxic releases in 1992. Users of the EIO-LCA model can use the different model dates to assess these types of changes over time for sectors of interest.

What can be done to reduce the uncertainty due to changes over time? One possibility is extrapolation from past estimates to the future. Individual impact values may be extrapolated linearly into the future from the values observed at year t and $t-1$:

$$R_{ii}(x) = (x-t)[R_{ii}(t) - R_{ii}(t-1)] + R_{ii}(t) \tag{4-1}$$

where $R_{ii}(s)$ is the impact value (in impact per dollar of output) of sector i in a time period s, x is the future target year for analysis, and t is the year of the latest estimate for R_{ii}. Input–output coefficients could also be extrapolated, subject to the constraints on estimated total production and output expected in year *x*. Given the relative volatility of the different parameters, it would likely be more useful to develop extrapolations of impact vectors, especially for sectors where significant change is occurring in pollution controls, rather than of input–output matrix coefficients.

Errors Due to the Model Form

The EIO-LCA model assumes proportionality in production, implying that there are no capacity constraints or scale economies. The environmental impact vectors use average impacts per dollar of output, even though the incremental or marginal effects of a production change might be different. For example, a new product might be produced in a plant with advanced pollution control equipment.

The linear assumptions of the input–output model may be thought of as providing a first-order, linear approximation to more complicated nonlinear functions. If these underlying nonlinear functions are relatively flat and continuous over the relevant range, then the first-order approximation is relatively good. If the functions are changing rapidly, are discontinuous, or are used over large changes, then the first order approximations will be relatively poor.

To reduce errors from this source requires some effort on the part of the LCA user. A simple approach is to alter the parameters of the EIO-LCA model to reflect the user's beliefs about their actual values. Thus, estimates of marginal changes in environmental impact vectors may be substituted for the average values provided in the standard EIO-LCA model. This requires substitution of the average emissions in particular sectors with the marginal emissions.

An analytically elegant approach to such updating is available through Bayes's Theorem, in which posterior parameter estimates are obtained by combining the existing EIO-LCA parameters with a user's beliefs about the actual parameter values (Morgan 1990). Unfortunately the formal use of Bayes's Theorem requires information about the distribution of the existing parameter estimates, which is not generally available from the underlying sources (as described in Chapter 5).

A second approach is to combine detailed analysis of processes not expected to follow the EIO-LCA model format with EIO-LCA for other inputs. For example, suppose a new product will be assembled in a new manufacturing plant. The expected air emissions from a new manufacturing plant may be used to replace the average emissions for the entire sector. This is more easily accomplished using a hybrid approach in which the manufacturing, use, and disposal of the new product is considered on its own, and the EIO-LCA model is used to estimate the environmental impacts of the inputs to manufacturing, use, and disposal. Relevant methods are described in Chapter 2.

Errors Due to Aggregation and Imports

Aggregation errors and imports are major sources of uncertainty in the EIO-LCA model. Aggregation errors arise from heterogeneous producers and products within any one input–output sector. For example, the battery sector contains tiny hearing aid batteries as well as massive ones used to protect against electricity blackouts in telephone exchanges. One million dollars spent on hearing aid batteries will use quite different materials and create different environmental discharges than $1 million spent on huge batteries. But the EIO-LCA model assumes that the products within a sector are uniform. Some sectors group a large number of products together, such as all industrial inorganic and organic chemicals in one sector. Again, the environmental impact of producing different types of chemicals may vary. Appendix I contains a listing of all the 1997 benchmark EIO sectors.

Leather shoes imported from China were probably produced with different processes, chemicals, and environmental discharges than leather shoes produced in the United States. Lacking data on the production of goods in other countries, the Department of Commerce assumes that the production is the same as in the United States. The magnitude of this problem is diminished by the fact that many imports are actually produced by processes comparable to those in the United States and with similar environmental discharge standards.

As a general note, the uncertainty associated with imports is larger as the fraction of imported goods increases within the economy generally or within a particular sector. International trade as a percentage of gross domestic production ranges from nearly 200% (Singapore) to 2% (Russia) (*Economist* 1990). The U.S. ratio is 12%. Smaller countries tend to have higher ratios. Sectors that have very little domestic production deserve particular attention since the EIO-LCA tables may be inaccurate.

The best means to compensate for these types of uncertainty is to use detailed information about particular products. Formally, this can be accomplished with the hybrid approach, as described in Chapter 2. Less formally, the environmental impacts or input requirements calculated by the EIO-LCA model may be adjusted to reflect actual information about specific products.

Errors Due to Incomplete or Missing Data

Incomplete and missing data certainly contribute to uncertainty in results, but reducing this uncertainty requires considerable effort.

Incomplete data occur if some firms do not have to report environmental impacts. Firms falling below size thresholds do not have to report their toxic emissions. As a result, the EIO-LCA estimates of toxic emissions for particular production levels are likely to underestimate the actual amounts. Fortunately, the survey methods used by the Department of Commerce for the input–output tables (and items such as energy inputs) do not have such threshold reporting limits.

The largest problem with missing data comes from data that are not collected. For example, roadway construction may result in ecological impacts on wildlife that are not evaluated in EIO-LCA. Roadway construction might even produce direct air emissions that are not estimated, such as volatile organics from asphalt pavements. In these cases, users must conduct side studies for the impacts of interest.

Overall Uncertainty and the Comparison of Products or Processes

Estimates developed in LCA studies inevitably have considerable uncertainty. Computers know nothing about uncertainty and will print estimates to as many significant figures as desired. We generally limit reports of impacts to two significant digits, and rarely believe that the estimates are this accurate. As one indication of the degree of uncertainty, Lenzen (2000) estimates that the average total relative standard error of input–output coefficients is about 85%. However, because numerous individual errors in input–output coefficients cancel out in the process of calculating economic requirements and environmental impacts, the relative standard errors of economic requirements are only about 10–20%.

Fortunately, deciding which of two products or processes is more environmentally desirable will be less uncertain than characterizing the impact of any single product. Because two competing alternatives share many characteristics, their associated uncertainty is usefully positively correlated (varying together), so that the impact differences between the two alternatives will be known with greater certainty than either impact separately. Suppose one product uses slightly less electricity than another. There is considerable uncertainty in the environmental impact of producing the electricity for either product. However, since the electricity use is less for the more energy efficient product, we can confidently predict that the environmental impact due to electricity use is better as well.

As a numerical example, Cano-Ruiz (2000) compared the environmental impact of chlor-alkali processes using a mercury cell, a membrane cell, and a diaphragm cell. If correlations among errors were ignored, then the difference in estimated impacts for the three methods was not statistically significant. However, if the positive correlations were considered, two alternatives were still similar in performance, but the mercury cell alternatives had only an 8% chance of being better than the others.

To numerically estimate the uncertainty of environmental impacts, a Monte

Carlo simulation is usually employed. Several steps are involved:

1. The underlying distributions, correlations, and distribution parameters are estimated for each input–output coefficient, environmental impact vector, and required sector output. Correlations refer to the interaction of the uncertainty for the various coefficients.
2. Random draws are made for each of the coefficients in the EIO-LCA model.
3. The environmental impacts are calculated based on the random draws.
4. Steps 2 and 3 are repeated numerous times. Each repetition represents another observation of a realized environmental impact. Eventually, the distribution of environmental impacts can be reasonably characterized.

Steps 2–4 in this process rely heavily upon modern information technology, as they involve considerable computation. Still, the computations are easily accomplished on modern personal computers. Appendix IV illustrates some simulations of this type on a small model for interested readers.

Step 1 is the difficulty in applying this method. We simply do not have good information about distributions, correlations, and the associated parameters for input–output matrices or environmental impact vectors. Over time, one hopes that research results will accumulate in this area.

A simpler approach to the analysis of uncertainty in comparing two alternatives is to conduct a sensitivity analysis; that is, to consider what level some parameter would have to attain in order to change the preference for one alternative.

Different LCA Approaches

Another useful approach to assessing uncertainty in LCA studies is to compare alternative approaches and assumptions. For example, in estimating the impact of nanotechnology on automobile catalysts (Chapter 8), we compare EIO-LCA results to those available from a commercial, process-based LCA tool, GaBi. The results are fairly close for each scenario analyzed, increasing our confidence in the conclusion.

Conclusions

Life cycle assessment inevitably involves considerable uncertainty. This uncertainty can be reduced with careful analysis of the underlying data and production processes. Fortunately, the relative desirability of design alternatives can be assessed with greater confidence than the overall impact of a single alternative because of the typical positive correlation between the impacts of alternatives. In general, we recommend that users of the EIO-LCA model use no more than two significant digits in considering results from the model.

5

Using the Economic Input–Output Life Cycle Assessment Model

As explained in the previous chapters, the EIO-LCA model traces the various economic transactions, resource requirements, and environmental emissions required to provide a particular product or service. The model captures all the various manufacturing, transportation, mining, and related requirements to produce it. For example, it is possible to trace out the implications of purchasing $46,000 of reinforcing steel and $104,000 of concrete for a kilometer of roadway pavement. Environmental implications of these purchases can be estimated using EIO-LCA. The model itself is available on the Web at www.eiolca.net, including a variety of input–output tables in addition to the 1997 U.S. benchmark table used extensively in this book.

In this chapter we explain how to use the EIO-LCA software. We list some frequently asked questions, give an example application of the software, provide a numerical example of the input–output calculations, list the various data sources for the model, and provide some sample problems.

Frequently Asked Questions for Using the EIO-LCA Software

How are sectors defined in the EIO-LCA model?

We use the sector definitions established by the U.S. Department of Commerce. All U.S. companies are grouped into standard categories. Formerly these were called standard industrial classifications (SIC), each with a numerical code. Now there is a standard coding system for North America, the North American Industry Classification System (NAICS). For example, "Fluid milk manufacturing" is NAICS sector code 311511 within the food manufacturing group (311) of manufacturing (3). Appendix I lists the 491 sectors used in the 1997 benchmark input–output model.

How do I use the www.eiolca.net software to do a life cycle assessment?

The software will identify the economic and environmental impacts of a purchase from a particular economic sector. The entire supply chain for producing this purchase is represented. The software does not automatically estimate the entire life cycle effects without some effort by the user. In particular, the environmental impacts for the use and disposal of products are not included. To assess the lifetime impact of a motor home costing $50,000:

1. Use the software to assess the environmental effects of producing $50,000 of motor homes in the motor home manufacturing economic sector (336213).
2. Add the environmental impacts of producing the petroleum and maintenance items that would be used by the motor home over its lifetime. Each of these items can be assessed.
3. Finally, estimate the direct air emissions from the motor home separately (as provided by the manufacturer and summarized in consumer magazines) plus any disposal impacts.

We provide examples of these types of calculations throughout this book.

When I use the EIO-LCA model, why does $1 million of purchases result in more than $1 million in economic activity?

The software reflects the entire supply chain of transactions to produce a good or service, including intermediate purchases. The purchase of an automobile will require purchases of steel, paint, plastics, and many other goods. The software estimates the total set of such transactions. The calculation of the gross domestic product omits these intermediate transactions; it includes only final demand (or $1 million in this case) in the total of national production. Note that purchase of $1 million of one good often results in more than $1 million of output for this sector because many sectors may use the good themselves in their production. For example, production of $1 million of truck transportation involves $1.146 million in purchases from this sector, because many parts of the supply chain use truck transportation for tasks such as transporting truck components to an assembly plant.

Where can I find price information for goods and services?

With the growth of e-commerce, price information for most commodities is available on the Internet. Current prices should be converted to $1997 by the

TABLE 5-1. Differences in Producers' and Purchasers' prices, 1997 (Millions of Dollars in Sector Output)

Item	Producers' Price	Transportation cost	Wholesale and retail trade margin	Purchasers' price	Producers' price / Purchasers' price (%)
Tobacco products	32,257	222	21,293	40,193	80
Shoes	18,333	179	21,748	40,259	45
Barber shops	31,246	—	—	31,246	100
Furniture	28,078	235	27,648	55,960	50

use of an appropriate economic index. A good source of price indices is the *Statistical Abstract of the United States*, available online (USCB 2001a). For example, the conversion from 2002 prices to 1997 prices using the consumer price index (CPI)is accomplished by finding the 2002 CPI value (180) and dividing it by the 1997 value (160.5), to get 1.12. Thus 2002 prices are on average 12% higher than 1997 prices. To convert to 1997, divide the 2002 price by 1.12.

In the EIO-LCA model, the price should be the price paid to producers (producer prices) rather than the price paid by consumers. For many services and utilities, the two are the same (Lawson et al. 2002). However, if there are significant transportation costs or retail markups on personal consumption expenditures, there would be a difference. Table 5-1 lists some typical differences between producer prices and consumer prices in the 1997 benchmark table.

Which input–output table is being used in this book?

We are using the 1997 benchmark industry-by-industry economic input–output model as supplied by the Department of Commerce (Lawson et al. 2002, BEA 2004b). It can be created from the underlying make and use tables for individual sectors with standard matrix manipulations (make and use tables are developed from census data and represent sales and purchases for the various sectors). The www.eiolca.net website provides a number of other models, such as the 1992 U.S. benchmark.

The Department of Commerce also provides commodity-by-commodity tables, reflecting the dollar transactions between industries, and commodity-by-industry models. We have chosen the industry-by-industry table since we are interested in assessing impacts for specific production processes. In calculations, the tables generally give similar results.

How does EIO-LCA account for imports?

Imports are assumed to have the same production characteristics as comparable products made in the United States. Thus, if a truck is imported from Japan or Mexico and used by a U.S. company, the environmental effect of producing the truck is expected to be comparable to those made in the United States. To the extent that overseas production is regarded as more or less of an environmental concern, the impacts developed from eiolca.net software should be adjusted by an appropriate factor.

An Example Application—Alternative Washing Machines

Problem

A household is considering purchasing a washing machine and has narrowed their choice to two alternatives. In addition to cost and other functional items, they wish to assess the energy consumption and greenhouse gas emissions over the lifetimes of the two alternatives:

- Machine 1 is a standard top-loading unit with a purchase cost of $500. This machine uses 40 gallons of water and 2 kilowatt-hours of electricity per load (assuming an electric water heater). The household would do roughly 8 loads of laundry per week with this machine.
- Machine 2 is a front-loading unit; it costs $1,000, but it can wash double the amount of clothes per load, and each load uses half the water and electricity.

    a. Estimate the total annual costs of water and electricity for each of the two machines. Use these values along with the manufacturing costs (assume this is equal to the price) to develop a purely cost-based comparison of the two machines over a 10-year period. Assume that electricity costs 8 cents/kWh and water is $2 per 1,000 gallons.

    b. Use the same cost values as inputs into EIO-LCA to estimate the relative energy consumption and greenhouse gas emission over their life cycles. Ignore the disposal phase. Be sure to express the comparisons of the two machines in terms of use versus manufacturing effects.

Solution

a. Calculate the total annual costs of water and electricity.

	Machine 1	*Machine 2*
Cost ($)	500	1,000
Water consumption per load (gal)	40	20
Electricity consumption per load (kWh)	2	1
Loads per week	8	4

Electricity cost ($/kWh)	*0.08*
Water cost ($/gal)	*0.002*

Total annual cost of water
Machine 1: $40 \times 8 \times 52 \times 0.002 = \$33.28$
Machine 2: $20 \times 4 \times 52 \times 0.002 = \$8.32$

Total annual cost of electricity
Machine 1: $2 \times 8 \times 52 \times 0.08 = \$66.56$
Machine 2: $1 \times 4 \times 52 \times 0.08 = \$16.64$

Total cost in a 10-year period
Machine 1: $\$332.80 + \$665.60 + \$500 = \$1,498.40$
Machine 2: $\$83.20 + \$166.40 + \$1,000 = \$1,249.60$

A more accurate cost comparison would calculate the present value of the annual costs using a realistic discount rate. In this case, discount rates below 8% imply a lower present cost for Machine 2, whereas higher discount rates would result in lower present costs for Machine 1.

b. Estimate the energy consumption and greenhouse gas emission over the life cycles of washing machines using www.eiolca.net software.

- Assume that the lifetime of washing machines is 10 years and we ignore the disposal phase in our calculations.
- We choose the household laundry equipment manufacturing sector to calculate the environmental effects of the manufacturing of washing machines, and use their purchase costs ($500 and $1,000) as producer prices. The results are summarized in Table 5-2.
- We use the water, sewage, and other systems sector in order to estimate the greenhouse gas (GHG) emission and energy consumption caused by the water used in washing machines. Table 5-3 includes the results from the software.
- We choose the power generation and supply sector to estimate the GHG emission and energy consumption caused by the electricity use of washing machines. Table 5-4 includes the results from the software.
- We consider the entire supply chain calculating the total effects. Table 5-5 shows the total GHG emission and energy consumption. Machine 2 has both lower overall cost and environmental impacts. However, if the life cycle costs are discounted at a rate above 8%, machine 1 has lower total present value cost.

This example illustrates the construction of a life cycle analysis for two alternatives using the EIO-LCA model. Both manufacturing and use phase impacts are included here. A full analysis would include differences pertaining to end-

TABLE 5-2. Greenhouse Gas Emission and Energy Consumption Caused by Manufacturing Two Alternative Washing Machines

	GWP (mt CO₂ equivalent)	Energy consumption (TJ)
Machine 1	0.42	0.005
Machine 2	0.83	0.010

TABLE 5-3. Greenhouse Gas Emission and Energy Consumption Caused by Water Use of Two Alternative Washing Machines

	Water use ($)	GWP (mt CO₂ equiv.)	CO₂ (mt CO₂ equiv.)	CH₄ (mt CO₂ equiv.)	N₂O (mt CO₂ equiv.)	CFCs (mt CO₂ equiv.)	Energy consumption (TJ)
1	330	0.69	0.62	0.015	0.054	0.0019	0.0088
2	83	0.17	0.16	0.0036	0.013	0.00048	0.0022

TABLE 5-4. Greenhouse Gas Emission and Energy Consumption Caused by Electricity Use of Two Alternative Washing Machines

	Electricity use ($)	GWP (mt CO₂ equiv.)	CO₂ (mt CO₂ equiv.)	CH₄ (mt CO₂ equiv.)	N₂O (mt CO₂ equiv.)	CFCs (mt CO₂ equiv.)	Energy (TJ)
1	666	7.1	6.7	0.22	0.073	0.082	0.067
2	166	1.8	1.7	0.055	0.018	0.020	0.017

TABLE 5-5. Total Greenhouse Gas Emission and Energy Consumption Caused by Manufacturing and Use of Two Washing Machines

	GWP (mt CO₂ equivalent)	Energy consumption (TJ)
Machine 1	8.2	0.081
Machine 2	2.8	0.029

of-life disposal, although the differences are likely to be relatively small for these two washing machines.

A Numerical Example of the EIO-LCA Calculations

For those new to input–output calculations, it is often useful to see the calculations performed on a small scale problem. Consider a case where the reinforced concrete to pave a one kilometer road costs $150,000, and requires 3,680 metric tons of concrete ($104,000) and 78 metric tons of reinforcing steel ($46,000). In this example, only one environmental output is presented: hazardous waste regulated under Subtitle C of the Resource Conservation and Recovery Act (RCRA). This example is based on Hendrickson et al. (1998).

We will use a simplified input–output model for this example, representing only 10 sectors as shown in Table 5-6 and including only the direct inputs to steel and concrete. A column in Table 5-6 represents the required direct inputs from the other stages for a unit of output of this particular stage. For example, $1,000 of concrete production requires $120 of aggregate and $200 of cement production, and $1,000 of iron and steel production requires $40 of iron and ferroalloy ores mining.

The requirements matrix shown in Table 5-6 could be constructed with many units of measurement. For example, the entries in the concrete production column might represent the metric tons of aggregate and cement required for a metric ton of concrete. However, not all outputs are easily measured by units of mass; electricity generation is an example of an important product without mass. We have chosen to represent the requirements in terms of dollars which can, in turn, be converted into quantity outputs. Use of other units is discussed more fully in Chapter 18.

The direct supplier inputs for concrete production can be obtained by multiplying the matrix in Table 5-6 by the required output of reinforced concrete ingredients:

$$x_{\text{direct suppliers}} = (I + A)y \tag{5-1}$$

where $x_{\text{direct suppliers}}$ are the direct supplier inputs to reinforced concrete (in dollars), I is a unit matrix (to include the output of the concrete production stage itself), A is the requirements matrix (shown in Table 5-6), and y is a vector of desired output. For $150,000 of reinforced concrete roadway, y consists of $104,000 of concrete and $46,000 of reinforcing steel. The calculation of direct supplier output (in $1,000) would then be:

TABLE 5-6. Process Model Requirements Matrix for $1 of the Example Reinforced Concrete Product
(Rows represent inputs into the sectors named at column heads)

Inputs	Transportation[1]	Aggregates mining[2]	Iron and ferroalloy ores mining	Lime	Electricity	Coal mining	Chemical additives[3]	Cement production	Iron and steel production	Concrete production
Transportation[1]	0	0	0	0	0	0	0	0	0.03	0.10
Aggregates mining[2]	0	0	0	0	0	0	0	0	0	0.12
Iron and ferroalloy ores mining	0	0	0	0	0	0	0	0	0.04	0
Lime	0	0	0	0	0	0	0	0	0.005	0
Electricity	0	0	0	0	0	0	0	0	0.07	0.04
Coal mining	0	0	0	0	0	0	0	0	0.05	0.02
Chemical additives[3]	0	0	0	0	0	0	0	0	0.05	0.03
Cement production	0	0	0	0	0	0	0	0	0	0.20
Iron and steel production	0	0	0	0	0	0	0	0	0	0
Concrete production	0	0	0	0	0	0	0	0	0	0

1. Motor freight transportation and warehousing
2. Sand and gravel
3. Industrial inorganic and organic chemicals

$$x_{\text{direct suppliers}} = (I + A)y =$$

$$
\begin{bmatrix}
1 & 0 & 0 & 0 & 0 & 0 & 0 & 0 & 0.03 & 0.10 \\
0 & 1 & 0 & 0 & 0 & 0 & 0 & 0 & 0 & 0.12 \\
0 & 0 & 1 & 0 & 0 & 0 & 0 & 0 & 0.04 & 0 \\
0 & 0 & 0 & 1 & 0 & 0 & 0 & 0 & 0.005 & 0 \\
0 & 0 & 0 & 0 & 1 & 0 & 0 & 0 & 0.07 & 0.04 \\
0 & 0 & 0 & 0 & 0 & 1 & 0 & 0 & 0.05 & 0.02 \\
0 & 0 & 0 & 0 & 0 & 0 & 1 & 0 & 0.05 & 0.03 \\
0 & 0 & 0 & 0 & 0 & 0 & 0 & 1 & 0 & 0.20 \\
0 & 0 & 0 & 0 & 0 & 0 & 0 & 0 & 1 & 0 \\
0 & 0 & 0 & 0 & 0 & 0 & 0 & 0 & 0 & 1
\end{bmatrix}
\begin{bmatrix}
0 \\ 0 \\ 0 \\ 0 \\ 0 \\ 0 \\ 0 \\ 0 \\ 46 \\ 104
\end{bmatrix}
=
\begin{bmatrix}
12 \\ 12 \\ 2 \\ 0.2 \\ 7 \\ 4 \\ 5 \\ 21 \\ 46 \\ 104
\end{bmatrix}
\quad (5\text{-}2)
$$

which implies that the $150,000 of concrete required $12,000 of aggregate mining activity, $2,000 of iron ore mining, and $21,000 of cement production.

More generally, a full analysis should take into account the entire supply chain for a product, including suppliers to a supplier (indirect suppliers). The total output including indirect suppliers as developed in Chapter 1 is:

$$x = (I - A)^{-1} y \qquad (5\text{-}3)$$

In the simple case shown in Table 5-6 in which only one level of suppliers exists, application of this general solution gives the same result as for the direct output:

$$x = (I - A)^{-1} y =$$

$$
\begin{bmatrix}
1 & 0 & 0 & 0 & 0 & 0 & 0 & 0 & 0.03 & 0.10 \\
0 & 1 & 0 & 0 & 0 & 0 & 0 & 0 & 0 & 0.12 \\
0 & 0 & 1 & 0 & 0 & 0 & 0 & 0 & 0.04 & 0 \\
0 & 0 & 0 & 1 & 0 & 0 & 0 & 0 & 0.005 & 0 \\
0 & 0 & 0 & 0 & 1 & 0 & 0 & 0 & 0.07 & 0.04 \\
0 & 0 & 0 & 0 & 0 & 1 & 0 & 0 & 0.05 & 0.02 \\
0 & 0 & 0 & 0 & 0 & 0 & 1 & 0 & 0.05 & 0.03 \\
0 & 0 & 0 & 0 & 0 & 0 & 0 & 1 & 0 & 0.20 \\
0 & 0 & 0 & 0 & 0 & 0 & 0 & 0 & 1 & 0 \\
0 & 0 & 0 & 0 & 0 & 0 & 0 & 0 & 0 & 1
\end{bmatrix}
\begin{bmatrix}
0 \\ 0 \\ 0 \\ 0 \\ 0 \\ 0 \\ 0 \\ 0 \\ 46 \\ 104
\end{bmatrix}
=
\begin{bmatrix}
12 \\ 12 \\ 2 \\ 0.2 \\ 7 \\ 4 \\ 5 \\ 21 \\ 46 \\ 104
\end{bmatrix}
\quad (5\text{-}4)
$$

Finally, the calculation of hazardous waste generation for the reinforced concrete product example would be:

$$b = Rx =$$

$$
\begin{bmatrix}
2.096 & 0 & 0 & 0 & 0 & 0 & 0 & 0 & 0 & 0 \\
0 & 0.002 & 0 & 0 & 0 & 0 & 0 & 0 & 0 & 0 \\
0 & 0 & 0.162 & 0 & 0 & 0 & 0 & 0 & 0 & 0 \\
0 & 0 & 0 & 0.025 & 0 & 0 & 0 & 0 & 0 & 0 \\
0 & 0 & 0 & 0 & 2.745 & 0 & 0 & 0 & 0 & 0 \\
0 & 0 & 0 & 0 & 0 & 0.027 & 0 & 0 & 0 & 0 \\
0 & 0 & 0 & 0 & 0 & 0 & 94.158 & 0 & 0 & 0 \\
0 & 0 & 0 & 0 & 0 & 0 & 0 & 13.866 & 0 & 0 \\
0 & 0 & 0 & 0 & 0 & 0 & 0 & 0 & 42.454 & 0 \\
0 & 0 & 0 & 0 & 0 & 0 & 0 & 0 & 0 & 0.0002 \\
\end{bmatrix}
\begin{bmatrix}
12 \\ 12 \\ 2 \\ 0.2 \\ 7 \\ 4 \\ 5 \\ 21 \\ 46 \\ 104
\end{bmatrix}
=
\begin{bmatrix}
25 \\ 0.03 \\ 0.3 \\ 0.005 \\ 19 \\ 0.1 \\ 471 \\ 291 \\ 1,953 \\ 0.02
\end{bmatrix}
\quad (5\text{-}5)
$$

where the elements of the R matrix are given in kilograms of RCRA Subtitle C hazardous waste generated per \$1,000 of output, the elements of x are in \$1,000, and the elements of the resulting b vector are given in kilograms of hazardous waste. For example, 0.027 kg of hazardous waste are generated per \$1,000 of output in the coal mining sector, thus for \$4,000 of coal mining demand 0.1 kg of hazardous waste are generated. Overall, 2,760 kg of hazardous waste are generated for the reinforced concrete example.

Data Sources for the www.eiolca.net Software

The data in the EIO-LCA software is derived from a variety of public datasets and assembled for the various sectors. For the most part, the data are self-reported and are subject to measurement error and reporting requirement gaps. For example, automotive repair shops do not have to report to the Toxics Release Inventory. Chapter 4 discusses major sources of uncertainty in the model. While more extensive explanations are available on the website, the major datasets include:

- *Input–output matrix:* The 491 sector 1997 industry-by-industry input–output (I-O) matrix of the U.S. economy as developed by the U.S. Department of Commerce (see Appendix I). Economic Impacts are computed from the I-O matrix and the user input change in final demand. Economic Impacts are reported in 1997\$ millions.
- *Electricity use* of manufacturing sectors is developed from the 1998 Manufacturing Energy Consumption Survey, and for mining sectors is calculated from the 1997 Economic Census (USCB 1997). Service sector electricity use is estimated using the detailed use table and average electricity prices for these sectors.
- *Fuel use* is calculated from commodity purchases (contained in the input–output model use table) and average 1997 prices.

- *Energy use* is calculated by converting fuel use per sector and 31% of electricity use into terajoules (31% is the amount of electricity produced in 1997 from non-fossil fuel sources).
- *Conventional pollutant emissions* are from the U.S. Environmental Protection Agency.
- *Greenhouse gas emissions* are calculated by emissions factors from fuel use.
- *Toxic releases* are derived from EPA's 2000 Toxics Release Inventory (U.S. EPA 2001a).
- *Weighted toxics releases*: CMU-ET is a weighting scheme for toxic emissions to account for their relative hazard (Horvath et al. 1995). It is computed from occupational exposure standards (called threshold limit values). The gross amount of toxic emissions is converted into metric tons of threshold limit value emissions equivalent, such as sulfuric acid.
- *Hazardous waste*: RCRA Subtitle C hazardous waste generation, management, and shipment was derived from EPA's 1999 National Biannual RCRA Hazardous Waste Report (U.S. EPA 2001b).
- *External costs* are calculated from conventional air pollutant emissions and estimates of pollution damage taken from the economics literature. Detailed information on these values is available from (Matthews 1999).
- *Water data* come from the Department of Commerce 1982 Census of Manufactures (U.S. DOC 1986).
- *OSHA safety data* come from the Bureau of Labor Statistics.
- *Employment data* come from the following sources:
  - 1997 Economic Census: Comparative Statistics for United States 1987, SIC Basis.
  - Bureau of Labor Statistics, Industry Illness and Injury Data 1997 (BLS 1997).
  - *Statistical Abstract of the United States* (1998–2000).
  - National Marine Fisheries Service, Employment, Craft, and Plants (Table) Processors and Wholesalers 1999 (NMFS 2000).
  - Bureau of Transportation Statistics
  - U.S. Department of Agriculture

Some Sample Problems Using the EIO-LCA Software

1. a. What are the greenhouse gas emissions associated with $1 million of university services in 1997 using the EIO-LCA 1997 benchmark model?
   b. Suppose a school purchases 8% of its electricity from wind power. How could you adjust the emissions found in part a for this fact? As a simplification, assume that no greenhouse gas emissions are associated with wind

power generation and the amount of wind power used in the estimate of part a is zero.

    c. Could your method in part b be used for other adjustments? If so, give one example. If not, explain why.

2. a. Use the 1997 benchmark EIO-LCA model to estimate the conventional pollutant and greenhouse gas emissions associated with electricity production in the United States in 1999.

    b. The Energy Information Administration estimates the following total environmental impacts of electricity production in the United States in 1999:

TABLE 5-8. EIA Estimates of Environmental Emissions Due to Electricity Production

Pollutant	Emissions (short tons)
Sulfur dioxide	13.3 million
Nitrogen oxides	7.91 million
Carbon dioxide	2,514 million

How does your answer in part a compare with the estimates in Table 5-8? What are the probable reasons for the discrepancies between your answer from part a and these other estimates?

3. Following is the direct requirements coefficients [A] matrix for the economy in 1997, at the nine-sector level (sector names listed below). The 500-sector version of the economy is available at www.eiolca.net.

	1	2	3	4	5	6	7	8	9
1	0.24	0.001	0.006	0.035	0	0.001	0.005	0.003	0.001
2	0.001	0.198	0.007	0.025	0.045	0	0	0	0.003
3	0.012	0.025	0.001	0.007	0.041	0.008	0.024	0.008	0.022
4	0.173	0.095	0.297	0.346	0.058	0.044	0.008	0.094	0.014
5	0.047	0.075	0.025	0.046	0.166	0.043	0.022	0.033	0.018
6	0.052	0.023	0.083	0.06	0.014	0.022	0.002	0.02	0.002
7	0.069	0.232	0.015	0.018	0.033	0.067	0.169	0.068	0.006
8	0.035	0.04	0.104	0.064	0.122	0.142	0.079	0.15	0.012
9	0.001	0	0.001	0.004	0.003	0.007	0.009	0.007	0.002

      1 Agricultural products
      2 Minerals
      3 Construction
      4 Manufactured products
      5 Transportation, communication, and utilities
      6 Trade
      7 Finance, insurance, and real estate
      8 Services
      9 Other

    a. Find the direct supply chain purchases from all nine sectors from a $100 million increase in agriculture.

b. Find the second-level supply chain purchases from a $100 million increase in agriculture (that is, the supply chain purchases for the purchases found in part a).

c. Find the total supply chain purchases from all nine sectors from a $100 million increase in agriculture. What percentage of the total purchases in each sector are direct? What percentage of the total purchases in each sector are second-level (found in part b)?

PART II

Example Applications

In Part II we have assembled a series of case studies of environmental life cycle assessments. They illustrate use of the EIO-LCA method and answer questions such as:

- Would buying a book from an e-commerce supplier have more or less environmental impact than traveling to a local bookstore?
- What is the relative environmental impact of generating electricity by burning coal?
- What are the environmental impacts of my automobile?

We have selected applications for a variety of goods and services to illustrate the potential range of application of the EIO-LCA model.

The case studies are all based on research published in the peer-reviewed literature. We have updated the impact estimates by using the 1997 benchmark input–output model at www.eiolca.net for each case study. As a result, the numerical estimates here may differ from earlier results in the literature, but the overall conclusions have not changed.

Despite the variation in application areas and scope, several general themes emerge from the case studies:

- Environmental impacts can occur in any phase of a product or process, so focusing on a single phase such as manufacturing can be misleading:
  - In Chapter 11, an examination of the service sectors finds that the supply chain for services has more impact than the service industries themselves. Environmental improvement may best come from better supply chain management.
  - In Chapter 7, we find that reducing the weight of a gasoline tank pays significant dividends in the use phase through reduced fuel consumption and air emissions.

- In Chapter 14, the environmental impact of residences arises substantially from heating, cooling, and electricity. Better design can reduce life cycle impacts and costs.
- New technology can have positive or negative environmental impacts, but a life cycle assessment can help pinpoint opportunities:
  - Nanotechnology has stirred considerable concern for the potential impacts of toxic or uncontrolled artificial particles released into the environment. However, Chapter 8 suggests that better placement of rare metals using nanotechnology in automobile catalytic converters can have substantial environmental benefits.
  - Conversion of coal to methane and transport via pipelines may be a good alternative to congested railroad lines or new electricity transmission lines. Chapter 13 considers several scenarios for the particular case of transporting energy from the Powder River Basin in Wyoming to Dallas, Texas.
- Drawing appropriate analysis boundaries and properly accounting for resources requires considerable care:
  - In Chapter 9, we consider the relative advantages of e-commerce and traditional retailing. Conclusions depend on whether private trips to stores are included or if inventory returns from stores are considered.
  - It is important to include the environmental impacts of fuel combustion for residential heating or running an automobile engine. In using EIO-LCA to estimate the effects of fuels, the purchases from a fuel sector (such as petroleum refineries) includes the impacts of providing the fuel, but not the impacts of burning the fuel itself after purchase. Chapter 6 on automobile impacts and Chapter 14 on residential buildings show how to account for them.
  - Comparison of two alternatives is often easier than performing an overall assessment of a product or process. First, any identical aspects of the alternatives can be ignored. Chapter 10 compares asphalt and reinforced concrete pavements; if the sub-base for both pavements is identical, then the impacts of making the sub-base can be ignored. Second, uncertainties in comparisons may be positively correlated, reducing the relative uncertainty of comparison as described in Chapter 4.

6

A Life Cycle Analysis of a Midsize Passenger Car

The economies of rich nations and the lifestyle of most of their residents are dependent on cars and light trucks—collectively, light-duty vehicles (LDVs). LDVs are gaining the same role in developing nations. They offer us the opportunity to go where we want when we want, subject to congestion, parking, and financial constraints. These vehicles are among our most important personal assets and liabilities, since they are typically the second most expensive asset we own, costing almost $100,000 over the lifetime of the vehicle. While LDVs are an essential part of our lifestyles and economy, the entire life cycle of an automobile, from extraction of raw materials, material production, and vehicle manufacture through vehicle use to end-of-life, is an environmental and public health concern (see Figure 6-1). Manufacturing, operating, maintaining, and disposing of the 210 million LDVs (more than one for every licensed driver) accounts for about 14% of economic activity in the United States, expressed as total commercial energy use and total materials use. Although legislation since the 1960s has eliminated much of the automobile's environmental discharges by reducing tailpipe emissions 90 to 95%, these vehicles continue to contribute significant portions of the carbon monoxide (CO), volatile organic compounds (VOC), and nitrogen oxides (NO_x) emitted in cities; counting discharges of engine coolant, windshield washer fluid, used motor oil, and gasoline, LDVs are responsible for a considerable amount of water pollution. Transportation accounts for 30% of total carbon dioxide (CO_2) emissions from fossil fuel combustion, with just under two-thirds resulting from gasoline consumption in motor vehicles (U.S. EPA 2002). LDVs are also responsible for considerable expenditures and environmental disruption due to construction and repair of highways and parking facilities. Finally, in the United States, LDVs are responsible for approximately 42,000 deaths and four million injuries each year (U.S. DOT 2004).

While progress has been made in recent decades improving the efficiency and lowering tailpipe emissions of regulated pollutants from LDVs, further reducing the environmental effects of these vehicles while preserving their attractiveness will be difficult. For example, the California Air Resources Board focused on tailpipe emissions in requiring zero-emissions vehicles, neglecting the other attributes of battery-powered cars, such as other environmental discharges, cost, consumer acceptance, and performance. The necessity of examining the whole life cycle and all the attributes is demonstrated by the fact that the California Air Resources Board had to rescind its requirement that 2% of new vehicles sold in 1998 and 10% sold in 2003 be zero-emissions vehicles.

If changes in the design of automobiles and associated products are to improve environmental quality, we need to consider the full life cycle of an LDV. It is easy to be deceived about the environmental benefits of a change in vehicle design that reduces the discharges of one aspect or stage of the life cycle but merely transfers them to another stage or medium.

In this chapter, we illustrate the use of the EIO-LCA model to assess the environmental impacts of a typical automobile. In this process, we define different life cycle phases and the various inputs required in each phase. The effects of producing these inputs are estimated from the EIO-LCA model. Air emissions from the automobile itself are estimated based on expected use. The next two chapters consider two automotive components in more detail.

Previous Automobile Life Cycle Assessment Studies

During the past decades, a number of LDV LCA studies have been completed, with the majority considering gasoline-fueled midsize North American automobiles or compact European automobiles. The studies have ranged from those that concentrate on a single resource such as energy or a particular material to comprehensive studies considering all life cycle stages and a large set of inputs and discharges (MacLean and Lave 2003).

The first applications of the EIO-LCA model to evaluate automobiles are by Lave et al. (1995). MacLean and Lave (1998) extend the automobile LCA analysis from manufacture to use for a gasoline-fueled Ford Taurus. Following this application, Lave et al. (2000) further expand their analyses to include alternative-fueled vehicle options such as diesel and compressed natural gas. MacLean and Lave (2003) review a large set of alternative-fueled vehicle LCA studies; almost all employ the SETAC LCA method.

Determining the overall impact on the environment and human health of a LDV requires a comprehensive, quantitative, life cycle approach. Encompassing more than "well-to-wheels," the analyses must include the extraction of all raw materials, fuel production, infrastructure requirements, component manufacture, vehicle manufacture, use, and end-of-life phases of the vehicle.

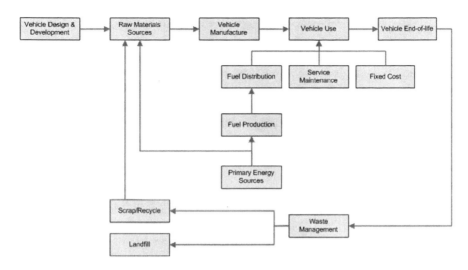

FIGURE 6-1. Simplified Automobile Life Cycle
Source: MacLean and Lave 2003.

Life Cycle Assessment Method

Since the EIO-LCA model is focused on the manufacture and production of products and services throughout the economy, it is possible to formulate the life cycle of a complex product such as an automobile through the use of sectors in the model that approximate the vehicle life cycle stages shown in Figure 6-1.

Boundary of the Analysis

A full LCA of an automobile would include the life cycle stages shown in Figure 6-1. In this analysis, we consider automobile manufacture and, over the vehicle lifetime, purchase of fuel (regular grade gasoline), maintenance and service, and fixed costs (including insurance, license fees, and depreciation). Since the EIO-LCA model does not have a sector that appropriately represents vehicle end-of-life, this phase is not included in this case study. Through the use of the EIO-LCA model the full set of activities throughout the U.S. economy associated with the production of each of the products or services included in the boundary is encompassed in our analysis. The functional unit selected for the study is the vehicle and its entire lifetime of operation.

Vehicle Description

We select a gasoline-fueled sedan, the model year 2002 Ford Taurus LX, a typical midsize domestic spark-ignition port-fuel-injection automobile. This vehicle has been on the market for some time, has significant market share, and is a representative vehicle for this analysis. It has a 3.0 liter 155 hp, V-6 engine with an EPA-rated fuel economy of 20 mpg city, 28 mpg highway, and 23.6 mpg combined city/highway (based on 55% city and 45% highway driving). The curb weight of the vehicle is 3,336 lbs. It is assumed to use U.S. federal conventional gasoline. The manufacturer's suggested retail price (MSRP) with no additional options is $19,035 (2002$) which does not include sales or other taxes, tags, or registration fees.

Application of the EIO-LCA Model

The first step in the life cycle inventory is to match each of the vehicle life cycle stages (components) with an EIO-LCA sector that corresponds to the relevant product or service purchased by the owner throughout the life cycle of an automobile (see Table 6-1). To determine the final demand for each sector, we estimate the average dollar amount spent by a consumer on the product or service over the vehicle lifetime (subtracting taxes and other relevant components) and then convert this value into 1997 dollars (to correspond to the year of the EIO-LCA model) using the implicit price deflator from 2002 to 1997.

Vehicle Manufacture

Vehicle manufacture is represented by the motor vehicle and passenger car bodies sector. This sector is responsible for car body manufacture and assembly of final vehicles. The final demand for this sector is calculated from the base invoice price of $17,697 (2002$). The base invoice is the amount Ford Motor Company charges its dealer for the vehicle, but it may not represent the actual dealer cost, as holdbacks, dealer advertising fund fees, shipping, and charges for gas may be included in the total invoice. To calculate the actual dealer cost (which is here used to approximate the producer price), a holdback of total MSRP is subtracted from the base invoice price (Ford Motor Company 2003), yielding $17,126 (2002$) and using the implicit price deflator results in $16,009 (1997$).

Vehicle Operation

The EIO-LCA model does not have a sector that corresponds to the operation (driving) of the vehicle during its lifetime and therefore we employ supplementary methods to estimate the energy use, air pollutants, and other environmental burden associated with this LC stage. The vehicle lifetime is estimated based on the average annual miles traveled by vehicles and the expected median lifetime for an automobile (16.1 years) in the United States (Davis and Diegel 2002) and is calculated as 193,800 miles.

TABLE 6-1. Automobile Life Cycle Stages, Corresponding EIO-LCA Sectors, and Final Demands

Life cycle stage	EIO-LCA Sector name	EIO-LCA Sector number	Final demand (1997$)
Vehicle manufacture	Automobiles and light truck manufacturing	336110	16,000
Fuel cycle (gasoline)	Petroleum refining	324110	5,700
Maintenance and repair	Automotive repair and maintenance	8111A0	10,000
Fixed costs: insurance only	Insurance carriers	524100	15,000
Vehicle operation	Not applicable	Not applicable	Not applicable

Energy Use

The energy required to operate the automobile over its expected lifetime can be calculated using the following equation:

$$E_{op} = (VMT \times E_{cmb})/MHFE \qquad (6\text{-}1)$$

where E_{op} is the operation energy of the vehicle, VMT is lifetime vehicle miles traveled (193,800 miles), E_{cmb} is the combustion energy of the fuel (regular grade gasoline, 127,000 Btu/gal), and $MHFE$ is the metro-highway fuel efficiency (23.6 mpg). Based on the assumption throughout the study that the vehicle fuel economy remains constant throughout the vehicle lifetime, we calculate the vehicle operational energy use as 1,043 million Btu (1.1 million MJ).

Vehicle Operation Emissions

Greenhouse Gases

$$E_{CO2} = VMT \times MHFE \times C_{content} \times 44/12 \qquad (6\text{-}2)$$

where E_{CO2} is the emissions of CO_2 for the vehicle lifetime in grams, VMT is the lifetime vehicle miles traveled, $C_{content}$ is the grams of carbon per gallon of fuel, and 44/12 is a factor to convert from grams of carbon to grams of CO_2. For the 2002 Taurus, the estimated greenhouse gas emissions for vehicle operation are 73,087 kg CO_2 over the vehicle's lifetime. Note that we do not subtract out the carbon in the fuel that becomes methane or carbon monoxide because of its small magnitude (MacLean and Lave 1998).

Regulated Pollutants. In this study we estimate only on-cycle emissions included in the standard federal test procedure (FTP). We do not include emissions resulting from off-cycle driving or those resulting from malfunctioning emissions control systems. We use a method based on the Tier I certification standards applicable for 2002 automobiles. For simplicity, we assume that the vehicle emissions meet the EPA standard during the vehicle's lifetime. The Federal Exhaust Emission Certification Standard for gasoline vehicles are hydrocarbons (HC) 0.41 g/mile, carbon monoxide (CO) 3.4 g/mile, nitrogen oxides (NO_x) 0.4 g/mile, and particulates 0.08 g/mile. These standard quantities are multiplied by the vehicle lifetime in miles to determine the emissions for the vehicle operation stage.

Fuel Cycle

The production of the vehicle fuel is a key component. Emissions and resource use resulting from the fuel cycle (activities from crude oil exploration and production through refueling of the vehicle) have become even more important as the burdens associated with the vehicle (e.g. exhaust and evaporative emissions) have been lowered.

We approximate the fuel cycle through gasoline production by the input–output sector for petroleum refining. The retail sector, which includes the sale of gasoline from service stations, also includes almost all retail outlets, so it is too aggregate to represent the petroleum industry; therefore this sector is not utilized. To determine the final demand for the petroleum refining sector, we compute the monetary value of gasoline using the producer price per gallon. The producer price is estimated by subtracting taxes (federal and state), distribution and marketing costs, and profits based on data from the Energy Information Administration (EIA 2004). We estimate the Taurus will use 8,212 gallons of gasoline over its lifetime. From the average retail price of $1.35 per gallon, we subtract federal and state tax (31%) and distribution and marketing costs and profits (13%), to get an estimated producer price of $0.76/gallon; the lifetime fuel cost in 1997$ is $5,700.

Automotive Service

Automotive service operations and their suppliers compose a significant portion of the U.S. economy: $49.8 billion in 1993. A major supplier to the industry, the motor vehicle parts and accessories sector, had a total value of shipments for 1992 of $75 billion (which is approximately half of the value of shipments of the motor vehicles and passenger car bodies sector).

Technical differences among vehicles, owner behavior patterns, environmental aspects, and regional requirements mean great variability in parts and fluids replaced as well as replacement prices. Published operating costs are usually based on data from a vehicle's first few years of life (Davis and Diegel 2002), which are lower than those for older vehicles.

Because of the lack of complete data covering vehicle lifetime, we combine several sources to obtain an estimated lifetime service expenditure of $12,580 (1997$) (MacLean and Lave 1998), based on average service for the first 75,000 miles of the vehicle's life. Replacement prices are dealer estimates; the labor rate is the national average; and estimates for auto-refinishing were obtained from industry personnel. Although we expect that the use of dealer prices and labor rates overestimates the total cost of service, there is substantial uncertainty in expenditures on service. For this analysis, a slight change in the cost of service does not have a significant effect on the final results. To avoid double counting the approximately 14% of an insurance premium that goes toward collision repair, this value is subtracted from service costs, yielding an adjusted estimate of $10,494 (1997$). Repairs covered under warranty are conceptually included in the vehicle price. Since warranty repairs compose a small portion of total repairs, and no estimate of the value is available, the amount remains included in service. To analyze these expenditures in the EIO-LCA model, we used the automotive repair and maintenance (excluding car washes) sector.

Fixed Costs

Fixed costs include insurance, license fees, depreciation, and finance charges. The Transportation Energy Data Book (Davis and Diegel 2002) reports fixed costs per year and per 10,000 miles. For a 2002 automobile, the annual fixed costs are $5,764 (2002$). Since depreciation reflects vehicle purchase price, its value ($3,721 in 2002$) is subtracted from fixed costs to avoid double counting, resulting in an annual fixed cost of $2,043 (2002$) or $1,876 (1997$).

The economic impact and total resources consumed for fixed costs are obtained using the insurance carriers sector. Finance charges and license fees are assumed to have few supplier impacts and are not included in the environmental analysis. An estimated insurance cost (2002$) of $1,014 per year is obtained from Davis and Diegel (2002), resulting in a lifetime insurance cost of $16,220 (2002$) or $14,897 (1997$). This assumes that insurance costs stay constant over the vehicle lifetime.

Comparisons of Life Cycle Stages

Economic Impact

Figure 6-2 shows the economic impact (1997$) over the vehicle lifetime resulting from the manufacture and use of the automobile. The economic impact associated with the industry itself (for example, insurance carriers) and that of all suppliers are differentiated. As shown in Figure 6-2, the manufacture of the vehicle causes significant resulting economic impact throughout the economy.

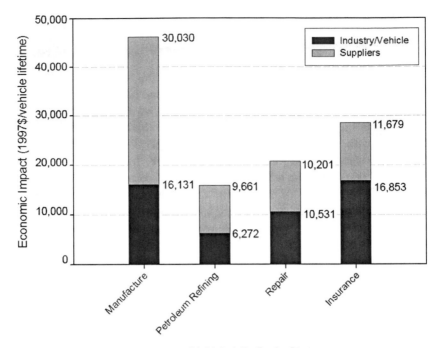

FIGURE 6-2. Economic Impact of the Stages of the Automobile Life Cycle
Note: Does not include fixed costs, with the exception of insurance.

The $16,009 final demand results in a small amount ($122) of additional economic activity within the automobile and light truck manufacturing sector, but the majority of impacts ($30,030) occur within other sectors. This results in a total of $46,161 of economic impact throughout the economy.

Summing the total economic impacts (industry sector and suppliers) for the use stage components (petroleum refining, maintenance, and insurance) results in a total use stage economic impact of $65,197. The use stage is more significant with respect to economic impact than the vehicle manufacture stage. Note that we have not included the fixed costs other than insurance (as they are not represented in the EIO-LCA model). To examine the entire set of life cycle costs of an automobile, these other fixed costs would have to be included.

Energy Use

The operation of the vehicle is by far the most energy intensive component of the life cycle of a gasoline vehicle, responsible for about 75% of total energy use (1,470,000 MJ) when the manufacture and use stages are considered. Including the energy required for petroleum refining raises the use phase to 85% of total energy use. Figure 6-3 shows energy use for each component of the life

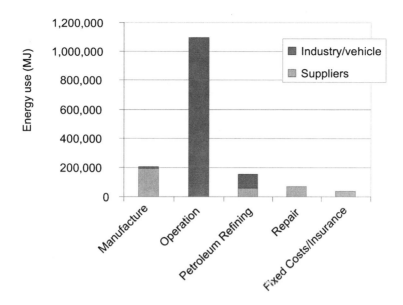

FIGURE 6-3. Energy Use in the Automobile Life Cycle

cycle over the vehicle lifetime. Vehicle manufacture is a distant second to operation, with 138,000 MJ. Only 17,000 MJ (12%) of this value result from the industry (motor vehicles and passenger car bodies), since this is mostly assembly. The remainder is utilized by suppliers. The implication is that materials or components that increase fuel economy are desirable, almost regardless of how energy intensive they are.

The petroleum refining sector rather than its suppliers is responsible for the majority of energy use (60%). The automotive repair and insurance industries use a small proportion of total energy.

Greenhouse Gas Emissions

Figure 6-4 shows the 110,000 kg (110 metric tons) of greenhouse gas emissions (weighted by their global warming potential) over the life cycle of the vehicle. This figure is similar to that of energy use, since the vast majority of energy comes from hydrocarbon fuels.

Conventional Pollutants

As shown in Table 6-2, considerable quantities of conventional pollutants result from the life cycle of the automobile. Vehicle operation results in higher quantities of the pollutant emissions (with the exception of sulfur dioxide) than do

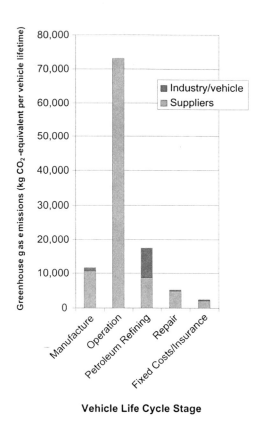

FIGURE 6-4. Greenhouse Gas Emissions in the Vehicle Life Cycle

TABLE 6-2. Conventional Air Pollutant Emissions Resulting from Automobile Life Cycle (Manufacture and Use Stages)

Life cycle component	SO_2	CO	NO_2	VOC	PM_{10}
Manufacture	23	124	23	24	7
Operation	NA	660	78 (NO_x)	79 (HC)	15
Petroleum refining	24	34	14	16	2
Maintenance	11	46	10	13	2
Fixed costs/ insurance	3	14	3	3	1

Notes: All values are in kg over the vehicle lifetime. SO_2: sulfur dioxide. CO: carbon monoxide. NO_2: nitrogen dioxide. VOC: volatile organic compound. PM_{10}: particulate matter 10 microns or less.

the other sectors. As emissions standards become stricter, the operation phase of the vehicle will continue to lessen its impacts on the environment and health. Vehicle manufacture results in the second highest quantities of the emissions. The majority of the 61 kg of SO_2 emissions result from the electric utilities sector.

Conclusions

The automobile sector is a major component of the economy, using large quantities of resources and discharging large amounts of residuals. Knowing the life cycle implications of particular designs and materials is essential for intelligent management and policy decisions. The results of the EIO-LCA model and supplemental methods indicate that driving an automobile uses much more energy and results in higher quantities of greenhouse gas and conventional air pollutant emissions than producing or servicing the vehicle.

7

Comparison of Steel and Plastic Fuel Tank Systems for Automobiles

Over the last two decades there has been a significant movement to make automobile components from lightweight composite materials, driven by increasingly stringent fuel efficiency standards and weight reduction goals. As a result, the percentage of plastic materials in a typical American passenger car has increased from 20.2% of weight in 1976 to 25.8% in 2000 (Joshi 1998). As a part of this continuing trend, traditional steel fuel tanks in automobiles are being replaced with tanks made from lighter plastic. The co-extrusion blow-molding process developed in the late 1980s has alleviated concerns over fuel permeation and safety associated with the early mono-layer plastic tanks. Plastic tanks can now be produced with multiple material layers that prevent fuel permeation and meet automotive evaporative emission standards. It is expected that almost 60% of all new passenger cars and light trucks produced in North America will have fuel tanks made from plastic materials (OSAT 1996).

In this chapter, we compare the life cycle environmental performance of steel and plastic automobile fuel tank systems using the EIO-LCA model. Which is better from an environmental perspective? Our comparison considers both manufacture of the tanks and the vehicle fuel efficiency impacts. We also illustrate a mixed analysis in which some impacts come from the EIO-LCA model and some are measured directly from processes such as tank welding. We compare the traditional steel fuel tank system on the Chevrolet GMT600 line of vans with the new blow-molded, co-extruded, multi-layer, high-density polyethylene (HDPE) plastic tank system that General Motors (GM) has introduced on select models. We chose these two systems as typical of an emerging trend. This chapter draws on earlier studies by Joshi (1998, 2000) and Keoleian et al. (1997), and updates the results using the 1997 EIO-LCA model.

Steel and Plastic Fuel Tank Systems

The GMT600 vehicle line, which includes several Chevrolet passenger and commercial vans, is built on a common General Motors truck platform. GM's passenger G-van uses a 31-gallon steel fuel tank. A 34.5-gallon multi-layer plastic tank is used in the cargo van, which is a modified version of the G-van. They share a common chassis and a front cabin, but the cargo section is fitted with application specific attachments such as ambulance cabins and campers in the modified G-van.

Each fuel tank system consists of three major components: the tank which holds the fuel, straps that secure the tank to the automobile frame, and a shield that serves different purposes in the two systems. The steel tank requires a plastic shield to protect it from damage and corrosion from exposure to humidity, road salt, stones and gravel, etc. The plastic tank, which is inherently more resistant to corrosion and damage, requires a steel heat shield in the GMT600 application. Such a heat shield may not be necessary in all applications. For the purpose of this comparative analysis, we do not include components such as fuel lines, fuel filters, and sending units, which are common to the two systems.

The steel fuel tank is made of plain carbon steel (conforming to American Iron and Steel Institute (AISI) standards 1008 or 1010), with a nickel-zinc coating and a coat of aluminum epoxy paint. The straps are made of hot-dipped galvanized steel with a painted finish. The tank shield is made of HDPE plastic. The plastic fuel tank is a six-layer co-extruded structure. The six layers from the outermost to the innermost, are made of virgin HDPE mixed with carbon black, a regrind layer which incorporates HDPE from flash and scrapped tanks, an adhesive layer, an ethyl vinyl alcohol copolymer permeation barrier, an adhesive layer, and finally a virgin HDPE inner layer. The straps for this tank system are hot-dipped galvanized steel with a polyvinyl chloride coating. The heat shield is made from plain carbon steel.

The life cycle of a fuel tank consists of four main stages as shown in Figure 7-1: fuel tank manufacture, use phase on the vehicle, shredding of auto hulk to recover ferrous scrap, and recycling scrap steel in an electric arc furnace. We develop detailed process descriptions for the manufacturing, use, and end of life disposal/recycling stages. In conducting the LCA of the fuel tank system, we draw a boundary around each of these stages and treat them as hypothetical new commodity sectors, which draw inputs from the economy and produce some desired output and undesired emissions. We estimate the value of inputs and direct environmental burdens at each stage. We assume that the inputs at each stage are well-approximated by their corresponding EIO sectors. The indirect economy-wide and hence life cycle environmental implications are then estimated using the EIO-LCA model. The aggregation of results from these stages provides a comprehensive life cycle inventory.

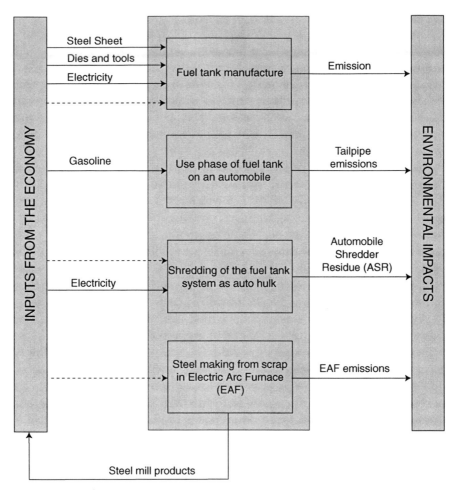

FIGURE 7-1. Life Cycle of an Automobile Fuel Tank System

Life Cycle Assessment of Steel Fuel Tank

Manufacture

The steel tank manufacturing process involves stamping, trimming and piercing of sheet steel, welding, washing, testing, and assembly operations using inputs such as sheet steel, electricity, dies, and lubricants. The estimated value of inputs and the U.S. input–output sectors by which these inputs are approximated are shown in the first part of Table 7-1. We estimate the life cycle environmental burdens of these inputs used in manufacturing by the economy-wide environmental impacts associated with corresponding increases in the final demand for the output of these sectors. Electricity and natural gas are directly used energy sources in the steel tank production process. We consider 73.53 MJ/tank from natural gas use as manufacturing energy, since energy use in electricity generation is already accounted for. Air emissions in steel tank manufacture are mainly from welding operations. Keoleian et al. (1997) report air emissions of 0.2651 g of zinc, chromium, manganese, and nickel, 1.841 g of particulates, and 0.684 g of volatile organic compounds per steel tank manufactured. We include emissions from the burning of 1.29 kg of natural gas for process heat and other requirements. Waterborne emissions in steel tank manufacturing are mainly from tank washing to remove the lubricant. The estimates of water emissions per steel tank based on the treatment plant data are 16.8 g of metals and 170.8 g of oil and grease. These metal emissions are included in the inventory of toxic chemical releases.

Use

The use phase environmental impacts include the life cycle burdens of inputs to the use phase and the direct emissions during use. However, there is no independent use phase for a fuel tank, except as a component of an assembled vehicle. We assume that the fuel tank contributes to vehicle use phase environmental burdens only in terms of additional fuel consumption because of its weight, and ignore possible incremental changes in maintenance services, lubricant and coolant use, tire wear, etc. over the lifetime of the vehicle. Keoleian et al. (1997) estimate the contribution of the steel tank system to vehicle lifetime fuel consumption to be 23.3 gallons, the producer value of which is $16.63 in 1997 dollars. We approximate the life cycle environmental burdens associated with production of gasoline by the economy-wide environmental impacts associated with an increase of $16.63 in the final demand for the output of the "petroleum refining" sector. The life cycle energy associated with the use phase is 3.37 GJ per steel tank, consisting of the heating value of 23.3 gallons of gasoline, and the life cycle energy of 316 MJ associated with the production of gasoline. Keoleian et al. (1997) estimate that the 1996 G-van emits 1969 kg of carbon monoxide, 101.2 kg of hydrocarbons, and 220 kg of nitrogen oxides over a lifetime travel of 110,000 miles. These emissions are allocated to the steel tank in proportion to its contribution to the lifetime vehicle fuel consumption of 6,707 gallons.

Scrap Processing

The scrap produced during steel tank manufacturing and the steel recovered from the auto hulk at the end of vehicle life are used as scrap input into steel production. A total of 21.26 kg of steel scrap per tank enters the shredding process and we assume that 100% of its weight is recovered as processed scrap. Processing a ton of auto hulk consumes about 53.6 kWh (0.193 GJ) of electricity, and $5.90 worth of tools and maintenance service (Sterdis 1997). Motor

TABLE 7-1. Steel Fuel Tank: Inputs for Different Life Cycle Stages, 1997$

Input	EIO sector	Input value ($)
Tank Manufacturing		
Carbon steel sheet	Blast furnaces and steel mill products	27.18
HDPE shield material	Plastics and resins (HDPE shield)	2.46
Stamping, trimming dies	Dies, tools, and machine accessories	3.75
Transportation of finished tanks	Motor freight transportation	1.32
Electricity	Electric utilities	1.06
Transportation of raw materials	Railroad transportation	0.31
Galvanizing and coating	Plating and polishing services	0.32
Natural gas for boilers	Gas distribution	0.22
Packing materials	Paper and paper board containers	0.21
Paints	Paints and allied products	0.16
Bearings and other repairs	Ball and roller bearings	0.14
Detergents for washing tanks	Soaps and detergents	0.02
Lubricants and coolants	Lubricants and greases	0.02
Use Phase		
Gasoline	Petroleum refining	16.63
Disposal: Auto shredding		
Electricity	Electric utility services	0.07
Transportation of hulks & scrap	Motor transportation	0.71
Shredder tools and repairs	Dies, tools, and machine accessories	0.13
Disposal: Steel recycling		
Limestone, Lime, Florspar	Lime	0.10
Refractories	Non-clay refractories	0.08
Electrodes	Carbon black	0.27
Ferroalloys	Electro-metallurgical products	0.08
Electricity	Electric utilities	0.61
Natural gas	Gas distribution	0.07
Maintenance of EAF supplies	Industrial process furnaces and ovens	0.17
Insurance	Insurance carriers	0.07
Recovered steel (credit)		
	Blast furnaces and steel mill products	-5.07

transportation costs per steel tank are estimated to be $0.614 (Keoleian et al. 1997). The estimated (1997) monetary values of these inputs and corresponding EIO sectors are also shown in Table 7-1. The life cycle environmental burdens of these inputs are estimated using the EIO-LCA model. Direct environmental burdens from the shredding operation include energy consumption in shredding (1.13 kWh per tank) and automobile shredder residue (ASR), which is landfilled. It is assumed that the HDPE shield will become ASR and landfilled as hazardous waste.

Steel Scrap Recycling

We assume that all the ferrous scrap recovered from the fuel tank systems is re-melted in an electric arc furnace (EAF) to produce steel mill products. Each steel fuel tank yields 21.26 kg of processed scrap, which can be processed into 20.24 kg of semi-finished steel mill products valued at $5.07. The various inputs required for EAF recycling and the U.S. input–output sectors by which they are approximated are shown in Table 7-1. Estimates of input requirements are based on a report on electric steel making by the Center for Metals Production (CMP 1987). This output of steel mill products is assumed to reduce the final demand for the output of the blast furnaces and steel mills sector by a corresponding amount. The environmental credits for recycled steel are the avoided environmental burdens (estimated by the EIO-LCA model) from $5.07 worth of steel mill products substituted by the recycled steel.

Summary environmental burdens for several environmental impacts over different life cycle stages of the steel tank are shown in Table 7-2.

Life Cycle Assessment of Plastic Fuel Tanks

We analyze the environmental burdens of the plastic fuel tank system over its entire life cycle covering production of input materials, manufacturing, use, and end-of-life management much as we did the steel tank. We estimate inputs and direct environmental burdens at each life cycle stage. We use the EIO-LCA model to calculate the economy-wide environmental burdens from these inputs approximated by their industry sectors. The input requirements at various life cycle stages of the plastic tank and corresponding sectors are shown in Table 7-3.

Manufacture

The first step in the plastic tank manufacturing process is mixing resin with appropriate additives in separate mixing vessels. These mixtures correspond to the six layers of the tank. They are fed through six individual extruders to produce layers just before entering the blow molder. The polymer layers are simultaneously blow-molded to the shape of the tank. The multi-layer tank is then sent to the piercing and machining station. Components such as rollover valves and clips are welded onto the tank, followed by assembly of the sending unit, straps, shield, and fuel lines. The finished tank is then packed, placed on a shipping rack, and sent to the vehicle assembly plant by truck. Table 7-3 shows the estimated monetary value of inputs from different commodity sectors for plastic tank manufacture. The major source of direct emissions in plastic tank manufacturing is the extrusion blow-molding process. We use emission factors for the HDPE blow-molding process from Barlow et al. (1996) to estimate

TABLE 7-2. Summary of Life Cycle Environmental Burdens of Fuel Tanks (per tank)

Environmental impact	Inputs to mfg.	Mfg.	Inputs to use	Use	Inputs to shredding	Shredding	EAF steel making	Credit for EAF steel	Row sum
Steel tank system									
Electricity used (kWh)	39	18	14	0	0.2	1	1	−6	67
Total energy (MJ)	1,100	74	360	3,100	25	4	84	−160	4,500
Conventional air pollutants released (g)	55	6	140	8,000	7	0	34	−77	8,600
Greenhouse gases released (kg CO$_2$ equivalent)	79	4	22	430	2	0	8	−11	530
Toxic releases and transfers (g)	140	0.3	9	0	0.2	0	33	−23	160
Weighted toxic releases and transfers (g)	540	0.2	17	0	1	0	120	−92	580
Plastic tank system									
Electricity used (kWh)	14	23	9	0	0.2	0.8	0.1	−1	47
Total energy (MJ)	500	160	230	2,000	17	3	11	−26	2,900
Conventional air pollutants released (g)	300	5	91	5,100	5	0	4	−12	5,500
Greenhouse gases released (kg CO$_2$ equivalent)	39	4	14	270	2	0	1	−2	330
Toxic releases and transfers (g)	58	0.5	6	0	0.1	0	5	−4	66
Weighted toxic releases and transfers (g)	110	0.2	11	0	0.8	0	19	−15	120

Notes: Inputs to manufacturing (mfg), use, and shredding are calculated from the EIO-LCA 1997 model, whereas manufacturing, use, and shredding impacts are estimated directly from process observations. Credit for electric arc furnace (EAF) steel represents reductions in environmental impacts from replacing new steel with recycled tank steel.

TABLE 7-3. Plastic Fuel Tank: Inputs for Life Cycle Stages, 1997$

Input	EIO sector	Input/tank ($)
Tank Manufacturing		
HDPE, PVC, EVOH	Plastics and resins	9.62
Steel straps and shield	Automotive stampings	4.00
Electricity	Electric utilities	1.71
Glycol and other supplies	Industrial org.& inorg.chemicals	1.31
Natural gas	Gas distribution	0.22
Packing materials	Paper and paper board containers	0.87
Molder spare parts	Special industry machinery parts	0.31
Carbon black	Carbon black	0.14
Adhesive layer material	Adhesives and sealants	0.21
Inputs To Use Phase		
Gasoline	Petroleum Refining	10.67
Inputs To Auto Shredding		
Electricity	Electric utility services	0.05
Transportation of hulks & scrap	Motor transportation	0.49
Shredder tools and repairs	Dies, tools, and machine accessories	0.09
Inputs to Steel Making		
Limestone, lime, florspar	Lime	0.02
Refractories	Non-clay Refractories	0.01
Electrodes	Carbon black	0.01
Ferroalloys	Electro-metallurgical products	0.00
Electricity	Electric utilities	0.10
Natural gas	Gas distribution	0.01
Maintenance of EAF supplies.	Industrial process furnaces and ovens	0.03
Insurance	Insurance carriers	0.01
Recovered steel(credit)		
	Blast furnaces and steel mill products	- 0.81

process emissions during plastic tank manufacturing. We also include emissions from burning natural gas for process heat and other requirements, estimated at 1.0 g of carbon monoxide, 3.25 kg of CO_2, 3.91 g of NO_x, and 0.08 grams of methane per tank.

Use Phase

As in the case of the steel tank, the life cycle impacts of gasoline production and exhaust emissions during vehicle use are allocated to the fuel tank. The lighter plastic tank results in allocated gasoline consumption of 14.95 gallons with producer value $10.67. The G-van fitted with a plastic tank consumes 6,699 gallons of gasoline over its lifetime (110,000 miles), and emits 1967 kg of carbon

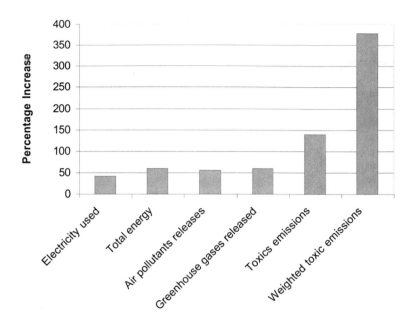

FIGURE 7-2. Steel Tank Impact Relative to Plastic Tanks

monoxide, 101 kg of hydrocarbons, 219.7 kg of NO_x and 58,733 kg of carbon dioxide (Keoleian et al. 1997). These use phase emissions are allocated to the plastic fuel tank based on its weight.

Scrap Recovery

For this analysis, we assume that the whole tank system is shredded without any disassembly of components prior to shredding. That is, the tank system weighing 14.6 kg enters the shredding operation, from which 3.41 kg of steel corresponding to the shield, straps, and prompt scrap are recovered and the balance, 11.2 kg, will be landfilled as automobile shredder residue. The input requirements for the shredding operation and the economy-wide environmental burdens are estimated as before. As in the case of the steel tank, all the ferrous scrap from the plastic fuel tank system is assumed to be processed into semi-finished steel mill products by re-melting scrap in an electric arc furnace. Steel scrap weighing 3.41 kg per tank entering the EAF process yields 3.25 kg of semi-finished steel mill products valued at $0.81. The credit for recycled steel is estimated similarly. A summary of the environmental burdens over the entire life cycle of the plastic fuel tank is also shown in Table 7-2.

Comparison of Steel and Plastic Fuel Tank Life Cycle Environmental Impacts

Table 7-2 and Figure 7-2 provide a summary comparison of the environmental impacts of the two fuel tank systems. It is clear that the total life cycle environmental burdens from the steel fuel tank are larger than those from the plastic fuel tank in all the dimensions shown. The environmental impacts from the steel tank range from nearly 50% higher for electricity use to 350% higher for weighted toxics releases and transfers. The environmental burdens from the steel fuel tank appear to be larger than those from the plastic fuel tank in most of the individual life cycle stages also. Higher gasoline consumption during the use phase, with associated environmental impacts, account for most of the difference. The manufacturing environmental burdens are also higher for the steel tank system. In this case, the lower weight of the plastic tank is important in that the gasoline tanks must be transported throughout the life of the car. Switching to a lighter tank results in fuel savings.

In conclusion, the EIO-LCA analysis suggests that if all other performance parameters are equal, the plastic tank is preferable.

8

Effects of Using Nanotechnology to Stabilize Platinum Group Metal Particles in Automotive Catalysts[1]

In this chapter, the value of using nanotechnology to improve platinum group metal (PGM) stability in automotive emission-control catalysts is evaluated. The study is parametric, in the sense that we hypothesize an improvement that could be possible with nanotechnology and estimate the resulting environmental savings. Large savings suggest that developing the new technology would be beneficial. We estimate savings both with the EIO-LCA model and with a commercial life cycle assessment tool based on detailed process models, providing an opportunity to compare results from these different approaches. Further detail appears in Lloyd et al. (2005).

Before 1966, emissions from automobile internal combustion engines were not controlled. Hydrocarbons (HC), oxides of nitrogen (NO_x), and carbon monoxide (CO) in automotive exhaust generated high levels of photochemical oxidants in many urban areas. The resulting pollution killed forests, damaged crops, ornamental plants, and materials, and caused health effects: eye irritation, respiratory disease, even premature death.

First California and then the U.S. government passed laws requiring 90% reductions in emissions. As expected, the first reductions were easily achieved, but further cuts became increasingly difficult and expensive. The platinum group metals—platinum (Pt), palladium (Pd), and rhodium (Rh)—have been used to make such reductions. In 1975, U.S. automakers introduced two-way catalytic converters, which employed Pt and Pd to convert carbon monoxide and hydrocarbons to less harmful carbon dioxide and water vapor. Three-way catalysts (TWC), introduced in 1981, also employ Rh to convert NO_x to nitrogen gas (N_2) and are still the primary method for controlling automotive emissions (U.S. EPA 1994a, 1994b; Gandhi et al. 2003).

---

[1]This chapter was originally written by Shannon Lloyd and Lester Lave.

In a catalyst, chemical reactions that reduce automotive emissions occur on the surface of PGM particles. Unfortunately, less than half of the available PGM surface area is exposed in new catalysts. To accomplish desired emission reductions, catalytic converters must be larger and contain more PGM than if a higher proportion of surface area were available. Other mechanisms further reduce PGM surface area during vehicle use: heat and vibration cause PGM particles to sinter and agglomerate; catalysts are poisoned by lead, sulfur, and phosphorous in fuel; and catalysts are deactivated by exposure to inorganic elements in lubricating oil or silicon residue in gasoline. One study found that after only 20,000 miles, 95% of available PGM surface area is no longer exposed to the vehicle's exhaust (Oh et al. 1993). As a result, the performance of the catalytic converters degrades over time.

There are currently no acceptable substitutes for PGM in this application, which accounts for roughly 50% of the global PGM market (Johnson Matthey 2004a). Both California and U.S. federal emissions standards are getting more stringent over time, requiring more effective catalysts that can function for most of a vehicle's life. Furthermore, new emissions standards around the globe and an expected surge in vehicle demand in developing countries will increase this market.

Study Boundary

Catalysts containing nanometer-dimensioned particles were one of the first nanotechnologies (Kung 2003). While conventional catalyst design relies on rational planning and lengthy trial-and-error testing, advances in nanotechnology are expected to offer increased understanding of and control over catalyst design and performance (Ying and Sun 1997; Kung 2003; NRC 2003). The ability to control the size, shape, and placement of PGM particles would increase the amount of PGM surface area in new catalysts. Furthermore, the ability to securely anchor particles in the catalyst would help maintain high surface area during vehicle use.

The life cycle diagram in Figure 8-1 illustrates the extraction, production, use, and disposition stages required for using PGM to control automotive emissions. A series of labor and energy-intensive procedures are employed to extract ore containing a few grams of PGM per ton, separate out a valuable metal concentrate, remove PGM from the concentrate, and remove impurities from the metal. Additional processes are required to prepare PGM liquid salts for use in automotive catalysts, apply the catalyst to a substrate, and assemble the catalyst canister. To recover PGM scrap from retired vehicles, the catalyst canister must be salvaged at an automotive scrap yard and sent to a collection center. Several specialized labor-intensive techniques are used to recover a PGM concentrate from the canister. The concentrate is then refined in processes similar to those used to refine virgin PGM.

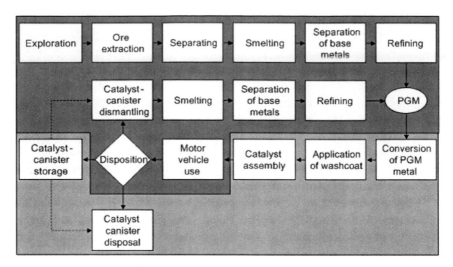

FIGURE 8-1. Life Cycle of Using Platinum Group Metals to Control Automotive Emissions

While it is possible to evaluate each life cycle stage based on current catalyst technology, it is difficult to evaluate each stage based on future technology. Rather than attempt to predict future catalyst composition and processing stages, we can estimate maximum possible reductions in PGM requirements. Hence, the goal of this study is to use EIO-LCA to perform a parametric analysis of the economic and environmental implications associated with producing PGM, which includes the stages shown in the dark area of Figure 8-1.

We estimate the amount of PGM required to meet U.S. vehicle emissions standards for light-duty vehicles, heavy-duty trucks, and nonroad diesel engines based on current catalyst technology. We then estimate the range of PGM that could be saved from potential nanotechnology advances. Finally, we employ EIO-LCA to estimate the direct and life cycle benefits from reducing PGM mining and refining. We model all results through 2030 to parallel the time horizon of EPA's regulatory impact analyses of new emissions standards programs (U.S. EPA 1999, 2000b, 2003). California sales are excluded since they are subject to different regulations.

Estimated Platinum Group Metal Requirements

Total PGM Requirements

PGM content levels vary considerably by manufacturer, vehicle type, model year, and motor vehicle destination. For each motor vehicle class we estimate total PGM requirements based on estimated content levels and motor vehicle

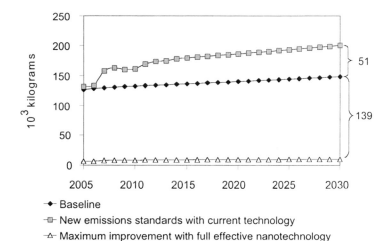

FIGURE 8-2. Estimated Annual PGM Requirements for Vehicles Sold in the United States (excluding California)

sales (U.S. EPA 1997b, 1999, 2000a, 2000b, 2003; Lloyd et al. 2005). As an upper bound PGM savings from nanotechnology advancements, we assume that content levels based on current technology could be reduced by 95% if all available PGM surface area is exposed and maintained throughout a vehicle's life.

Figure 8-2 shows estimated annual PGM requirements (including Pt, Pd, and Rh) for three scenarios. The "baseline" scenario shows expected annual PGM requirements for meeting current emissions standards using baseline loading estimates. PGM requirements increase with increased motor vehicle sales. The "new emissions standards with current technology" scenario shows expected annual PGM requirements for meeting new standards using current technology. PGM requirements increase substantially through 2008 to meet tighter emissions standards, drop slightly between 2009 and 2011 because of learning effects for the diesel vehicle classes, and increase thereafter with increased motor vehicle sales. Compared to the baseline scenario, an additional 51,000 kg of PGM would be required in 2030 to meet the stricter emissions standards. The "maximum improvement with fully effective nanotechnology" scenario applies a 95% reduction over loading levels used in the new standards scenario. Compared to the baseline scenario, an annual PGM savings of 139,000 kg would be realized in 2030 while still meeting stricter standards.

While the baseline and new emissions standards scenarios provide expected PGM use for specified emissions standards and technology, the nanotechnology scenario provides a hypothetical performance improvement for a fully effective deployment of nanotechnology. Since catalyst technology will improve over time, the new emissions standards scenario can be viewed as a lower performance bound. Since a fully effective deployment is unlikely to be realized, the nanotechnology scenario is viewed as an upper performance bound. Hence, PGM demand is likely to fall between the new standards and nanotechnology scenarios.

Recycled PGM Use

Retired automobiles are the primary source of secondary PGM for automotive catalysts. However, the economic viability of recycling PGM has been limited by the complexity of collecting catalysts and the amount of labor required to recover PGM. The average recycling rates for Pt, Pd, and Rh are estimated to be 54%, 61%, and 40% (Lloyd et al. 2005). Secondary PGM makes up approximately 16% of PGM used in current automotive catalysts (Johnson Matthey 2004a).

Recycled and virgin PGM prices are equal under current market conditions (TIAX LLC 2003). Since the EIO-LCA model estimates economic and environmental impact based on economic purchases, this implies that aggregate implications of purchasing virgin and recycled PGM are the same. Therefore, it is not necessary to determine the amount of PGM requirements that will be met with recycled content.

Environmental Impacts using EIO-LCA

We use the "primary nonferrous metal, except copper and aluminum" sector (sector 331419), which includes primary PGM refining. For each year, we estimate economic activity associated with purchasing PGM for motor vehicles. We use the 1997 average market price for Pd, $5.92/g (Johnson Matthey 2004b). To adjust for high price volatility, we use the average 1997 adjusted market price from 1992 through 2002 for Pt, $13.85/g, and Rh, $32.97/g. Assuming effects occur in the same year vehicles are sold, we input total PGM purchases for each scenario into the primary nonferrous metals sector to estimate expected energy use and environmental burden.

We estimate expected changes in each effect from meeting new standards with current technology and with a fully effective deployment of nanotechnology by calculating the difference between each of these scenarios and the baseline scenario. Table 8-1 summarizes expected changes for 2005 and 2030 using the EIO-LCA model. A negative result indicates a reduced environmental effect. For example, producing additional PGM to meet new emissions standards with current technology would require an additional 12,700 TJ of energy in 2030. However, a fully effective deployment of nanotechnology would enable manufacturers to meet new standards using less PGM, saving 24,100 TJ of energy in 2030.

TABLE 8-1. Environmental Impacts from Producing Platinum Group Metal to Meet New Emissions Standards, Relative to the Baseline Case of No New Standards

	Using current technology		Fully effective deployment of nanotechnology	
	2005	2030	2005	2030
Energy used (terajoules)	1,000	13,000	−19,000	−22,000
Fuels used (terajoules)	910	11,000	−17,000	−20,000
Electricity used (million kWh)	100	1,300	−1,900	−2,200
Conventional pollutants (million kg)	2.7	33	−50	−58
Greenhouse gases (million kg CO_2 equivalent)	94	1,200	−1,800	−2,000
Toxic releases and transfers (million kg)	4.0	50	−76	−87

Comparing EIO-LCA to Other LCA Model Results

GaBi Process-Based LCA Model

Given the high level of uncertainty associated with life cycle modeling, it is often useful to compare results across models. Here, we compare the results using the EIO-LCA model to those using GaBi LCA software. The GaBi software system, developed by the University of Stuttgart in cooperation with PE Product Engineering GmbH, is a process-based LCA model (SETAC 1993; ISO 1997; GaBi 2004). A noble metal extension database for the current version, GaBi 4, includes life cycle inventories for producing virgin Pt, Pd, and Rh. These "cradle to gate" inventories estimate total required inputs and resulting environmental burdens from mining to obtaining pure metal. The data sets are based on input from industry, technical, and patent literature, and on other sources.

Recycled PGM Use

Where the EIO-LCA model derives environmental burden based on economic purchases, the GaBi model uses the mass of materials consumed. Therefore, it is necessary to determine the amount of PGM requirements that will be met with recycled content.

For the baseline and new emissions standards scenarios, we estimated expected virgin and recycled PGM use based on expected PGM availability from retired motor vehicles and historical recycling practices (Lloyd et al. 2005). While recycling is influenced by many factors, such as market price, recovery capacity, and amount of PGM in catalysts, we estimate future recycled PGM use by assuming constant rates of recycling secondary PGM.

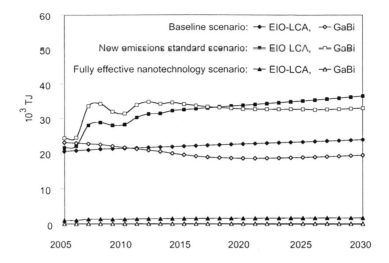

FIGURE 8-3. Estimated Annual Energy Required to Produce Platinum Group Metals with EIO-LCA and a Process Model (GaBi) for Three Scenarios

It is impractical to estimate expected recycled PGM use in the nanotechnology scenario since it estimates maximum possible PGM savings rather than expected use over time. Realistically, performance improvements would take a long time to be realized and would occur incrementally rather than in a dramatic leap. Furthermore, such low PGM content in catalysts may make recovery impractical. We maintain an upper bound performance estimate by assuming complete virgin PGM use in the nanotechnology scenario. Whether or not this is practical depends on when and to what extent performance improvements are realized.

GaBi's noble metal database does not provide inventories for recycled PGM. However, Amatayakul's recent (1999) life cycle assessment of catalytic converters compiles data for several environmental effects associated with producing both virgin and recycled PGM. Amatayakul obtains process information from a primary producer of PGM in South Africa and uses economic information to allocate environmental effects to Pt, Pd, and Rh. The most complete inventory, energy use, indicates that 93% less energy is required to produce recycled PGM (93.8% less for Pt, 83.1% less for Pd, and 94.1% less for Rh). Lacking data for other inputs or environmental burdens, we apply the energy-specific comparison across the GaBi inventory to estimate effects from using recycled PGM.

Comparison between the EIO-LCA and Process Model Results

Figure 8-3 graphs the estimated energy that would be required each year to produce PGM for motor vehicles sold in the United States using both the EIO-LCA and process models. The crossover between the baseline and new emissions standards scenarios occurs because of the different methods of accounting for recycled PGM use. The EIO-LCA results increase linearly with total PGM use since we used the same price for all PGM requirements. This implies that aggregate implications of purchasing virgin and recycled PGM are the same. In contrast, our adjustment to GaBi's noble metal inventory results in much lower effects for producing recycled PGM. Thus, with a higher percentage of recycled PGM use, total effects decrease even though total PGM requirements increase.

Conclusions

Results using EIO-LCA and the process based GaBi models are comparable, providing reasonable first approximations of life cycle effects from producing PGM.

For regulations aimed at reducing environmental burden, life cycle analysis can be used to estimate life cycle costs and benefits of utilizing technologies to comply with standards. In the emissions abatement programs considered here, vehicle emissions reductions offer large environmental benefits. However, a more detailed analysis is required to evaluate life cycle costs associated with all effects from producing PGM, as well as other emission control components. Better technology predictions and life cycle-based benefit–cost analysis could help design emissions programs and phase-in schedules that optimize environmental benefits.

Dramatic resource and environmental burden savings could be realized from reducing PGM in automotive catalysts while holding performance constant. The small amounts of PGM in ore mean that substantial quantities of rock must be mined, crushed, and processed in order to produce the few grams used in an automotive exhaust catalyst. The resulting expense and environmental damage provide a powerful incentive to reduce the amount of PGM in catalysts. Furthermore, similar design and synthesis processes are used to construct catalysts used in other applications, resulting in inefficient material use. The life cycle environmental benefits associated with advancing catalyst technology to overcome current design and synthesis inefficiencies are far-reaching.

9

E-Commerce, Book Publishing, and Retail Logistics

Use of the Internet for shopping (Business-to-Consumer or B2C retailing) is increasing steadily. In 1999, only 0.7% of retail sales were via the Internet (U.S. DOC 2004). By 2004, the percentage was 1.9%, with overall sales of $15.5 billion in the first quarter alone. It is tempting to assume that sales on the Internet are beneficial to the environment; emissions from vehicles driven to shopping malls can be avoided, retail space can be reduced, and inventories and waste can be avoided.

However, a product ordered online may be shipped partially by air freight across the country and requires local truck delivery. It is likely to be packaged individually, and the packaging may not be reused. The adverse impacts on the environment of such transportation can be significant, and the net effect of different logistics systems is not obvious.

Book publishing is an excellent industry to study when assessing the environmental impacts of e-commerce. Books are regularly purchased online as well as in retail stores. The high number of books produced but not sold also makes the publishing industry an interesting case study. After sales have peaked, these extras are discarded, recycled, or sold to a discount bookstore. Selling books by e-commerce allows for lower inventories (since there is only one inventory point) and fewer extras, thus reaping environmental benefits due to avoided warehousing and book paper production.

This chapter compares just two life cycle stages. We assume that the use phase of books (that is, reading the book) is identical with either e-commerce or traditional retailing. We ignore any differences in leisure pleasures that may result from purchasing the book, even though buying it at a bookstore may enhance the reader's satisfaction. As a result, we can focus upon the logistics of moving a book from a central publisher's warehouse to a consumer. This analysis requires some side calculations for items such as emissions from private vehicles that are not included in the EIO-LCA model. Also, the number of returned books (or extras) must be considered, so impacts due to the production of extra books and of packaging materials are within the boundaries of the analysis. We will leave to the reader the opportunity for comparing new book technologies, such as on-demand local printing or use of e-books.

Comparison Framework and Analysis Boundaries

Two generic models of logistics networks will be considered in this case study (Matthews et al. 2001). First, traditional retailing involves selling a book through a "brick-and-mortar" retailer (such as a mall bookstore). In this method, the book is shipped from the publisher through various distributors and warehouses and finally to the retail outlet. The customer then purchases the book at the retail store and brings it home. Second, the e-commerce model involves shipping the book from the publisher to a single warehouse by truck and then air freighting to a regional hub, from which the book is delivered by truck to the customer.

The monetary costs incurred in each model will be evaluated first. The calculations are based on the comparative costs involved in selling a million dollars worth (at production) of hardcover books, or roughly 286,000 books at an assumed production cost of $3.50 each. We assume each book is $9 \times 2.25 \times 6.25$ inches in size and weighs 2.4 pounds. As the issue of extras is especially significant for bestsellers because of the extra volume of books printed, our calculations will focus on the costs associated with bestsellers. Following this, the environmental impacts of each of the logistics models can be estimated.

Traditional Retailing

The traditional method of retail, where books are sold through retail stores, can be modeled as a series of transport links among organizations and facilities as shown in Figure 9-1.

Books are transported from the printer to a national warehouse and then shipped again to a regional warehouse. From the regional warehouse, they are transported to a retail store, and a customer purchases a book and takes it home. In addition there is a return link for unsold copies, as roughly 35% of bestsellers are not sold (*Publishers Weekly* 1997). An assumption of our model for this method is that all transportation is carried out by truck in the traditional distribution network. We assume the distance between all destinations (for example, warehouses and stores) is separated into segments of 500 miles. This allows the model to be easily adjusted for differing distances. The average consumer lives roughly 10 miles away from a bookstore. However, as consumers tend to buy more than one item at a bookstore (or as part of a larger

FIGURE 9-1. Traditional Book Publishing Logistics Chain

shopping trip), only a round-trip distance of 5 miles was allocated for the round-trip distance to the bookstore.

We assume that 35% more copies are printed than sold due to traditional retailing methods (or a total of 386,000 books). All of these books are transported in boxes of 10 to bookstores through the network in Figure 9-1. Assuming that each empty box is 20 x 16 x 16 inches and weighs 2 pounds, the cost of each box is $1.33. Thus the total cost of the packaging used in traditional retail is roughly $51,000.

The environmental effects of the automotive trips made by consumers to bookstores to purchase books must also be taken into account. Taking the fuel economy of a passenger car to be 22.5 mpg, and the fuel economy of a light truck to be 15.3 mpg, we can calculate that the energy required per mile for a passenger car is 5.8 MJ/mile and for a light truck is 8.6 MJ/mile. A weighted average of the environmental impacts caused by passenger cars and light trucks can be taken into account, given that the percentage of light trucks in the passenger fleet is approximately 35%. The environmental impacts of an average trip to the bookstore are shown in Table 9-1.

Returns of unsold books from retailers in the traditional model are an important issue. Shipping of returns involves an additional truck leg, which we again assume to be 500 miles. We ignore returns from customers after purchases; we assume they would involve similar personal trips for both traditional and e-commerce retailing.

TABLE 9-1. Environmental Impacts of Round-trips to Bookstores in Passenger Vehicles

Type of environmental impact	Impact/mile (passenger car)	Impact/mile (light truck)	Impact for 5-mile round trip (passenger car)	Impact for 5-mile round trip (light truck)	Total impact for 286,000 trips (65% cars, 35% trucks)
Energy use	5.8 MJ/mile	8.6 MJ/mile	29 MJ	43 MJ	9.7 TJ
Hydrocarbons	2.9 g/mile	3.7 g/mile	15 g	19 g	4,600 kg
Carbon monoxide	22 g/mile	29 g/mile	110 g	150 g	35,000 kg
Nitrogen oxides	1.5 g/mile	1.9 g/mile	7.5 g	9.5 g	2,400 kg
Carbon dioxide	360 g/mile	540 g/mile	1,800 g	2,700 g	610,000 kg

Source: U.S. EPA annual emissions estimates (U.S. EPA 1994a).

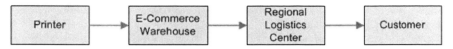

FIGURE 9-2. E-Commerce Book Retailing Logistics

E-Commerce Retailing Logistics

We assume that the e-commerce method of selling a book (where a book is marketed and sold online) has fewer links but involves air freight from the e-commerce warehouse to a regional logistics center (Figure 9-2). We also assume that this warehouse is located near an air hub of a major carrier (for example, UPS or FedEx), so transfer from warehouse to the carrier is not included. As not all orders are shipped by air, this assumption is intended to represent a worst-case scenario for analysis.

The books are shipped from the printer to the company's major distribution warehouse via truck; we assume 500 miles for this link. The books are then air freighted to a regional center (again assuming the same distance) from which the books are delivered by local courier truck to the customer's residence.

The packaging used in e-commerce tends to be corrugated cardboard boxes. Assuming a box size of $12 \times 9 \times 4.5$ inches, a weight of 0.7 pounds, the cost of each box to be $0.41 and that the books are packaged individually, we can calculate the cost of individually packaging $1 million worth of books as $117,000. We assume no extra printing or returns in this model. However, the cost of the bulk packaging of 286,000 books—$38,000—also needs to be included, for a total of $155,000.

Comparative Costs of Traditional and E-Commerce Logistics

Now we compare the different categories of costs for the two generic logistics systems for the sale of $1 million of books. We calculate approximate costs, without including small categories of costs or items such as external congestion costs. Selling $1 million of books in the traditional model requires 386,000 to be produced and shipped given the 35% return rate. The total weight of shipments in the traditional model is 501 short tons, including 463 short tons of books and 38 short tons of bulk packaging. A base production of $1 million of bestseller books in the e-commerce (no returns) model requires only 286,000 books to be shipped; this means a total of 372 tons in bulk (including 343 tons of books and 29 tons of packaging) and a total of 443 tons individually. A comparison of these costs is shown in Table 9-2. We present estimates for two traditional models—with and without extras. We use the 35% return rate to scale up costs.

TABLE 9-2. Comparative Estimated Costs of Logistics and Returns for Traditional versus E-Commerce Book Retailing

| | *Traditional retailing* | | | *E-Commerce retailing* | |
| | | No returns ($1,000) | 35%* Returns ($1,000) | | ($1,000) |
Item	*Calculations*			*Calculations*	
Packaging	$1.33 x 286,000 books/10 books per box	38	51*	($1.33 x 286,000 books /10 books per box) + ($0.41 x 286,000 books)	60
Bulk truck shipments to warehouse	3 trips x 500 miles per trip of 338 metric tons (501 short tons) at $0.26/ton-mile	140	200*	One 500-mile shipment of 338 metric tons (371 short tons)	48
Air freight	None	0	0	One 500-mile trip of 403 tons (443 short tons) at $0.80/ ton-mile (*Publisher's Weekly* 1997)	180
Local delivery/ pickup	Allocate 5 miles at $0.33/mile for 286,000 book pickups	470	470	Local delivery charge of $1.50 for 286,000 books	440
Retailing overhead cost	12% of revenue with average $15/book for 286,000 books	520	700*	4% of revenue with average $15/book (Uline 2001) for 286,000 books	170
Return shipping from retailer	500 miles of 35% returns (100,000 books x 10 books/box x $0.26/ton-mile	0	17		
Return production cost	$3.50 of 100,000 books	0	350		
Total without returns and without private auto		700	940		990
Total without private auto but with returns		700	1,300		990
Total without returns but with private auto		1,200	1,400		990
Total with returns and private auto		1,200	1,800		990

* Some estimates for traditional model with returns were found by multiplying the traditional model without returns by 1.35

Our results indicate that the fraction of returns is critical in assessing relative overall costs. With a zero return rate, the traditional system has a slightly higher overall cost than e-commerce but can provide immediate service to customers. But generally a certain proportion of the books published will remain unsold, and will be either returned to the publisher to be recycled or sold to discount stores. Assuming the average return rate for bestsellers of 35%, our estimate of e-commerce retailing costs is far lower than the traditional system.

TABLE 9-3. Comparison of Costs for Models of Overhead Operating of Traditional Versus Online Bookstores

	Traditional book superstore	*Online bookstore*
Titles per store	175,000	2,500,000
Occupancy cost (% of revenues)	12%	<4%
Revenue per operating employee	$100,000	$300,000
Inventory turns	2-3×	40-60×
Sales per square foot	$250	$2,000
Rent per square foot	$20	$8

Source: Kellogg 1998.

General booksellers have a lower overall average return rate of 11.2%, while specialty booksellers have an average return rate of 6.4% (ABA 2000).

Several items are not included in these retail and logistics costs that affect the benefits and marketing effectiveness of the two retailing modes. First, our estimates do not include any costs associated with stock-outs in the traditional system; the e-commerce model places books not immediately available on back-order for eventual delivery. Second, there are benefits associated with being able to peruse and purchase books in person. Third, online booksellers may have a wider selection than conventional bookstores.

The personal (but not corporate) costs associated with personal automobile travel are also an important factor in the relative costs of the two delivery systems. The cost estimates above do not include any time cost associated with driving, on the assumption that shopping trips may be pleasurable.

A final important factor affecting the relative costs is the relative efficiencies of the overhead operations of the two systems. Table 9-3 gives one comparison from the literature of the difference between the conventional and online retail operations.

Comparative Environmental Impacts

Turning to environmental implications, the e-commerce logistics systems involve more reliance upon air freight service than truck or rail modes. Table 9-4 shows some supply chain environmental effects from $1 million of trucking, air freight, and book publishing taken from the EIO-LCA 1997 model. Combining the data from Tables 9-1, 9-2, and 9-4, Tables 9-5 and 9-6 show the use of energy, emissions of conventional air pollutants, and greenhouse gas emissions for the trucking, air freight, packaging, fuel production, and book production for the retail models described earlier. Conventional air pollutants include sulfur dioxide, carbon monoxide, nitrogen dioxide, volatile organic compounds, lead particulate emissions, and particulate matter (less than 10 microns in diameter). These emissions data are combined with the cost esti-

TABLE 9-4. Some Effects of $1M of Trucking, Air freight, and Book Publishing Production

Effect	Trucking	Air freight	Book production	Paperboard containers and boxes	Fuel production
Energy (TJ)	10	21	9	14	26
Conventional air pollutants (mt)	150	13	13	19	16
Greenhouse gas emissions (CO_2 equivalents, mt)	910	1,900	700	1,100	3,100

TABLE 9-5. Comparative Effects of Trucking, Air freight, and Returns Book Production for Traditional Retailing (with and without returns)

		Energy (TJ)	Conventional air pollutants (mt)[a]	Greenhouse gas emissions (CO_2 equivalents, mt)
Traditional retail (with 35% returns)	Trucking (inc. returns)	0.195(10) + 0.017(10) =2.2	0.195(150) + 0.017(150) = 32	0.195(913) + 0.017(913) = 194
	Production	1.35(9)=11.6	1.35(13) = 17.8	1.35(700) = 945
	Packaging	0.051(14)=0.7	0.051(19) = 1.0	0.051(1142) = 59.
	Passenger trips	9.7	4.55 + 35 + 2.35 = 42	611
	Passenger fuel production	0.0644(26) = 1.7	0.0644(16) = 1.0	0.0644(3066) = 197
	Total	26	94	2003
Traditional retail (no returns)	Trucking	0.144(10) = 1.5	0.144(150) = 22	0.144(913) = 132
	Production	1(9)=9	1(13) = 13	1(700) = 700
	Packaging	0.038(14)=0.5	0.038(19) = 0.7	0.038(1142) = 43.
	Passenger trips	9.7	4.55 + 35 + 2.35 = 42	611
	Passenger fuel production	0.0644(26) = 1.7	0.0644(16) = 1.0	0.0644(3066) = 197
	Total	22	78	1682

a. For passenger trips, this figure includes only carbon monoxide, nitrogen oxides, and hydrocarbons. For all other categories, the figure includes carbon monoxide, nitrogen dioxide, sulphur dioxide, volatile organic compounds, lead, and PM_{10}.

mates to determine estimated environmental effects in Table 9-7.

In order to quantify the environmental impacts associated with the production of the fuel used in passenger vehicles, a producer price of $0.90/gallon was assumed for our calculations. This figure was then combined with the values for the fuel efficiencies of passenger cars and light trucks of 22.5 mpg and 15.3 mpg respectively to arrive at the dollar amount of fuel used for passenger

TABLE 9-6. Effects of Trucking, Air Freight, and Returns Book Production for E-Commerce Retailing

	Energy (TJ)	*Conventional air pollutants (mt)*	*Greenhouse gas emissions (CO_2 equivalents, mt, two significant digits)*
E-commerce retail			
Trucking	$0.048 \times 10 = 0.5$	$0.048 \times 150 = 7.2$	$0.048 \times 913 = 44$
Air freight	$0.177 \times 21 = 3.7$	$0.177 \times 13 = 2.3$	$0.177 \times 1{,}910 = 338$
Production	$1 \times 9 = 9$	$1 \times 13 = 13$	$1 \times 125 = 125$
Packaging	$0.155 \times 14 = 2.2$	$0.155 \times 19 = 2.9$	$0.155 \times 1{,}142 = 177$
Delivery trips	$0.440 \times 10 = 4.4$	$0.440 \times 150 = 66$	$0.440 \times 913 = 402$
Total	20	91	1,086

TABLE 9-7. Relative Effects of Retail Delivery Methods

	Energy (TJ)	*Conventional air pollutants (mt)*	*Greenhouse gas emissions (CO_2 equivalents, mt)*
Difference between traditional with returns and e-commerce	7	4	352
% Difference	27	4	18
Difference between traditional without returns and e-commerce	3	−12	31
% Difference	14	−15	2

trips to the bookstores. Using a fleet composition of 65% passenger cars and 35% light trucks, the dollar cost of fuel for one round trip to the bookstore is $0.225. For 286,000 trips to the bookstore, the monetary cost of the fuel used is $64,350.

Our results indicate significant differences between the retail fulfillment modes, with e-commerce having less of an environmental impact in all categories compared to the traditional model with returns. The comparison between e-commerce and the traditional model without returns is less clear.

Overall, emissions from passenger vehicle trips (including fuel production) contribute significantly to the environmental impacts. By eliminating these trips, emissions of greenhouse gases and conventional air pollutants are significantly reduced in the e-commerce model. However, the increased air freight and packaging of the e-commerce system reduce much of the benefits from reduced passenger trips. It can also be seen that the environmental savings due to the omission of production and transportation of the extras are significant and again help to offset the environmental impacts caused by air freight. Table 9-8 summarizes impacts per book sold.

TABLE 9-8. Effects of Traditional and E-Commerce Logistics, per Book

	Traditional with returns	Traditional no returns	E-Commerce
Energy (MJ)	90	77	68
Conventional air pollutants (g)	330	270	320
RCRA hazardous waste (g)	650	480	560
Greenhouse gas emissions (CO_2 equiv, g)	7,000	5,900	5,800

As seen in Tables 9-7 and 9-8, the e-commerce impacts lie roughly between the zero and 35% return traditional models. For energy use and greenhouse gas emissions, e-commerce has less impact than the traditional retailing model even with no returns. Thus, the e-commerce model is at worst comparable to the traditional model, and under normal conditions superior.

As noted above, this chapter assumes that all shipping of e-commerce book orders is done by air freight (the worst case). However, many orders are shipped exclusively by truck. This means that the actual effects from e-commerce delivery are generally lower. This makes e-commerce even more competitive when comparing energy and environmental effects.

Conclusions

We have analyzed a generic scenario for traditional versus e-commerce retailing of a single commodity, best-selling books. Our analytical approach can be adjusted for different assumptions about shipping distances, return rates, or shopping allocations. By altering these critical parameters, e-commerce can be found to be more or less costly than the traditional system. Nevertheless, our base analysis case suggests that e-commerce sales have a cost advantage and environmental benefits.

10

Construction Materials for Roads and Bridges

The rate of industrial development over the past century has been remarkable. The world's industrial production has increased a hundredfold, while population has nearly quadrupled. Our social infrastructure has likewise expanded, with continuing construction and maintenance of buildings, roads, and other facilities. Entirely new types of infrastructure have appeared and are being built, usually associated with new technologies such as air transportation and telecommunications.

Materials for roads and bridges (asphalt, concrete, and steel) constitute a large fraction of construction materials use, which in turn account for about 80% of all materials use in the United States (Horvath and Hendrickson 1998a, 1998b). In many applications, several materials are cost-competitive. Major bridges are often designed and bid in reinforced concrete and in steel, with the final selection based upon the overall cost. As environmental quality becomes more important to society, the environmental burdens of construction in general and construction materials in particular need to be assessed, analyzed, and reduced (Horvath 2004).

This chapter estimates some of the life cycle impacts of roads and bridges, and the associated comparative design and materials issues. We focus on production of the material inputs to the facilities, as the construction impacts are relatively low compared to the material inputs and are similar for the different materials. In pavement applications, for initial cost, an equivalent design appears to have lower energy demand and global warming potential when reinforced concrete is used instead of asphalt. However, annualized impacts may result in more comparable environmental assessments. For bridge girder designs, reinforced concrete appears to be a better environmental choice than steel. End-of-life options that involve recycling of asphalt and concrete and reuse or recycling of steel may contribute to lower overall environmental impacts of construction.

Life Cycle Inventory Assessment of Asphalt and Concrete Pavement Material Manufacturing

We compare newly constructed one kilometer-long asphalt and cement concrete pavement sections that represent equivalent designs and have the same functionality (Horvath and Hendrickson 1998a). The designs are based on the guidelines of the American Association of State Highway and Transportation Officials (AASHTO 1972). The pavement cross-sections are 720 cm wide and sit on 15 cm of high-quality cement-treated soil sub-base, and are typical of heavily traveled two-lane U.S. highways designed for 10 or more years of use. The concrete pavement section is continuously reinforced (CRCP) with steel bars, and is 22 cm thick. The steel content of the CRCP section is 78,066 kg, and is estimated to cost $23,420 in 1997. The asphalt pavement is 30 cm thick, and a 1 km-long section uses 5,018 metric tons of asphalt paving material. A similar CRCP section requires 3,680 metric tons of concrete. The materials cost for the asphalt pavement section is estimated to be $145,500, whereas the CRCP is $130,100 ($106,700 for the concrete and $23,400 for the steel). For the asphalt pavement analysis, the EIO-LCA asphalt paving mixture and block manufacturing sector (324121) was used. For the concrete content of the pavement, the ready-mix concrete manufacturing sector (327320), and for the steel reinforcement, the iron and steel mills sector (331111) were analyzed using 1997 data. Only the environmental effects of the manufacturing of pavement surface materials were analyzed since the road sub-base is the same for both pavements. The transportation and construction stage environmental burdens were assumed to be comparable.

The price of pavement materials is a source of considerable uncertainty in our calculations. Pavement material prices can vary substantially from place to place, over the course of a year, and with respect to the quantities purchased. We use national average prices for 1997, but the actual price for a particular project may be different.

Table 10-1 shows some environmental effects associated with the asphalt and concrete pavement example. The total energy use is larger for asphalt. The global warming potential is also higher for asphalt, reflecting the higher energy input. Sulfur dioxide, nitrogen oxide, and volatile organic compound (VOC) emissions are roughly comparable, whereas particulate matter emissions are higher for asphalt.

We have previously conducted a similar analysis with 1992 data (Horvath and Hendrickson 1998a). The earlier study did not include global warming potential, but accounted for some other environmental burdens such as the use of ores and emissions of toxic substances. For the same set of environmental metrics found in Table 10-1, the 1992 results differed mainly in SO_2 and VOC emissions (higher for the concrete option) and the energy use analysis showed a less substantial difference between the two materials.

TABLE 10-1. Environmental Impacts Associated with Asphalt and Steel-Reinforced Concrete Manufacturing for One Kilometer of Pavement

Environmental effects	Unit	Asphalt	Concrete and steel	Ratio A:C
Total energy	terajoule	11	2.9	3.8
Global warming potential	mt CO_2 equivalent	960	290	3.3
Sulfur dioxide (SO_2)	metric ton	0.7	0.8	0.9
Nitrogen oxides (NO_x)	metric ton	0.7	0.9	0.8
Volatile organic compounds (VOC)	metric ton	0.6	0.7	0.9
Particulate matter (PM_{10})	metric ton	0.4	0.2	2.0

End-of-life Options for Pavement Materials

The recycling of both asphalt and concrete pavements is thought to save energy and resources. The reclaimed materials are typically reused on or near a site, or stored at a nearby mixing plant, with relatively little transportation involved (Horvath and Hendrickson 1998a). The recycling of steel reinforcing bars in concrete pavements has been problematic since substantial labor is typically involved in separating the bars. Newer concrete crushers have been able to separate steel reinforcing bars after the crushing process.

Asphalt. According to a survey of 29 state highway agencies (U.S. DOT 1993), approximately 80% of the reclaimed asphalt pavement, around 100 million tons per year, gets recycled into highway applications.

Concrete. Only about 3 million metric tons of concrete are recycled annually (U.S. DOT 1993), even though recycled concrete can be used in several applications such as road base, embankments, or new pavements. Recycled concrete amounts could also be significantly underestimated. Also, concrete pavements are often left in place after they become structurally or functionally obsolete to serve as a road base, and are overlaid with a new asphalt course.

Discussion

The above summary compares the environmental effects of materials extraction and manufacturing, without taking into account the other life cycle stages or different service lives of the pavements. Comparing the annualized environmental burdens would be more helpful. However, it is challenging to determine the actual or average service life of pavements because they vary from one region to the next because of local factors such as climatic effects, traffic volumes, construction and material quality, and construction practices. According to Marland and Weinberg (1988), the interstate highways "are designed to last 20 years before major repairs are necessary, but many do not." Throughout their service lives, pavements are repaired many times, whenever a pavement distress occurs. Therefore, maintenance requirements are important to the life cycle assessment, and the overall environmental performance of the two pavement types depends on how much repair is needed for one pavement type or the other. One material may have capital and operating cost advantages in a specific geographic area. With regular maintenance, asphalt pavements are thought to last 10 to 15 years on average before a major reconstruction is necessary, while concrete pavements could last for 25 years. However, there are examples when asphalt pavements have outlasted concrete (Cross and Parsons 2002).

Life Cycle Inventory Assessment of Concrete and Steel Bridge Girders

The following example is based on designs for a 428 meters long and 14.7 meters wide bridge on U.S. 231 over the White River in Indiana first used in a similar analysis using an early version of EIO-LCA (Horvath and Hendrickson 1998b). The bridge girders could be made of either steel or steel-reinforced concrete. In either case, the bridge deck would be made of concrete, resulting in similar costs for the deck as well as the cross girders under the deck. The cost of the substructure for the concrete bridge was 13% less expensive than the steel. The expansion joints cost $53,000 for the steel design and $35,000 for the concrete design. The cost of bearings was $94,000 for the steel design and $20,000 for the concrete design. The total cost of the steel design was $1,756,000, while the reinforced concrete girders cost $781,000. Because there was a substantial difference in the costs of girder materials, but not in other bridge parts, the analysis extended only to the manufacturing of the girders.

For the concrete girder, the other concrete product manufacturing sector was used (327390). For the steel girder estimate, the fabricated structural metal manufacturing sector (332312) was analyzed.

Environmental Impacts of Alternative Bridge Materials

As shown in Table 10-2, concrete has lower environmental impacts for all categories analyzed, with the exception of VOC emissions, for which the materials are roughly equal. Our first analysis (Horvath and Hendrickson 1998b) draws a similar conclusion in favor of concrete.

Use Phase Environmental Effects

In addition to materials manufacturing and construction, a life cycle assessment should also account for maintenance operations during the lifetime of a bridge. Unfortunately, publicly available records of maintenance are typically hard to find. Concrete girders are not expected to have substantial maintenance needs that would require additional materials. Conversely, steel girders have to be

TABLE 10-2. Environmental Effects Associated with Steel-reinforced Concrete, Steel Girder, and Paint Manufacturing for an Example Equivalent Bridge Design

Environmental effects	Unit	Concrete	Steel	Ratio C:S	Paint
Total energy	terajoule	9.6	20	0.5	0.1
Global warming potential	mt CO_2 equivalent	1,000	1,500	0.7	8.7
Sulfur dioxides (SO_2)	metric ton	2.2	3.5	0.6	0.01
Nitrogen oxides (NO_x)	metric ton	2.5	2.8	0.9	0.01
Particulate matter (PM_{10})	metric ton	0.4	1.2	0.3	0.005
Volatile organic compounds (VOC)	metric ton	1.8	1.8	1.0	0.02

painted regularly to protect them from corrosion. We estimated that approximately 6,040 m^2 of the steel girder needs to be painted by a product of the paint and coating manufacturing sector (325510). At \$0.10 per ft^2, or \$1.08 per m^2, the cost is estimated at \$6,500. Repainting is required about every 8 years, or 10 times during the design life of this bridge (80 years).

The results in Table 10-2 indicate that environmental effects of paint manufacturing during the life of the bridge amounts to merely 0.2% to 1% of the effects of steel girder manufacturing. Our 1992 analysis found the paint effects to be in the 5–15% range. The difference is likely due to paint and painting process improvements.

End-of-life Options for Bridge Materials

Data are available from a joint FHWA-EPA survey (Bloomquist et al. 1993) of bridge girder reuse and recycling practices of state highway agencies in the United States. While this was a good first effort, the available data have gaps in them, and it is unclear in what year the data were collected. For example, the report collected data on beams and decks, not just on steel structural members; thus reuse or recycling rates are difficult to determine for steel girders alone. To various degrees, reuse of obsolete bridge steel superstructures has been reported by 20 states, recycling by 9 states. Steel superstructure recycling includes cutting, breaking, or modifying the steel superstructure for use in a different highway application, or reusing or storing it for subsequent use after straightening, painting, or minor repair. Obsolete steel becomes property of the contractor in 11 states, and it is unclear whether that steel is reused or recycled eventually. Most bridge material is disposed of, but it does not automatically mean landfilling. Options include sale as scrap, landfilling, giving the superstructure to a contractor or to others, and disposing of unusable or unsuitable items. Therefore, the reported 17% reuse and 21% recycle rates are actually minimum rates. For example, 100% of a dismantled steel superstructure was "disposed of" in Virginia, when in fact it was recycled as scrap. Instead of the reported zero rate, it should have been reported as 100% recycled.

Bloomquist et al. (1993) is a data source on concrete girder recycling as well. Most concrete girders are landfilled. Only 6 out of 27 reporting states noted any reuse. Four states report various recycling rates. As is the case with steel, concrete girders given to contractors may have been recycled or reused.

Discussion

Concrete appears to be the cheaper as well as the environmentally preferable material, based on the assessment of materials extraction, processing, and manufacturing stages for bridge girders in this example. The maintenance phase adds to the environmental effects of steel girders. However, the reusability and especially the recyclability of steel girders have been much more prominent than that of concrete girders. Steel is 100% recyclable, and has been recycled profitably since it was first manufactured. The EIO-LCA analysis accounts for steel recycling because recycled steel is part of the raw materials input for steel mills (20–30% in the feedstock). Further, electric arc furnaces are increasingly the source of steel plates used to fabricate structural members. These furnaces use 90% or more steel scrap to produce steel. Therefore, with more efficient manufacturing, the results would be more favorable for steel than in the current analysis.

This analysis compared bridge girders based on initial environmental effects. A comparison based on the actual or average service lives and annualized environmental effects would be more realistic. The service life of bridges in Belgium, Japan, Sweden, and Switzerland has been estimated (Veshosky and Nickerson 1993) at 47–76 years for steel, and 47–86 years for reinforced concrete (21–86 years for prestressed concrete) bridges. In the United States, the service life has been estimated (Bonstedt 1998) at 55–68 years for steel, and 66–102 years for reinforced concrete (69–83 years for prestressed concrete) bridges. While the service life appears to be longer for concrete bridges, parts of steel bridges can survive for 100 years or more with regular maintenance, extensive repair, and modifications. In addition, factors other than time may also influence the useful life of bridges: floods, fire, wind, foundation scour, etc. (Marland and Weinberg 1988). Traffic increases and changing societal demands may result in a bridge becoming obsolete long before its physical end-of-life would dictate its closing. For that reason, all other criteria (engineering, aesthetic, economic) being equal or similar, it is worth reconsidering how we design bridges and other structures. We should build them from materials that have the least environmental effects throughout their life cycle, where that life cycle may be shorter than originally anticipated.

11

Environmental Impacts of Services[1]

A s economies of industrialized nations become increasingly service-ori-
ented, more attention to the environmental impacts of providing such
services is warranted. In the United States, roughly 60% of the 1997 gross
domestic product (GDP) is associated with the service sectors, which excludes
manufacturing, mining, agriculture, forestry and fishing, government services,
electric, gas, sanitary services, and transportation (USCB 2001a). With transportation, government, electric, gas, and sanitary services added, this fraction
jumps to 80%. Traditional manufacturing companies are developing a substantial presence in the service sector, such as the financing, information technology,
and real estate subsidiaries of automobile companies, and new service domains
are emerging, such as e-commerce. Environmental engineering and policy has
tended to focus on processes with a high concentration of pollution as measured
by emissions to different media, or quantity of emissions per unit of production.
Service industries have tended to be ignored for environmental policy because
of their relatively low emissions at their point of generation. In addition, services often lack a well-defined unit of production, so it is difficult to assess their
relative performance over time or between companies.

The service sector can influence environmental performance in some important ways:

1. Influencing suppliers to provide more environmentally conscious products
   and services.
2. Reducing resource inputs in their operations, for instance through energy
   efficiency programs and cutting business travel.
3. Educating consumers about the relative merits of different products (particularly in the retail sales sector).

[1]This chapter was originally written by Jeff Rosenblum, Chris Hendrickson, and
Arpad Horvath (Rosenblum et al. 2000).

4. Reducing resource use on the part of consumers by substituting more environmentally beneficial services or activities (like substituting teleconferencing services for business travel).

Measurement and assessment of these various activities can be difficult, especially in category 4, substitution on the part of consumers. Telecommuting services may reduce travel, but may lead to increased resource uses at home and sprawl as telecommuters opt for ex-urban residences. Measuring the benefits of telecommuting is further complicated by rebound effects if reduced work-related commuting time is used for increased pleasure travel (such as more trips for shopping or vacations).

In this chapter, we focus on the effects of categories 1 and 2, and attempt to trace both the direct and the indirect supply chain environmental effects for several important service industries. In particular, we examine four representative service sectors: truck transportation, retail trade, colleges and universities, and hotels and motels.

Impacts of Services Compared with Other Major Sectors of the Economy

Formally, the 485 commodity industries, as defined by the U.S. Department of Commerce in 1992, consist of manufacturing (352 industries), services (79), construction (15), agriculture (20), mining (10), and special industries (10). For this analysis, we grouped the 485 industries into four sectors: Manufacturing, Utilities, Services, and Other. We grouped electric services (utilities), natural gas transportation, natural gas distribution, and water supply and sewerage systems in a utilities category as their outputs are more of a product than a service. The construction, agriculture, mining, and special industries sectors are grouped into a category called other. Figure 11-1 shows each major economic sector's contribution to the 1992 U.S. economic output. Services represent over half of the overall economy. Note that the total economic output for the United States is higher than the GDP because total output includes costs of material, energy, etc., while the GDP is an economic indicator that sums only the value added (employee compensation, indirect business taxes, and property-type income) or, in another definition, the total final demand (largely, domestic private and government purchases, and exports). The sectors for the 1997 input–output model are similar and are listed in Appendix I along with their 1997 contributions to GDP.

Table 11-1 compares the impacts of the service industries to other sectors of the economy for energy use, global warming potential (converted to CO_2 equivalents), and RCRA hazardous wastes generated. Results are presented for total sector economic output as well as normalized by million dollars of output. The service sector contributed about half the direct energy use and global

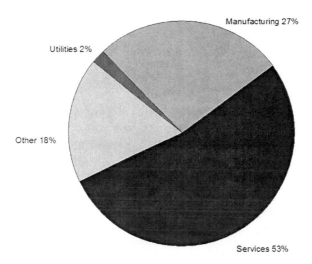

1992 Total Output = $11 Trillion

FIGURE 11-1. Relative Contribution of the Major Economic Sectors to the 1992 U.S.
Economic Output
Source: Rosenblum et al. 2000.

TABLE 11-1. Direct and Indirect Environmental Implications of the Major Sectors of
the U.S. Economy in 1992

For Total Sector Economic Output

	Manufacturing		Services		Utilities		Other	
	Direct	Indirect	Direct	Indirect	Direct	Indirect	Direct	Indirect
Energy (106 TJ)	9.9	53	9.8	28	21	11	21	12
RCRA hazardous wastes (106 metric tons)	190	170	6.7	75	0.05	4.2	.04	41
Global warming potential (106 mt CO$_2$ equiv.)	680	2700	660	2600	1900	610	1100	1800

Per Million Dollars of Economic Output

	Manufacturing		Services		Utilities		Other	
	Direct	Indirect	Direct	Indirect	Direct	Indirect	Direct	Indirect
Energy (TJ)	3.4	18	1.8	5.0	80.	41.	11	6.2
RCRA hazardous wastes (metric tons)	63	58	1.2	13	0.2	16	.02	21
Global warming potential (mt CO$_2$ equiv.)	230	920	120	460	7000	2300	580	910

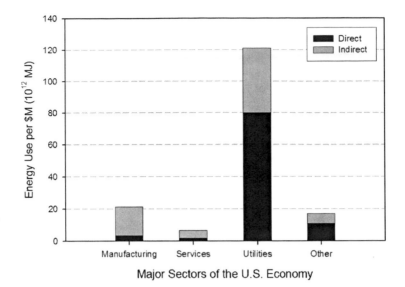

FIGURE 11-2. Direct and Indirect Energy Use (Electricity Plus Fuels) by the Major Sectors of the U.S. Economy, 1992

warming potential, and about one-fiftieth the RCRA hazardous wastes of the manufacturing sector per million dollars. However, because the service sector has twice the total economic output of manufacturing, the service industries have about the same energy use and global warming potential as the manufacturing sector on a total sector economic basis (see Figure 11-2). (Note that the utility category has a large energy use contribution because the use of fuels to generate electricity creates significant direct emissions.)

For some environmental metrics, the contribution of non-manufacturing sectors appears significantly smaller. For example, the manufacturing sector is responsible for the direct generation of nearly all of the RCRA hazardous wastes (see Figure 11-3). This does not present the full picture because service industries are responsible indirectly, through their supply chain, for a significant amount of RCRA wastes generated. In general, service industries have significant environmental effects on an economy-wide basis even when their direct emissions are negligible. With a large share of the economy, the direct and indirect environmental effects of the service sector become a significant component of overall U.S. emissions, wastes, and energy use.

Consumer Impacts

The above analysis focuses on the overall environmental effects of the service sector in 1992. Indirect consumption effects are also interesting. The U.S. Con-

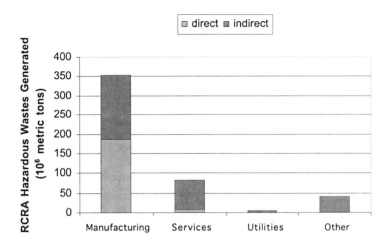

FIGURE 11-3. Direct and Indirect Generation of RCRA Hazardous Wastes by the Major Sectors of the U.S. Economy, 1992

sumer Price Index, a widely recognized economic indicator published by the Bureau of Labor Statistics, relies on a "market basket" to determine the goods and services (in about 200 subcategories) purchased by the average consumer. The I-O sector numbers have been mapped against each subcategory (Matthews 1999) and the 1992 EIO-LCA model is used to determine the annual total (direct and indirect) environmental effects of average U.S. household expenditures ($29,850 in 1992). The results are presented in Table 11-2. Each subcategory is given one of four classifications: manufacturing, service, utilities, or property rental. Though the amount spent on manufactured goods is about 25% greater than that spent on services, the environmental effects associated with manufacturing are about two to three times higher than that of services.

Direct and Indirect Impacts of Four Service Sectors

To illustrate the environmental effects of particular service industries, we have selected representatives of four major categories of services in the U.S. economy: truck transportation, retail trade, colleges and universities, and hotels. The 1997 EIO-LCA model is used to estimate the environmental outputs, both direct and indirect. A purchase of one million dollars of services from these four sectors is simulated. The results are presented in Table 11-3.

Of the four sectors, truck transportation has the largest energy input, but lower electricity use per dollar than the other three sectors. With this high energy input, it is not surprising that trucking has larger emissions than the other sectors. The fraction of direct energy is relatively high for each of the sec-

TABLE 11-2. Selected Environmental Emissions of Major Consumer Spending
Categories for $29,850 of Average Consumer Demand, 1992

	Expenditure	CO	NO_2	PM_{10}	SO_2	VOC	GWP
Total (lb/year)	—	220	210	25	280	57	80,000
Manufacturing	38%	59%	46%	34%	30%	63%	41%
Services	30%	25%	15%	21%	14%	25%	15%
Utilities	5%	6%	31%	21%	48%	6%	37%
Property rent	27%	10%	8%	23%	8%	7%	7%

TABLE 11-3. Resource Inputs and Environmental Outputs of Four Service Sectors for
One Million Dollars of Demand in Each Sector, 1997

	Trucking		Retail trade		Colleges and universities		Hotels	
	Total	% Direct	Total	% Direct	Total	% Direct	Total	% Direct
Resource Inputs								
Electricity (million kWh)	0.21	18%	0.40	70%	0.25	32%	0.64	86%
Energy (terajoules)	10	53%	5.5	27%	4.5	12%	5.6	27%
Environmental Outputs								
TRI total releases (metric tons)	0.21	0%	0.13	0%	0.15	0%	0.13	0%
SO_2 (metric tons)	1.1	35%	1.2	8%	0.66	0%	1.4	16%
NO_x (metric tons)	10	91%	4.3	81%	0.65	0%	1.0	9%
CO (metric tons)	130	97%	6.0	70%	2.2	0%	1.8	0%
VOC (metric tons)	10	95%	0.8	63%	0.45	0%	0.33	1%
PM_{10} (metric tons)	0.4	51%	0.25	48%	0.15	0%	0.16	5%
GHG (metric tons CO_2 equiv)	910	49%	450	16%	400	12%	470	15%

tors, with the exception of colleges for which the supply chain uses 88% of its
total energy input per dollar of output.

The overall environmental impact of the sectors is summarized in Table 11-4
for various indicators. To obtain these figures, a purchase from each sector
equal to its 1997 contribution to GDP is calculated. Retail trade is the largest of
these four sectors, so we expect its environmental impact to be substantial. The

TABLE 11-4. Resource Inputs and Environmental Outputs of Four Service Sectors for Total Output of Each Sector

	Trucking	Retail trade	Colleges and universities	Hotels
Total output ($ million)	169,397	729,824	55,821	70,574
Resource inputs				
Electricity (billion kWh)	35	290	14	45
Energy (million terajoules)	1.7	4	0.25	0.4
Environmental outputs				
Toxic total releases (thousand metric tons)	35	92	8.5	9.4
SO_2 (thousand metric tons)	180	880	37	100
NO_x (thousand metric tons)	1,700	3,100	36	72
CO (thousand metric tons)	22,000	4,400	130	130
VOC (thousand metric tons)	1,700	580	25	24
PM_{10} (thousand metric tons)	73	180	8.6	12
GHG (million metric tons)	150	330	22	33

retail trade energy inputs and environmental emissions are larger than those of the other sectors.

Table 11-5 provides more detail on the important sectors in the supply chain for the four analyzed sectors. It summarizes contributions to total toxic releases and greenhouse gas emissions. The impact of power generation and supply is apparent, with this sector appearing among the top five for each category. The use of total toxic releases as an emissions indicator emphasizes the impact of mining sectors with their substantial amount of land and underground releases. With other indicators, different sectors would appear on a top five list. For the college sector, the top five contributors to toxic air releases (rather than the total releases shown in table 11-5) would be power generation and supply (38%), pulp mills (10%), paper and paperboard mills (7%), primary nonferrous metals (3%), and plastic plumbing supplies (3%), with only power generation and supply and pulp mills on both lists.

The supply chain environmental effects associated with services appear to be significant, and merit further consideration. In particular, trucking displays significant direct and indirect impacts from combustion of fuels, both on a total and per-dollar basis. Retail trade is a large sector with significant supply chain resource and energy demands. Hotels consume significant amounts of electricity directly, though most of total energy use is consumed in the supply chain. Relative to the three other examples, the hotel industry requires large direct electricity inputs per dollar of output. Colleges and universities are a relatively small sector with small direct impacts, except for emissions presumably associated with laboratory work.

TABLE 11-5. Top 5 Supply-Chain Sectors Associated With Four Selected Service Sectors for Total Toxics Releases (TRI) and Greenhouse Gas (GHG) Emissions

	TRI		*GHG*
Trucking	%		%
Copper, nickel, lead, and zinc mining	38	Trucking	49
Gold, silver, and other mining	11	Power generation and supply	10
Power generation and supply	10	Petroleum refining	8
Waste management and remediation	8	Scenic transportation and transportation support	5
Petroleum refining	5	Oil and gas extraction	5
Retail trade			
Power generation and supply	35	Power generation and supply	42
Copper, nickel, lead, and zinc mining	27	Retail trade	16
Waste management and remediation	6	Real estate	7
Gold, silver, and other mining	4	Natural gas distribution	4
Pulp mills	4	Waste management and remediation	4
Colleges and universities			
Copper, nickel, lead, and zinc mining	40	Power generation and supply	26
Power generation and supply	15	Real estate	20
Waste management and remediation	7	Colleges and universities	12
Gold, silver, and other mining	6	Waste management and remediation	5
Pulp mills	4	Natural gas distribution	4
Hotels and motels			
Power generation and supply	37	Power generation and supply	44
Copper, nickel, lead, and zinc mining	25	Hotels and motels	15
Waste management and remediation	12	Waste management and remediation	7
Gold, silver, and other mining	4	Natural gas distribution	6
Pulp mills	2	Transit	3

Conclusions

This chapter provides a macroscopic view of environmental impacts of resource consumption and environmental outputs of the service sector of our economy in general (focusing on a comparison with manufacturing), as well as a life cycle environmental assessment of four representative services.

Services contribute about twice the economic output of manufacturing, making their overall economy-wide direct environmental impact in areas such as energy consumption much more significant than expected when looking at the effect normalized by output. Thus, the potential for reducing the environmental effects of services is significant, and warrants increased attention.

When assessing and analyzing service industries, the supply-chain effects must be considered along with their direct environmental impacts. This is especially the case for certain environmental emissions that are not directly associated with services (for example, TRI emissions) but are significant when indirect supply-chain impacts are considered.

For the four services detailed in this chapter, EIO-LCA can be used to determine where the majority of indirect supply-chain impacts occur. Similar analysis of other service industries is warranted. Greening the service industries has to include the greening of their supply chains.

12

Life Cycle Assessment of Electricity Generation[1]

Widespread electrification was selected as the top engineering achievement of the twentieth century in a survey conducted by the National Academy of Sciences (Constable and Somerville 2003). Electricity makes possible numerous labor and time saving mechanisms for us all. At the same time, generation of electricity has numerous environmental consequences, and there is considerable debate about the best mix of generation technologies. In this chapter we investigate impacts from several prominent generation technologies.

Net energy analysis (NEA), one of the precursors of life cycle assessment, was developed to assess the energy input–output ratio of energy supply and conservation technologies, significantly motivated by the petroleum shortages in the 1970s. Early studies focused on fossil fuel technologies (Chapman et al. 1974; Chapman 1975), and later assessments focused on renewable energy (Haack 1981; Herendeen and Plant 1981). The adoption of NEA in the United States was supported by the Non-Nuclear Energy Research and Development Act of 1974 (Leach 1975).

Fuel cycle studies during the 1980s were an extension of NEA that attempted to include environmental considerations in the assessments. Total fuel cycle studies capture the whole chain of energy and material inputs and pollution releases during the life cycle of power plants (Meridian 1989; San Martin 1989; Uchiyama 1992). Results should be normalized to the electricity output of the power plants so that different technologies can be compared.

Life cycle assessment (LCA) of competing energy technologies reveals the potential of an alternative to achieve increased performance and decreased emissions (Niewlaar et al. 1996). Indeed, LCA is fundamental to assessing any kind of technology, and is especially suitable in the study of climate change

---

[1]This chapter was originally written by Sergio Pacca and Arpad Horvath (University of California, Berkeley).

because the location of the emission sources does not affect the potential impacts. That is, while the effects of many pollutants are local or regional, the effect of greenhouse gases (GHG) is global. In addition, the share of GHG emissions from electricity generation is highly relevant. Worldwide, 38% of GHG emissions are related to electricity production. The United States is responsible for almost one third of that (Metz et al. 2001).

An LCA attempts to capture impacts from every phase of a process that may lead to the production of a product or delivery of a service. The inventory phase of an LCA maps all materials and energy inputs needed to produce electricity. Because energy is consumed in every step, greenhouse gas emissions are intrinsically associated with each step. The contribution of each step to the overall emissions varies as a function of technology, environmental resources, and the analytical period. LCA has been applied to address the use of energy and materials over the lifecycles of power plants (Uchiyama 2002; Gagnon et al. 2002), but more detailed quantitative studies have not been widely publicized.

LCA Applied to Electricity Generation

GHG emissions are usually of interest for electricity generation LCAs. All GHG emissions are added over the life cycle of a power plant, and the total is normalized by the electricity output over the same period.

Different electricity generation technologies are currently available, and the final energy use and the availability of resources determine the design of a specific project. Although many technological choices are at the discretion of the investors, other analytical choices are at the discretion of the analysts. The more choices and parameters are explicit in an LCA, the more relevant the assessment is because it can be compared with other LCAs. The first step in assessing GHG emissions from power plants is identifying and quantifying the major energy and materials consumed by each facility over its life cycle. In addition, complete LCAs also draw on land use change and its effects on the carbon cycle.

A bias in the comparison between results from different published LCA assessments arises because of the use of different boundary conditions. How far the analysis extends into the chain of processes and products consumed in electricity generation, and what the characteristics are of environmental loads ascribed to such processes, make substantial differences in the analysis and conclusions.

Hydroelectric Power Plants

The purpose of the reservoir, hydrology, and local topography affect the total energy output of the power plant. A hydroelectric power plant supplying base load power relies on the storage capacity of its reservoir to produce a constant energy output over time. Alternatively, the plant can use its storage capacity to maximize the amount of power supplied over a limited amount of time (peak load). Some run-of-river hydroelectric power plants need only a small reservoir to divert water to the intake, and feed the turbine.

Local geography and topography are strategic to determining the design that maximizes the energy output of a hydroelectric plant. Indeed, not all hydroelectric plants are the same, and each one should be assessed based on its own characteristics (Koch 2002). Arch and gravity dams are two basic designs for damming rivers and creating reservoirs. When a river runs through a canyon, an arch dam blocks the water passage through a high wall of steel-reinforced concrete. In contrast, gravity dams rely on massive earth- and rock-filled structures to retain water.

The choice of a specific design affects the results of an LCA in several ways. The amount of resources needed to build the dam and the power plant vary. The operation mode and the electricity output vary. In addition, environmental constraints may impose changes in the operation of the power plant, and its respective electricity output, in order to restore the natural flow of the river (Brouwer 2002).

Hydroelectricity was for a long time considered a renewable energy source free of GHG emissions. In the early 1990s, the contribution of reservoirs as a source of carbon emissions became an object of investigation for researchers concerned with the comparison between hydroelectric plants and fossil-fueled power plants (Rudd et al. 1993; Gagnon and Chamberland 1993; Rosa and Schaeffer 1994).

The filling of the reservoir inhibits activities that depend on oxygen consumption and leads to the decomposition of the flooded vegetation. Thus, carbon that was previously stored in biomass and soils is subject to mineralization by microorganisms. Mineralization transforms organic carbon into carbon dioxide (CO_2) or methane (CH_4). Emissions from reservoirs depend on the carbon available and the rate of decomposition, which relates to the amount of standing organic carbon characteristics of the ecosystem (St. Louis et al. 2000).

Besides the decomposition of flooded material, the loss of an active ecosystem implies the loss of a net flux of carbon to the soil. The net ecosystem productivity (NEP) measures this flow for different ecosystems. The NEP loss triggered by the filling of reservoirs can be compared to carbon emissions of fossil-fueled power plants (Pacca and Horvath 2002).

In summary, land-use changes affect the carbon balance and need to be included in any LCA of impacts on climate change.

Photovoltaic Systems

Photovoltaic (PV) modules convert solar energy directly into electricity. The need to prove that PV installations were net energy sources promoted the first

LCA applied to this energy source. Energy payback assessments included the indirect energy used in the production chain of the modules and other parts of the PV systems. The energy payback time indicates the time necessary to match all energy inputs to the facility with its lifetime energy yield (Alsema and Nieuwlaar 2000).

Although several LCAs in the literature show carbon dioxide (CO_2) emissions normalized by electricity output of PV systems, different assumptions used in each study make results hard to compare. The range of results published is ample. Variability arises from local solar radiation, the boundary setting of each analysis, the energy mix used in the manufacturing of system components and its respective GHG emissions, and the choice of the PV technology, which is not homogeneous. Currently, PV module production is based on three types of technologies: monocrystalline, polycrystalline, and amorphous.

The balance of the system (BOS) refers to all the other components in the PV installation besides the modules. The BOS depends on the end use of the electricity and local conditions, and includes the structure to support the modules and hardware, batteries to store and deliver energy during electrical load periods, and inverters to convert direct current into alternate current.

Wind Farms

Although the technology of most modern wind turbines is similar, results from LCAs of their energy and CO_2 emissions vary (Lenzen and Munksgaard 2002). One basic difference is the location of wind turbines, which can be on land or offshore. The foundation requirements for offshore wind turbines are different from land-based turbines. The energy intensity of a turbine's tower is associated with the type of materials used in its construction. A concrete tower requires less energy than a steel tower. Offshore support structures require more material and are more energy-intensive to install.

A review of the literature shows that CO_2 emission factors for wind power plants range from 7.9 to 123.7 g of CO_2/kWh, capacity factors are 7.6%–50.4%, and the lifetime of the facilities is 15–30 years (Lenzen and Munksgaard 2002).

The technology of wind turbines is changing rapidly. In past decades, the most efficient turbines were in the 50–200 kW range, but by 2000 they were in the 1–3 MW range. Both their weight and cost per installed capacity have been decreasing (Johnson 2003). The weight of a 1.65 MW turbine per installed power is similar to the weight of a 600 kW turbine per installed power; however, the percentage of materials by weight depends on the size of the turbines, therefore GHG emissions during the manufacturing phase are a function of the size of the turbines selected.

One factor in the comparison between different renewable energy sources is the expected life of the major components of the installation. Emissions normalized by electricity output vary according to the lifetime of components and the analytical period of the study. The lifetime of wind turbines is usually assumed to be 20 years; however, they can operate for longer (Krohn 1997), and the expected life of larger turbines is on the order of 25 years (Kuemmel et al. 1997). The consideration of retrofits and partial replacement of the infrastructure and equipment of the wind farm also affect the LCA results.

Coal-fired Power Plants

In 2001, 51% of all electricity produced in the United States was generated by coal-fired power plants (EIA 2003b). Electricity production from coal typically involves a sequence of life cycle phases, and all phases release GHGs. However, the majority of the environmental impacts are associated with the operation of the power plant.

In a conventional coal-fired power plant, a boiler produces steam that powers a turbine generator set. More advanced designs, such as integrated gasification combined-cycle plants, maximize the conversion efficiency of coal by gasifying the coal and using a combined-cycle scheme, which involves the use of two turbines in series and the reuse of the heat in the exhaust of the first turbine to power a second steam turbine.

Published LCAs show that over 93% of the GHG emissions from electricity generated by coal power plants are released during fuel combustion (Spath et al. 1999; Lombardi 2003).

Despite the dramatic contribution of combustion to the life cycle emissions of coal power plants, other phases such as coal mining, transportation, materials manufacturing, construction, maintenance, and end of life should also be considered in an LCA.

There are two variants of mining: surface mining (also known as strip mining) and underground mining. It is estimated that every year 3.6 million metric tons of methane (CH_4) are released from coal mining activities in the United States, most of which come from underground mining (Longwell and Rubin 1995).

GHGs are also released from transportation of coal. Coal is usually transported by ships, barges, or rail (Davis and Diegel 2002); Chapter 13 analyzes the impacts of transportation in detail.

The capacity of a coal power plant affects its life cycle emissions because it drives the total electricity output. However, a higher capacity factor may imply shorter lifetime for some parts of power plants.

Natural Gas-fueled Power Plants

Natural gas accounts for 22% of all energy consumed in the United States, and its role in energy production is becoming increasingly important because of environmental concerns (Spath and Mann 2000). In comparison with a coal-

TABLE 12-1. EIO-LCA Sectors Used in the LCA of Electricity Generation Technologies

		Energy Technologies				
EIO-LCA sector #		*Hydro.*	*Coal*	*PV*	*Wind*	*Natural gas*
212100	Coal mining		X	X		X
212320	Sand, gravel, clay and refractory mining		X	X		
211000	Oil and gas extraction					X
325211	Plastics material and resin manufacturing				X	
324110	Petroleum refineries		X	X	X	X
324121	Asphalt paving mixtures			X	X	
32721A	Glass and glass products			X	X	
327320	Ready-mixed concrete	X			X	X
331111	Iron and steel mills	X			X	X
331411	Primary smelting and refining of copper	X		X	X	
331312	Primary aluminum	X		X	X	X
333611	Turbines and turbine generator sets	X				
335311	Transformers	X				
482000	Rail transportation		X			
221100	Power generation		X	X	X	X
221200	Natural gas distribution					X

fired power plant, a natural gas-fueled power plant does not have the problem of SO_2 emissions, and because the conversion to electricity is more efficient, less CO_2 is emitted per unit of electricity output. In contrast to coal, natural gas is a much more homogeneous fuel which contains 90% to 98% of CH_4 (Hayhoe et al. 2002).

Using EIO-LCA for Electricity Generation Assessment

It is useful to combine information on the energy and material inputs for generating electricity by different technologies with EIO-LCA data. This renders more compatible results because of the economic boundary of EIO-LCA and its methodological consistency in factoring in environmental stressors. This technique has been applied to an LCA of different electricity generation technologies based on hydropower, solar, wind, coal, and natural gas (Pacca and Horvath 2002).

Several EIO-LCA sectors are used in inventory assessment of both the construction materials used in each technology, and the acquisition of fossil fuels (Table 12-1). All technologies are compared in a case study based on the Glen Canyon hydroelectric plant on the Colorado River on the border of Utah and Arizona. Lake Powell, the reservoir formed by this power plant, is the second largest in the United States; in 1999 the power plant output was 5.5 TWh (Pacca and Horvath 2002). The other power plants included in the analysis are located in the same geographical area and scaled to meet the output of the hydroelectric facility. The assessment of the other alternatives is based on published data, which includes materials and energy input for power plants.

Information from EIO-LCA is used to find the amount of GHG emissions associated with the major commodities consumed over the lifecycle of the individual power plants.

The analysis moves one step further from the inventory phase of GHG emissions and provides environmental impact assessment based on the global warming potential (GWP) method. Because the location of GHG emissions does not affect impacts on global climate as much as the timing of such emissions, the global warming effect (GWE) method is proposed to aggregate GHG releases at different times in the life of power plants.

The GWE sums all GHG emissions (such as CO_2, CH_4 and N_2O) M_j weighted by the specific GWP calculated over the period between the actual emissions and the end of the period of the analysis *TH*:

$$\sum M_j \times GWP_{j,TH} \tag{12-1}$$

Changes in the period of analysis may change the ranking of the alternatives compared. The period of analysis may not coincide with the decommissioning of the power plant. The GWE method is intended to carry out comparative assessments.

The time scale of interest in the analysis is a discrete series of annual intervals. Therefore, the GWP for each GHG j and corresponding to a time horizon *TH* is calculated using Equation 12-2:

$$GWP = \frac{\int_0^{TH} a_x \left[x(t) \right] dt}{\int_0^{TH} a_r [CO_2(t)] \, dt} \tag{12-2}$$

where:

a_x is the radiative efficiency of any GHG that is being compared to CO_2

a_r is the radiative efficiency of CO_2, which equals 1 because all the effects of other GHGs are compared to the effect of CO_2

$x(t)$ is an exponential decay function with the characteristic residence time of the GHG being compared to CO_2.

The calculation of the GWP is explained in the Third Assessment Report of the Intergovernmental Panel on Climate Change (IPCC). The volume containing the scientific basis devotes Chapter 6 to the "radiative forcing of climate change," and Section 6.12 explains the GWP method in detail (IPCC 2001). The report provides all values used in Equation 12-2; the function representing the denominator of Equation 12-2, which relates to the approximation of the out-

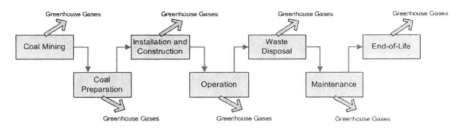

FIGURE 12-1. Green House Gas Emissions of Power Generation Technologies for Four Different Analytical Periods
Source: Pacca and Horvath 2002.

put of the Bern model and denotes the airborne fraction of CO_2 over time, is available in footnote 4 of the IPCC special report on land use, land-use change, and forestry (Equation 12-3) (Watson 2000):

$$[CO_2(t)] = 0.175602 + 0.137467^{-t/421.093} + 0.185762^{-t/70.5965} \\ + 0.242302^{-t/21.42165} + 0.258868^{-t/3.41537} \qquad (12\text{-}3)$$

In the case of the Glen Canyon plant, detailed construction records provide the major materials volumes used in the construction of the dam. This information is combined with estimates of the construction energy and their respective emissions using equipment productivity and fuel use factors. Besides construction, other effects due to land-use changes are also addressed. GHG emissions modeled from flooding of the reservoir are estimated at 2,000,000 to 5,000,000 Mg of CO_2 equivalent (CO_2eq) measured 20 years after construction. The loss of NEP and forgone carbon uptake amount to 400,000 Mg of CO_2eq over the same period. The total emissions from the hydroelectric power plant, including emissions from construction, range from 3,000,000 to 6,000,000 Mg of CO_2eq 20 years after construction.

The final results in Figure 12-1 showing the CO_2 equivalent values are normalized by the electricity output and calculated for four different analytical periods. All GHG emissions, including CO_2, are aggregated over time using Equation 12-3. Electricity produced using wind turbines is the alternative with the lowest emissions.

Conclusions

There is a range of technologies and design options for each alternative, which need to be explicit in any LCA. Sometimes local conditions dictate a given choice, especially in the case of renewable energy that relies on natural resources such as insolation (solar radiation), wind patterns, water flows, topography, etc.

Electricity generation technologies are not homogeneous. The selection of options within a given technology also affects the results of LCAs. For example, there are different types of PV modules with different energy conversion efficiencies and lifetimes, which require different material and energy inputs in their fabrication.

The displacement of a terrestrial ecosystem and the consequent GHG emissions and imbalances should be factored into a comparative analysis of technologies responsible for large footprints such as hydroelectric plants and PV installations. In the case of hydroelectricity, the assessment of impacts from the aquatic ecosystem should also be considered. The new equilibrium between the aquatic ecosystem and the atmosphere also needs to be part of the analysis.

Economies of scale also affect the performance of the alternatives. The size of a wind turbine or a solar power plant affects the carbon emission intensity of the alternatives. The load curve, which should be met by electricity produced by a power plant, also influences the final result because sometimes storage capacity is needed to match supply and demand.

The assessment of electricity production and climate change impacts demands a flexible framework that considers periodical retrofits and maintenance in the life cycle of a power plant. For fossil fuel plants, gains in efficiency and carbon sequestration technologies will be important. For renewable technologies, reductions in emissions related to the manufacturing of materials, construction, and land use will play a major role.

This assessment does not deny the importance of other stressors or environmental impacts caused by electricity generation technologies. The GWE method is an analytical framework to assess the impacts of competing technologies on the global climate.

13

Comparison of Energy Transportation Modes

Coal by Rail, Methane by Pipeline, and Electricity Transmission

The United States mines over one billion tons of coal each year to produce 51% of its electricity supply (EIA 2003a, 2003b). Since coal deposits are distant from population and electricity demand, shipping coal generates hundreds of billions of freight transportation ton-miles each year. This transport requires large amounts of energy, generates pollution emissions, and results in the death of about 400 people each year at rail crossings. A major increase in shipments would require new transportation capacity, which is costly to build and maintain.

Here, we explore the economic and environmental impacts of alternative options for delivering electricity to demand centers. We focus on one of the largest U.S. shipments: coal from the Powder River Basin (PRB) in Wyoming to Dallas, Texas. In 2000, unit trains carried 50 million tons of PRB coal to Texas. We focus on shipping 3.9 million tons a year from the PRB 1,000 miles to Dallas. While diesel electric locomotives are relatively efficient, this shipment expends 10 million gallons of diesel fuel and releases many air emissions. Shipping electricity from the coal mine to customers through transmission lines is a possible alternative. However, shipping the energy in the form of electricity requires substantial new infrastructure, consumes energy because of line losses, and has numerous aesthetic, health, land use, and environmental implications.

Coal from the PRB is in high demand because of its low cost and sulfur content (<0.4%) (EIA 1999). Although the heat content of PRB coal is lower (8340 Btu/lb) than in bituminous coal, it occurs in massive shallow formations that are inexpensive to extract by surface mining. Thirty percent of U.S. coal is mined in the PRB (BLM 2000). In 2000, 330 million tons of PRB coal was shipped to 27 states, with Texas receiving 50 million tons (see Figure 13-1). The

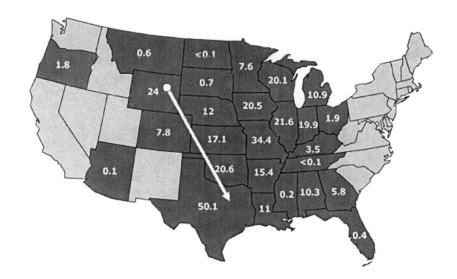

FIGURE 13-1. Wyoming to Texas Coal Transport
Source: http://smtc.uwyo.edu/coal/WyomingCoal/customers.asp

67 billion tons of extractable coal in Wyoming is 200 times the current extraction rate (EIA 2000), so there is considerable coal available for future generations.

The price of coal at the mouth of a PRB mine is approximately $7/ton, or $0.42/million Btu (EIA 2003c); the delivered price in Texas is $17 to $29/ton (but most often between $20 and $26/ton, which is $1.17–1.52 per million Btu). The cost of shipping coal is greater than the extraction cost.

Several studies have investigated the environmental impact of transmission (DeCicco et al. 1992; Kalkani and Boussiakou 1996), the tradeoffs between alternating current and direct current power (Hauth et al. 1997; Linke and Schuler 1988), and the costs and feasibility of new transmission development (Wiese and Kaltschmitt 1996; Hirst and Kirby 2001). One recent study investigated the environmental tradeoffs between transmission and rail (Amphlett et al. 1996), but did not consider costs.

We compare four scenarios to provide 6.5 billion kWh of electricity in Dallas from PRB coal. The first scenario is a pulverized coal power plant in Texas, fueled by unit trains carrying PRB coal. The second is a pulverized coal power plant in Wyoming close to the mine; transmission lines carry the electricity to Texas. In the third scenario, the coal is gasified and converted to methane in Wyoming and then transported by pipeline to Dallas to generate electricity in a combined-cycle power plant. The fourth gasifies the coal, converts it to methane, and then generates electricity near the mine, sending the electricity to Texas via transmission lines.

In this case study, we illustrate the development of comparative life cycle environmental assessments as well as life cycle costs. In many investment decisions, both costs and environmental impacts are of interest. To simplify the analysis, we consider only a restricted range of possible environmental impacts and power plants. For more extensive analysis and discussion, see Bergerson and Lave (2005).

Analysis Assumptions and Boundaries

We assume that new generation plants, transmission lines, rail lines, and gas pipelines can be built, despite siting problems often characterized as "not in my backyard" (NIMBY) opposition. All plants are assumed to satisfy stringent emissions regulations. The location of the plants is assumed not to affect either the plant costs or emissions. Thus, we examine only costs and emissions relative to the current situation where coal is shipped to a pulverized generation plant in Dallas. Location matters in that additional capacity and coal is required to make up for transmission and gas pipeline losses.

Although the plants are identical, the public health implications differ by location, since many more people are exposed to emissions from the generation plant located in Dallas. Life cycle analysis is used to assess the economic and environmental impacts associated with every stage of the production of electricity, from extracting ore to final disposal of unwanted residuals.

The capital costs (amortized over the life of the capital investment), operating, and maintenance costs, as well as societal costs, are calculated and represented in terms of an annual cost. These costs are then divided into economic sectors. The monetary values associated with each sector are then used in the EIO-LCA model to estimate the environmental emissions from these scenarios.

To estimate the costs and environmental impacts associated with the power plant (considered primarily in terms of the impact associated with the additional capacity required to compensate for the losses through the transmission line and pipeline) a software tool titled "Integrated Environmental Control Model" (IECM 2001) was used. Using this model, a power plant can be built "virtually" to specifications such as the fuel type, control technologies, boiler type, etc. The output of this model describes the costs associated with this plant as well as the stack emissions that result from a particular configuration.

Table 13-1 summarizes general assumptions for the four scenarios. In the base case, 3.9 million tons of coal is transported to generate 6.5 billion kWh. Four main alternatives are explored to transport the energy from the PRB to Dallas:

1. *Coal by rail.* Ship coal by rail to Dallas and generate electricity in Dallas at a

TABLE 13-1. General Assumptions for Four Transport Scenarios

Item	Quantity
Distance from PRB to Dallas	1,000 Miles
Coal heating value	8340 Btu/lb
Total electricity delivered to Dallas	6.5 billion kWh
Cost of capital	8%
Amortization period	30 years
Pipeline losses	3%
Transmission line losses (±408 kv HVDC line)	7%

"subcritical" pulverized coal power plant. Subcritical plants have boilers operating at close to atmospheric pressure with steam that is pressurized at roughly 16 MPa and a temperature of 550° C, whereas "supercritical" plants operate at almost double the pressure. This alternative has two sub-options: existing capacity is sufficient for the required transport, or new track must be built. The differences between the two are the capital costs and environmental impacts of new rail line construction.

2. *Coal by wire.* Generate electricity at a subcritical pulverized coal power plant located at the mine mouth. Electricity is then transmitted via wire on an interstate transmission line (± 408 kv HVDC line).

3. *Coal to gas by pipeline.* Gasify coal at the mine mouth, convert it to methane, ship the methane through a new interstate gas pipeline, and generate electricity in Dallas at a combined-cycle generation plant.

4. *Coal to gas by wire.* Gasify coal at the mine mouth, convert it to methane, and generate electricity at a combined-cycle plant located at the mine mouth. Electricity is transmitted via wire as in the coal by wire scenario (± 408 kv HVDC line).

The base case assumes that no infrastructure exists. This means that 1,000 miles of either rail, transmission lines (including converter stations), or gas pipeline must be built. The economies of scale in the three systems mean that costs would be lower if the transport systems were built and used to capacity, especially for rail and gas pipelines. This is less relevant for the transmission line, since increasing the power flows increases the losses and costs.

Assumptions for each scenario are summarized in Table 13-2. The gross plant capacity is different for each scenario because of the plant characteristics and the additional power required to compensate for line losses. The IECM software used to model the pulverized coal plant assumes it meets "new source performance" emissions standards and has an efficiency of 34%. The gasification and methanation process is modeled after the Lurgi gasifier and methanation process currently in operation in North Dakota. This plant uses lignite and is likely to be more suited to gasify PRB coal than the Texaco IGCC systems (which would run sub-optimally due to the moisture and ash content

TABLE 13-2. Some Assumptions for Each Transport Scenario

Power plant	Coal by rail Pulverized coal	Coal by wire Pulverized coal	Coal to gas gas by pipeline Gasifier and combined cycle	Coal to gas gas by wire Gasifier and combined cycle
Gross plant capacity (MW)	1,100	1,200	1,000	1,100
Overall efficiency (%)*	34	32	33	31
Total coal required (million tons)	3.9	4.2	4.1	4.3
Natural gas produced (B cu.ft./year)	—	—	48	50
Net annual output (B kWh)	6.5	7.0	6.5	7.0

*Overall efficiency includes transport, generation, and transmission energy losses.

of the PRB coal). The NGCC unit is modeled using the IECM software, which calculates an efficiency of 49%.

Fuel Consumption

As shown in Table 13-3, the base case uses 10 million gallons of diesel fuel, while the other three cases use 280,000, 150,000, and 330,000 tons of coal in order to deliver the stipulated amount of electricity to Dallas. At $10.8/million Btu, diesel fuel is much more expensive than coal at $0.42/million Btu.

Inputs to the EIO-LCA Model

Using the assumptions above, the various resource requirements are calculated for each scenario and the environmental impacts estimated. For a few cases such as coal gasification, there is no appropriate sector to represent the impacts, so separate calculations are performed for these requirements. For capital investments, costs and environmental impacts are annualized to facilitate com-

TABLE 13-3. Annual Fuel Consumption for Each Scenario

	Fuel		Energy			CO_2	
	Additional coal (million tons)	Diesel (million gallons)	Coal (trillion Btu)	Diesel (trillion Btu)	Total (trillion Btu)	Emissions from fuel only (tons of CO_2 eq)	Fuel cost ($ million)
Coal by rail	—	10	—	1.3	1.3	0.13	15.0
Coal by wire	0.28	—	4.7	—	4.7	0.51	2.0
Coal to gas by pipeline	0.15	—	2.5	—	2.5	0.23	1.1
Coal to gas by wire	0.33	—	5.5	—	5.5	0.54	2.3

TABLE 13-4. Sectoral Purchases Used in EIO-LCA for Coal by Rail and Coal by Wire Transport

Item	EIO-LCA sector	Purchase ($ millions)
Coal by rail		
Railroad investments	Railroad rolling stock manufacturing	124
	Other new construction	2,500
Fuel consumption	Petroleum refineries*	9
Maintenance	Railroad rolling stock manufacturing	11
	Other new construction	8
	Ferrous metal foundries	7
	Architectural and engineering services	4
Coal by wire		
Transmission line	Architectural and engineering services	97
construction	Truck transportation	11
	Iron and steel mills	200
	Aluminum rolling and drawing	140
	Plastics materials and resin manufacturing	9.0
	Ready-mix concrete manufacturing	54
	All other electronic component manufacturing	290
	Plastics, plumbing fixtures, and all other plastics products	5.3
	Lighting fixture manufacturing	2.0
	Other new construction	43
	Real estate	91
Additional capacity	Other new construction	72
Additional coal	Coal mining*	2.3
Maintenance	Other new construction	5.0

*Emissions from diesel fuel and coal combustion are estimated directly from quantities burned and rail or boiler emission factors.

parisons. Tables 13-4 and 13-5 summarize the various sectoral calculations used in the EIO-LCA model for the different scenarios.

Life Cycle Costs and Environmental Impacts

Annual Costs

Figure 13-2 summarizes the annual costs associated with the four scenarios. Plant costs are added to the transport costs for the annualized capital cost. Operating and maintenance (O&M) costs include transportation and incremental costs of energy production for differing transportation efficiencies. Fuel includes the base amount of coal required (3.9 million tons), the fuel used in transport, including additional coal needed to deliver the electricity to Dallas.

TABLE 13-5. Sectoral Purchases Used in EIO-LCA for Coal to Gas by Pipeline and Coal to Gas by Wire Transport

Item	EIO-LCA sector	Purchase ($ millions)
Coal to gas by pipeline		
Pipeline construction	Water, sewer and pipeline construction	1,500
Additional coal mining	Coal mining	1.2
Pipeline operation	Pipeline transportation	58
Support services	Other maintenance and repair construction	12
Additional Capacity	Other new construction	30
Coal to gas by wire		
Transmission line	Architectural and engineering services	97
construction	Truck transportation	11
	Iron and steel mills	200
	Aluminum rolling and drawing	140
	Plastics materials and resins manufacturing	9.0
	Ready-mix concrete manufacturing	54
	All other electronic component manufacturing	290
	Plastics, plumbing fixtures, and all other plastics products	5.3
	Lighting fixtures manufacturing	2.0
	Other new construction	43
	Real estate	91
Additional capacity	Other new construction	110
Additional coal mining	Coal mining	2.6

Note: Impacts of coal gasification and coal combustion are estimated separately.

Externalities include the deaths experienced throughout the construction and operation periods of the life cycle, as well as the social cost of environmental emissions including GWP, SO_2, NO_2, PM_{10}, VOC, and CO. The total costs are the sum of the four categories of cost.

The annualized costs of the capital investments dominate the costs for each scenario. The rail scenario is the most costly in this base case, in which we assume that there is no current infrastructure so a new rail line must be constructed. The two transmission scenarios are slightly cheaper than the pipeline scenario because of lower construction costs for transmission lines. However, this scenario does not use the available capacity of any of the scenarios: Much more coal could be shipped on the rail system, the right of way could accommodate more power, and a larger pipeline could be built that would handle much more methane. In each case, the unit costs would fall as the capital costs were spread over more shipments. However, increasing throughput would lead to congestion, with higher costs and losses.

The rail infrastructure is the most costly system to operate once built, whereas the transmission network is the cheapest to maintain. The fuel costs in

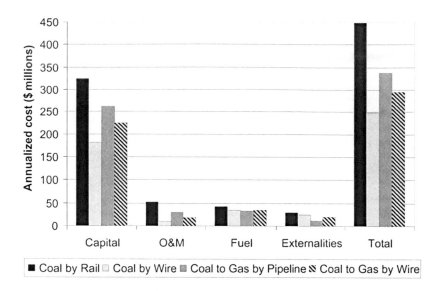

FIGURE 13-2. Summary of Annual Costs for Four Methods of Transporting Energy from the PRB to Dallas, Assuming New Infrastructure Required for Each Scenario

the rail scenario were for 10 million gallons of diesel fuel. In the other scenarios, the fuel costs consist of the additional coal required to deliver that assumed level of electricity to Dallas.

U.S. rail shipments kill close to 1,000 people each year (BTS 2004). We estimate that coal transport in the base case would result in 1.4 fatalities per year, but these costs do not significantly affect the results of this analysis. Other societal costs include injuries and lost work days due to nonfatal collisions. We find that these unfortunate events do not affect our conclusions.

The social costs from air pollution emissions are important, but do not affect the conclusion. Chapter 3 describes the valuation process for these air emissions.

Environmental Life Cycle Assessment

Figure 13-3 shows emissions expected from each case, excluding the level of emissions from burning the base level of 3.9 million tons of coal. These are cumulative emissions for construction and 30 years of operation for each scenario. The results are mixed. For nitrogen dioxide (NO_2), volatile organic compounds (VOCs), and small particulate matter (PM_{10}), coal to gas by wire has less emissions; for global warming potential (GWP) and carbon monoxide (CO), rail and coal by wire, respectively, have the lowest. The GWP is made up of the sum of greenhouse gases converted to metric tons of CO_2 equivalent.

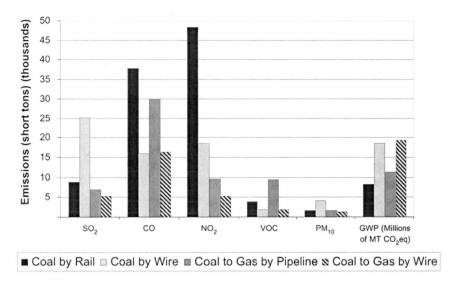

FIGURE 13-3. Comparison of Emissions for Four Methods of Transporting Energy from the PRB to Dallas Over 30 Years

The main reason that PRB coal is shipped by rail an average of 1,100 miles across the United States is its low mining cost and low sulfur content. Current regulations limit SO_2 emissions. Achieving the reductions through burning low sulfur coal is generally cheaper than installing SO_2 emission control technologies. The power plant in this scenario is assumed to be a subcritical plant with a lime spray dryer, burning PRB coal with a sulfur content of 0.4%. This configuration meets the New Source Performance Standards. Since the 1990 Clean Air Act capped the total SO_2 emissions from power plants, this new plant would have to purchase allowances each year equal to their mass emissions.

Although the controls greatly reduce pollution emissions, there are still externalities. We translate the emissions into dollars using estimates of the social cost of air emissions as described in Chapter 3. While difficult to quantify and full of uncertainty, these estimates help to internalize the externalities of environmental discharges.

Between 17,000 and 24,000 acres would be cleared for the transmission towers and lines, but much of this land could be used for other purposes (for example, farming or ranching). This is not the case for the railroad bed.

Mining a ton of coal would be the same in all scenarios, so we have neglected the impacts of coal mining. But the scenarios require slightly different amounts of coal. Emissions from mining are quantified, but we neglect miner safety, environmental disruption, and other impacts.

Breakeven Distances

The U.S. rail infrastructure, particularly from the PRB to Texas, is extensive. Just over one unit train per day would be required to carry 3.9 million tons of PRB coal to Dallas. It seems unlikely that one train per day would add much to congestion, but if there were bottlenecks, triple or quadruple track could be added. We estimate that perhaps 100 miles of new track would be needed. If more than 200 miles of rail bed had to be added, building a transmission line would be cheaper. While more energy is required to transport electricity 1,000 miles than transporting coal, the cost of transporting coal is greater than the cost of transporting electricity. Thus, transporting coal by rail would be efficient only if the vast majority of the rail network were already in place.

Transmission line losses across 1,000 miles can be large, but the capital costs of the lines are more important than the cost of the lost energy. High voltage direct current (HVDC) lines have lower losses, but are more expensive than high voltage AC lines. However, converting AC to DC costs energy. If the line were longer than roughly 500-600 miles, HVDC lines would be cheaper.

Diesel fuel is an important cost in the base case. If petroleum costs increased, the cost of using unit trains would increase. However, the price of diesel would have to increase from $1.50 per gallon to at least $4 per gallon before shipping coal by rail would be more expensive than shipping electricity, assuming that only 100 miles of new rail would have to be built.

Although the United States backed away from the Kyoto Protocol for greenhouse gas reductions in 2001, it is likely to implement some form of carbon management within the next 30 years. When that occurs, the additional CO_2 emitted in the transmission scenario will raise the costs. If 1,000 miles of rail is required, a carbon tax as high as $400/ton is necessary to make this an economically preferred scenario.

One way to decrease the number of fatalities due to rail traffic is to have the train go over or under the highway at each rail crossing. The average cost associated with these upgrades is $9 million. Assuming that only 100 miles of new rail bed were required, having to upgrade more than 10–11% of the current grade crossings would make coal transport more expensive than shipping electricity.

Coal to Gas Options

While converting coal to methane is not a commonly discussed option, the results of this analysis show that it is a competitive option. Gasifying PRB coal using a Lurgi gasifier requires development, but appears to be feasible. Transporting the methane by pipeline is attractive since only 3% of the methane is needed to power the compressors along the 1,000-mile stretch of gas pipeline. In contrast, 7% of the electricity goes to line losses for the transport by wire scenarios. The cost of this "coal to gas" scenario would fall if the separated byproducts of the synthetic gas were sold. This scenario produces smaller greenhouse gases than the transmission scenario. Finally, gasifying the coal could be taken a step further to produce pure streams of hydrogen and CO_2; the latter might be sequestered, eliminating nearly all of the CO_2 emissions.

General Applicability of the Case Study Results

Getting energy from coal mine to the customer is a major problem throughout the United States, not just for PRB coal bound for Texas. Several factors specific to the source and demand for electricity are relevant to determining the best method. Distance from the mine to the customer is important, as well as the ruggedness of the terrain. The quality of the coal is important; 50% more lignite would have to be shipped than bituminous coal because of the heat content. Low quality coals, as a general rule, should be burned or gasified at the mine rather than shipped.

Siting power plants, rail beds, transmission towers, or gas pipelines can be difficult in some areas. Pipelines are less obtrusive and may be the only feasible alternative if there is opposition to transmission towers or rail beds.

Building a power plant in one location to serve customers in a different location can be problematic. Should Wyoming (and surrounding states) suffer the environmental impacts of generating electricity for Texas? The population of Wyoming is 2% that of Texas. Therefore fewer people would be affected by the emissions from the power plant if the power plant were built in Wyoming. However, it is difficult to assign the impact of these emissions to people who are not benefiting from the electricity generated. Wyoming would benefit from additional jobs, but it is unclear whether they would welcome the environmental degradation, crowding, and noise.

Conclusions

The best way to get energy from the PRB to Dallas seems clear from our analysis. Since 50 million tons a year of PRB coal is already being shipped to Texas, there appears to be sufficient capacity to handle one additional unit train a day. If more capacity had to be added, perhaps a few hundred miles of rail bed could be double- or triple-tracked.

If PRB coal were used for supplying electricity to a place 1,000 miles away that did not already have rail capacity, a generator at the mine and a transmission line would be the cheapest alternative, with gasifying the coal and shipping the methane by wire a close competitor. Gasifying the coal and generating the electricity in a combined-cycle plant has similar costs as a pulverized coal plant and has environmental advantages. We did not evaluate a coal slurry pipeline, a potentially competitive technology.

If much greater amounts of electricity were needed by the distant customers, the new infrastructure would be used more intensively, reducing the cost. For sufficiently high demand (more than 9 GW), it would be cheaper to build a new rail line than to construct multiple transmission lines. Gasifying the coal and shipping it via pipeline might be an even more competitive alternative.

Ultimately the answer to the question of shipping coal, methane, or electricity depends on the distance, the amount of spare capacity in infrastructure already in place, and the amount of energy to be shipped. Longer distances and greater amounts of energy favor rail and pipelines over transmission. Since the capital costs are the largest part of total costs, not having to build a large part of the infrastructure by relying on existing rail, transmission lines, or pipelines is likely to be the cheapest alternative.

While the social costs do not change the recommendation, internalizing the externalities associated with emissions serves to strengthen the case for rail over transmission. Burning additional coal to make up for transmission losses leads to larger pollution emissions than from the diesel locomotives. Accounting for these social costs strengthens the argument for gasifying the coal and using a combined-cycle plant.

14

Life Cycle Assessment of Residential Buildings in the United States[1]

Residential buildings are significant within the U.S. economy, not only in construction, but in maintenance and operation. The value of new construction of residences in 2000 was about 4.2% of the gross domestic product (USCB 2001a). By 1999, there were 105 million occupied residential units in the United States, and the residential sector consumed 18 trillion Btu of direct energy, representing about 19% of total U.S. energy consumption. In this chapter, we estimate overall environmental impacts of U.S. residences and discuss some approaches to ameliorate these impacts.

Residences have associated environmental impacts in consumption of non-renewable resources, and emission of toxic and nontoxic substances to subsoil, land, water, and air. New residential single-unit structure construction contributed 5% to the total U.S. global warming potential emissions (Hendrickson and Horvath 2000), and 6% to U.S. total equivalent toxic air releases (Horvath et al. 1995). These construction impacts are significant alone, even without considering use, maintenance, and disposal of the buildings.

This chapter makes a quantitative and qualitative environmental assessment of the relative importance of the residential buildings sector in the whole economy of the United States, considering the role that the complete life cycle of these buildings plays, including construction, use, and disposal as shown in Figure 14-1. Figure 14-2 summarizes relative impacts in five categories for the three life cycle stages. Figure 14-3 summarizes the relative share of national totals derived from residences, with nearly 40% of all electricity used for residences while only 4% of GDP is derived from the sector. We comment on possibilities for environmentally conscious design, pollution prevention, and sustainable development, through better selection of construction materials,

---

[1]This chapter was originally written by Luis Ochoa, Chris Hendrickson, and Scott Matthews (Ochoa et al. 2002).

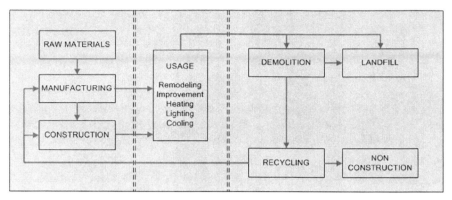

FIGURE 14-1. Life Cycle Phases for Residential Buildings

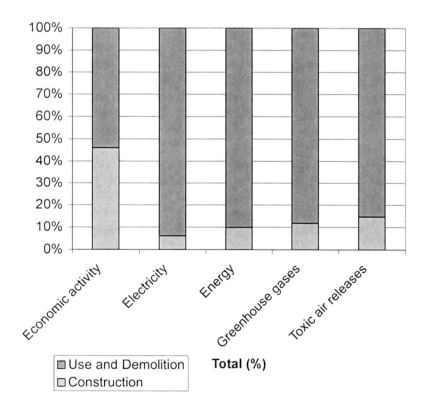

FIGURE 14-2. Comparative Impacts of Different Life Cycle Phases for U.S. Residential Buildings, 1997

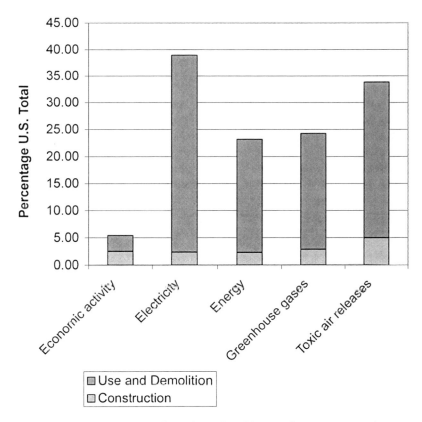

FIGURE 14-3. Relative Impact of Residential Buildings Relative to U.S. Totals, 1997

energy efficiency techniques, improved construction equipment, reductions in construction waste, and public policies.

Life Cycle Analysis and Boundaries

Construction Phase

For 1997, the value of new residential buildings put in place for the category single-unit residential buildings was $175 billion. This excludes the cost of land but includes overhead and profits. We use this amount to estimate the supply chain effects of this construction. The results from the EIO-LCA analysis appear in Table 14-1. In 1997, multi-family residential buildings represented $22 billion in new construction (USCB 2001a, No. 1191) and public housing $6.2 billion, so the total amount of construction in this category is $28 billion. In the 1992 EIO benchmark, multi-family residential housing construction was split into several sectors, but for the 1997 EIO benchmark, they are consolidated into a single sector, new multi-family housing structures, non-farm.

Use Phase

For characterizing use phase resources, we consider remodeling, improvement, and energy consumption of all existing residential buildings within the United States in 1997. The U.S. Census Bureau (USCB 2001b) reports expenditures for improvement of residential properties in 1997 of $120 billion for maintenance and repairs, additions and alterations, and major replacements. We model this economic activity in EIO-LCA with the sector "new residential additions and alterations, non-farm." See Table 14-1.

The U.S. Census Bureau (USCB 2001a, No. 961) reports 1,100,000 MkWh (or 3,800,000 TJ) for total electricity utility sales to residences in 1997. The average cost of electricity was 6.9 cents per kWh (EIA 2001a, Table 8), suggesting expenditure of $89 billion input for the matching power generation and supply sector (see Table 14-1). The consumption of electricity and energy require an additional step in this case. The EIO-LCA output for producing the $89 billion of electricity is just the electricity required by the supply chain to produce the electricity consumed by the households. We must add the actual electricity consumed in residences (1.1 MkWh) as shown in Table 14-1.

Natural gas is another major component in the energy consumption of households. The Energy Information Administration (2001b) reports consumption of 4,984 billion cubic feet in 1997 for the residential sector and notes the natural gas production price in 1997 of $6.9 per thousand cubic feet. With these data, the total increased economic activity that drives the assessment in Table 14-1 for the natural gas distribution sector is $35 billion. Again, we must add the energy content of the natural gas consumed in the residence (6 million TJ) to the supply chain energy calculated in EIO-LCA.

Disposal Phase

For this stage, we estimate emissions due to the demolition process and debris transportation. The Census of Construction Industries (USCB 1995) reports a total of $117 million of demolition activity in 1992. Inflating this to 1997 and assuming a 3% growth rate results in an estimate for demolition of $136 million. We estimate environmental impacts of this activity using the other Construction sector that includes SIC 1795, wrecking and demolition work. This is probably an underestimate since specialty contractors do not undertake some demolition. However, even if the demolition activity were two or three times larger, the estimated impact of demolition would still be small relative to construction or use.

TABLE 14-1. EIO-LCA Direct and Indirect Impact Results for Residential Buildings, 1997

EIO-LCA sector	Increased economic activity ($million)	Electricity used (MkWh)	Energy Used (TJ)	Greenhouse gases released (GWP, CO_2 equiv. million mt)	Toxic air releases (TRI, mt)
(a) *Construction*					
New residential single-unit structures, nonfarm	180,000	65,000	2,000,000	170	27,000
New multifamily housing structures, nonfarm	28,000	9,200	270,000	24	2,900
Total	210,000	74,000	2,300,000	190	30,000
(b) *Use*					
New residential additions and alterations, nonfarm	120,000	49,000	1,800,000	160	21,000
Electrical services, utilities*	89,000	1,100,000	13,000,000	950	150,000
Natural gas distribution*	35,000	1,100	6,000,000	320	1,700
Total	240,000	1,200,000	21,000,000	1,400	175,000
(c) *Demolition*					
Other construction	136	33	1500	0.1	11

*EIO-LCA result plus actual consumption.

U.S. Economy Benchmark

To show the environmental impact of the residential buildings sector within the whole economy, we established the U.S. benchmarks that appear in Table 14-2. Based on these data, we compare the economic and environmental performance of residential buildings along their life cycle with the U.S. economy, identifying the contribution of each of the three phases within the residential buildings total (Figure 14-3).

Discussion of Life Cycle Assessment Results

As shown in Figure 14-2, the construction phase represents nearly half of the economic activity among the three phases, but construction electricity and energy consumption is about 5% of the total consumption of residential buildings, and its contribution to global warming effects is also small. The disposal phase plays a minor role, with a negligible share of economic activity and environmental emissions. The use phase is important for the consumption of electricity and energy, and for greenhouse gas releases. The energy consump

TABLE 14-2. U.S. Economy Benchmarks, 1997

Item	Value	Source
Gross domestic product (GDP)	$8,318,400 billion	USCB (2001a)
Electric utility total sales	3,140,000 MkWhr	USCB (2001a, No. 961)
Total energy	99,500,000 TJ	USCB (2001a, No. 942)
Greenhouse gas total emissions	6,678,000,000 metric tons of CO_2 equivalents	U.S. EPA (2001a)
Total toxic air emissions	604,575 metric tons	U.S. EPA (2001c)

tion profile of the use phase is closely related to some important features in the construction phase: materials and HVAC, assembling techniques, design and orientation of windows and openings, shading and glazing, etc. This profile can be significantly reduced by a proper redesign of these features, which typically implies higher construction costs but savings in electrical and gas bills and reductions in emissions to the environment. The payback time may vary considerably, depending on utility prices and discount rates (Blanchard and Reppe 1998).

Using our estimates from Table 14-1 and the benchmarks in Table 14-2, we calculate the impact of residences relative to the entire economy. In Figure 14-3, we note the considerable portion (5%) that residential buildings contribute to the whole economy. Residential impacts in other areas are much higher, with electricity at 39%, energy at 23%, greenhouse gas emissions at 24%, and toxic air releases at 34%. The high toxic air releases reflect the relatively recent requirement for electric utilities to report them.

Governmental rules that require new central air conditioners in the market to be 20% more efficient by the year 2006 (Wald 2001a) would "eliminate the need for 27 power plants of 400 megawatts each, nationwide, by 2030," with total savings—considering cost—of $2 billion over the next 30 years. For clothes washers, the newly approved standard requires a 22% increase in efficiency for 2004, and 35% by 2007 (Wald 2001b), with estimated savings of "7,100 gallons of water a year for the average consumer, along with $48 in electric bills...equal to the output of a dozen 400-megawatt power plants." There is a federal voluntary program "Energy Star" to assist consumers in choosing more energy-efficient appliances. Another proven energy-saving technology is the "geothermal heat pump," which is part of a "home heating and cooling system that circulates fluids through underground coils but otherwise uses conventional technologies" (Kahn 2001). This system saves electricity and eliminates the use of natural gas for water heating.

In this aggregate study, we find that electricity consumption for the use stage of residential buildings is 95% when considering the construction and disposal phases altogether. This includes direct and indirect contributions of the whole supply chain of materials and service suppliers, and is based on rough figures for the whole residential buildings sector. A detailed analysis of a single-family house (Keoleian et al. 2001) concluded that the use phase accounted for 91% of the total life cycle energy consumption over a 50-year home life.

The contribution of residential buildings to global warming is also important, with the use phase as the main actor. This would diminish with a reduction in the consumption of energy by homeowners. Cleaner technologies for generating electricity (solar, wind, biomass, and geothermal) may also help. Hazardous waste is also considerable for residences. Substituting hazardous construction materials is a possible strategy, as well as minimizing materials off-cutting when designing for construction, and making improved waste management plans. Bans on lead and asbestos are other good examples. One government-sponsored initiative to promote the use of more sustainable materials is the National Institute of Standards and Technology Building for Environmental and Economic Sustainability system (Lippiatt 2000), which offers the community information and software tools to judge the sustainability of construction materials. TRI air emissions from residential buildings are roughly proportionate with their economic activity, with major sources in off-road construction equipment, dump trucks, and particles emitted during the manufacturing of materials and the production and consumption of energy. More stringent emissions standards for diesel fuel and engines have been proposed (Marquis 2001). This would cut air pollution by 95%, gradually reducing the sulfur content of highway diesel by 97% by 2010.

Another effort toward sustainability of buildings is known as LEED (Leadership in Energy and Environmental Design). This program of the U.S. Green Building Council evaluates the environmental performance of the building's life cycle in areas like sustainable site, water efficiency, energy and atmosphere, materials and resources, and indoor environmental quality (GBC 2001).

Conclusions

This chapter assesses electricity consumption and environmental emissions (greenhouse gases, hazardous waste, and TRI air emissions) for the residential buildings sector of the U.S. economy in 1997. The method is an online economic input–output life cycle assessment, which includes direct and indirect contributions of the whole supply chain of materials and service suppliers and provides fast and comprehensive results based on the remainder of the U.S. economy model. We find that in the life cycle of residential buildings, the construction phase is the largest contributor to economic activity, hazardous waste, and toxic air emissions, while the use phase accounts for disproportionate electricity consumption, energy use, and greenhouse gas emissions. The contribution of the disposal phase is negligible. The residential buildings percentage of hazardous wastes, toxic wastes, and global warming potential and energy is larger than the fraction of the gross domestic product generated, suggesting it should receive particular attention for research, support, and regulation.

PART III

Further Developments in the EIO-LCA Method

Parts I and II described the EIO-LCA model and presented a number of applications as examples. Part III develops some extensions and alternative models.

Chapter 15 extends EIO-LCA to include examination of safety risks by adding a safety vector to the basic model. This type of extension could be used for any case in which impacts can be estimated by industrial sector. For example, employment impacts of investments are often of interest.

Chapter 16 introduces some regional EIO-LCA models. A region may be a state, a portion of a state, or a group of states. Regional models are of interest to obtain estimates of the local impacts of changes. Of course, the availability of data for regions is a major concern. Often, regional models are derived from national input–output tables.

Chapter 17 describes a Canadian EIO-LCA model. The same techniques used for EIO-LCA can be used for any country with input–output models and appropriate environmental impact data. While most countries have economic input–output models, they tend to be at a more aggregate level than the 480-sector U.S. model. As a result, aggregation errors can arise (see Chapter 4 and Appendix IV). Also, many countries do not publish environmental impact data, although these data are becoming more readily available. Many countries have implemented Pollutant Release and Transfer Registers, similar to the U.S. Toxics Releases Inventory.

As an example of the types of results possible from input–output models from different regions, Table 17-1 shows some estimated impacts for a reinforced concrete roadway section using the U.S. model from Chapter 10, a Pennsylvania model described in Chapter 16, and a Canadian model described in Chapter 17. The results are surprisingly close, despite numerous differences between the three application areas and quite different data sources.

Chapter 18 develops input–output models at the enterprise level. Material flow models in manufacturing plants are widely used, and an input–output formulation can aid quantitative analysis of plant changes. These models are typically based on proprietary information and used solely for internal company purposes.

Most of the extensions described in this section are available on the EIO-LCA website: www.eiolca.net. For example, fatality and safety impacts are available from Occupational Safety and Health Administration data. Readers can use these various extensions or create their own.

15

Occupational Safety Risks in an Input–Output Framework

Improving occupational safety has been a significant policy goal in state-enacted workers' compensation laws throughout this century. By 1965, Congress judged state regulation to be insufficient to protect workers and so created the federal Occupational Safety and Health Administration (OSHA). Despite efforts of employers and regulators, workplaces are inherently risky. OSHA and its state counterparts continue to seek reduction in workplace injuries and illnesses. The current safety regulations involve detailed descriptions of personal protective equipment, protective equipment for machines and facilities, and training requirements. Inspections target facilities with poor safety or compliance records. Fines are levied to punish the employer and to force actions to eliminate or at least reduce the hazard. Major incidents that involve death or severe injury garner headlines and an immediate investigation by OSHA, generally followed by fines and orders to remedy the situation. However, companies have exhibited little concern for the safety records of the companies from which they purchase goods and services.

We conjecture that safety concerns have not reached up into the supply chain because there are no estimates of the occupational injuries embodied in a product or service. We expect that manufacturing companies and consumers will react to data on the occupational injuries embodied in a product or service by seeking alternatives that cause fewer injuries and deaths to workers. For example, we examine the OSHA data on injury rates for coal and iron ore mining, transportation of these minerals, iron and steel making, and automobile manufacture. The occupational injuries embodied in a car are not just those associated with assembling the vehicle. Rather, the injuries accumulate from the mining and transport of coal and iron ore, making, rolling, and casting steel, and making the components that are assembled into the automobile. The occupational injuries associated with assembling a car are a small fraction of the total occupational injuries from the entire supply chain.

This chapter focuses on the performance of sectors with respect to occupational safety. First, we consider the injuries, illnesses, and fatalities that occur within each sector, as reported to OSHA. We translate these "direct" injuries, illnesses, and fatalities into the occupational injuries associated with every sector through their own safety record and the safety record of the suppliers to the sectors. Finally, we discuss the policy implications of these calculations and new approaches for data analysis from regulations in the future. This chapter has been adapted from Matthews and Lave (2000).

The use of the economic input–output model for safety risk analysis illustrates one pathway for broadening and extending the use of the model system. As shown in previous chapters, we can broaden an economic input–output model to estimate environmental life cycle impacts by adding environmental impact vectors to the model. By adding occupational safety impacts, we can estimate supply chain safety risks. A similar extension can be used to estimate employment effects from new purchases with an employment vector.

Current Design of Safety Data and Regulations

OSHA data are summarized and published by the Bureau of Labor Statistics (BLS) and published on the Internet (OSHA 2005). Individual companies and facilities report the data to OSHA; they include such information as the type of injury or illness that occurred, the cause of the incident, and the resulting work restrictions of the injured or ill employee. Businesses submit annual summaries of incidents based on the rate of injury and illness experienced per 100 fulltime workers. Fatal and nonfatal injuries are reported separately. The overall number of nonfatal injuries and illnesses for private industry is approximately 5 to 6 million annually, or about 5 to 8 per 100 fulltime workers. The injury and illness rates are a relative estimate of safety and are somewhat comparable across industries and facilities of different scope and size. However, the rates do not distinguish between job types within an industry (for example, within the mining industry a machine operator and a clerical worker have very different safety risks).

Although the cause of an industrial incident resulting in injury or illness is reported to the BLS, the severity of the injury or illness is difficult to assess. A fall could result in an injury as mild as a minor bruise or as serious as quadriplegia. One means to assess severity of safety incidents is lost workday data. Lost workday cases include incidents that resulted in an employee missing one or more days of work (excluding the day of the injury or illness) or an employee being placed in a restricted work activity, or both. An injury or illness that results in lost workdays or restricted work activity can be assumed to be more severe than an incident that does not. The rate of lost workday cases per 100 fulltime workers has fallen from around 4 in the mid-1990s to about 3 in 2002.

About one-half of all workplace injury and illness result in some lost work or restricted work activity. Lost workdays consider only individual incidents with restricted work or time away from work, and do not consider the length of time. Thus, the data do not give a complete picture of injury and illness severity. However, since the rate data are comparable across industries, these data are used in this analysis with annual average employee figures to calculate the total number of lost workday cases for each industry sector.

Data on incidents involving fatal injuries are published separately in the Census of Fatal Occupational Injuries. Deaths in private industry caused by workplace hazards have hovered around 6,000 per year for the past decade. Unlike injuries or illnesses, the occurrence of a fatality in some sectors is extremely rare.

Although the data on safety incidents are collected and reported regularly, the data have some limitations. The data are self-reported, which likely leads to underreporting. Since the rate data are the basis for OSHA auditing, facilities have some incentive to underreport to avoid scrutiny by regulators. Audits completed by OSHA estimate that total injury and illness cases are underreported by about 10%, and that lost workday cases are underreported by about 25% (Conway and Svenson 1998). Also, illnesses due to occupational exposures are much more difficult to identify. The cause of an illness may not initially be connected to workplace conditions, or may have a delayed onset and is not recognized as caused by the workplace. These unidentified illnesses do not affect the rate of incidence for a facility, but do affect the costs sustained by companies.

The rate data collected by OSHA have been used to focus on reducing incidents in industries where rates are high, while ignoring industries where rates are generally low. The stagnant overall rates of both nonfatal and fatal injury and illness over the past decade may be due to the limitation of the regulatory design and how performance of industries is measured. The focus on high rates of injuries has led to regulatory control tailored to situations in a specific industry. Only recently has OSHA begun collecting the cause of injuries or illness from the annual reports of businesses (Abraham et al. 1996). By analyzing the root causes of incidents across industries, OSHA is now attempting to address problems that are common in different workplaces.

Safety Risks in the EIO-LCA Model

In this chapter the EIO framework is augmented with occupational lost workday cases and fatalities to estimate the total occupational risk across the economy associated with increasing demand for a given sector. However, BLS does not report occupational safety data down to the level of the 480 sectors in the detailed EIO model. In the absence of disaggregate data, we use the 1992 economic input–output total requirements matrix at the 80 × 80 sector level as a basis in this chapter. The matrix was aggregated to a 38 × 38 standard industrial classification (SIC) sector level to match the sector divisions used with the published safety data. The aggregation was based on the proportion of output of each of the industry sectors included in the major sector categories. Note that the 1992 EIO model is based on SIC rather than the new North American Industrial Classification System (NAICS) categories.

Injuries and Illnesses

Table 15-1 lists the results of the analysis using lost workday case data and economic output of the various industries for 1992. The data in the third column show the direct lost workday rate per 100 fulltime workers ranging from a high of 9.5 in food and kindred products (SIC 20) to a low of 1.8 for communications (SIC 48). Other sectors with high rates are those usually thought to be risky, including coal mining (SIC 12) at 7.7 and lumber and wood products (SIC 24) at 7.6. As indicated earlier, these rate data are comparable across sectors and give an indication of the risk involved for all employees in an industry. Again, since only a small proportion of workers have the dangerous jobs at the mine face or felling trees, the rate for an industry is decreased by averaging the much safer jobs of clerks, for example.

The safety impact per dollar of output tells a different story. The direct lost workday cases per million dollars of output, shown in the fourth column of Table 15-1, estimates risk based on the products and processes of an industry. The services sector (SIC 70, 72, 76) now tops the list with 0.77 lost workday cases per million dollars of output, followed by furniture and fixtures (SIC 25) and eating and drinking establishments (SIC 58), each with 0.73 cases. Using the EIO model to calculate supply chain effects across all industry sectors, the total (direct plus indirect) lost workday cases per million dollars of output for an additional million dollars in final demand is calculated and given in the seventh column of Table 15-1. Leather and leather products (SIC 31) now tops the list with 1.25 lost workday cases throughout the economy per million dollars of the sector output.

The lost workday cases directly attributed to an industry sector can be compared to the indirect lost workday cases—those occurring in other industry sectors. Shown in column six of Table 15-1, the ratio of indirect to direct lost workday cases gives the relative risk in other industries due to production in an industry. A value of one indicates an equal number of lost workday cases inside and outside the industry. Numbers larger than one indicate higher numbers of lost workday cases in supplier industries. Petroleum and Coal Products (SIC 29) is significantly higher in indirect lost workday cases than other industries with a ratio of 10.7. We infer that the high ratio means that great care is taken to protect worker health and safety in this sector, although suppliers are notably

TABLE 15-1. Lost Workday Risk per Million Dollars of Output

SIC	Industry	Direct lost workday rate per 100 workers	Direct lost workday cases per $M output	Indirect lost workday cases per $M output	Ratio: indirect to direct	Total lost workday cases per $M output
1, 2, 7-9	Agriculture, forestry, and fishery	5.4	0.278	0.363	1.305	0.641
10	Metal mining	3.3	0.163	0.327	2.001	0.490
12	Coal mining	7.7	0.359	0.264	0.735	0.623
13	Oil and gas extraction	3.0	0.100	0.180	1.805	0.280
14	Nonmetallic materials	3.7	0.274	0.246	0.897	0.521
15-17	Construction	5.8	0.382	0.407	1.066	0.789
20	Food and kindred products	9.5	0.385	0.532	1.383	0.917
21	Tobacco	2.4	0.029	0.174	5.953	0.203
22	Textiles	4.2	0.369	0.477	1.295	0.846
23	Apparel	4.0	0.567	0.481	0.849	1.048
24	Lumber and wood products	7.6	0.590	0.564	0.956	1.154
25	Furniture and fixtures	6.6	0.731	0.435	0.595	1.166
26	Paper and allied products	5.0	0.261	0.430	1.647	0.692
27	Printing and publishing	3.2	0.238	0.273	0.949	0.561
28	Chemicals and allied products	2.8	0.104	0.330	3.183	0.434
29	Petroleum and coal products	2.8	0.031	0.327	10.695	0.357
30	Rubber and miscellaneous products	6.8	0.532	0.339	0.637	0.872
31	Leather and leather products	5.4	0.688	0.558	0.811	1.246
32	Stone, clay, and glass products	6.1	0.514	0.353	0.686	0.867
33	Primary metal industries	7.1	0.351	0.463	1.320	0.814
34	Fabricated metal industries	6.6	0.532	0.408	0.768	0.940
35	Industrial machinery and equipment	4.2	0.325	0.402	1.236	0.727
36	Electronic and electric equipment	3.6	0.264	0.368	1.392	0.632

(continued on next page)

TABLE 15-1. (Continued) Lost Workday Risk per Million Dollars of Output

SIC	Industry	Direct lost workday rate per 100 workers	Direct lost workday cases per $M output	Indirect lost workday cases per $M output	Ratio: indirect to direct	Total lost workday cases per $M output
37	Transportation equipment	7.1	0.344	0.530	1.539	0.875
38	Instruments and related products	2.7	0.193	0.286	1.486	0.479
39	Miscellaneous manufacturing	5.0	0.440	0.403	0.916	0.843
40-47	Transportation	6.7	0.612	0.293	0.479	0.904
48	Communications	1.8	0.096	0.212	2.202	0.308
49	Electric, gas, and sanitary services	3.6	0.121	0.247	2.033	0.368
50-57, 59	Wholesale and retail trade	3.6	0.621	0.145	0.233	0.766
58	Eating and drinking establishments	3.1	0.729	0.365	0.501	1.094
60-64, 67	Finance and insurance	1.9	0.224	0.202	0.901	0.425
65	Real estate	3.1	0.039	0.096	2.432	0.135
70, 72, 76	Services	3.8	0.767	0.226	0.295	0.992
73	Business services	2.6	0.284	0.164	0.578	0.449
75	Auto repair, services, and parking	3.3	0.209	0.291	1.388	0.500
79	Amusement and recreation services	4.4	0.424	0.243	0.574	0.567
80-83	Health, legal, education, and social services	3.4	0.427	0.175	0.411	0.502

unsafe. The tobacco industry (SIC 21) has about half that at 5.9, and chemical and allied products (SIC 28) follows with a ratio of 3.2. These results indicate that while an industry may be perceived as fairly safe based on reported data, as these three sectors are with lost workday rates per 100 fulltime employees less than 3.0, the overall risk created throughout the economy can be very high. In the case of real estate (SIC 65), which ranks fourth with a ratio of 2.4, the transfer of property involves generally safe clerical office work; but sales include development of property by the construction sector (SIC 15-17), a high-risk industry.

Fatalities

The analysis is repeated using the data on fatalities in the workplace. Results per $100 million of output are given in Table 15-2. The fatality rate per 1,000 employees, provided in column 3, ranges from a high of 0.68 for agriculture, forestry, and fisheries (SIC 1, 2, 7-9) to a low of 0.01 for five different sectors. The leather and leather products sector (SIC 31) had no recorded fatalities from 1992 to 1998. When considering the number of fatalities normalized to $100 million of output, agriculture, forestry, and fishery (SIC 1, 2, 7-9); lumber and wood products (SIC 24); and services (SIC 70, 72, 76) rank as the top three sectors for both direct and total fatalities, as shown in the fourth and seventh columns of the table.

The allocation of direct and indirect fatalities among the different categories, however, reveals important differences among industries. The ratio of indirect to direct fatalities in column six indicates that three sectors—petroleum and coal products (SIC 29), food and kindred products (SIC 20), and tobacco (SIC 21)—have a much higher proportion of fatalities occurring in the supply chain than directly within the industry. For every fatality within the petroleum and coal products sector (SIC 29), a dozen fatalities occur in other sectors in order to supply that sector with input materials. Not surprisingly, sectors normally considered as having high risk—agriculture, forestry, and fishery (SIC 1, 2, 7-9), mining (SIC 10 and SIC 12), and construction (SIC 15-17)— are at the bottom of this list. These are the most dangerous sectors and so the sectors they buy from are necessarily less dangerous. In fact, the 10 most risky sectors by fatality rate are in the bottom 15 in the ratio of indirect to direct fatalities, and all have ratios less than one. Many fatalities within these sectors are due to providing sectors further down the supply chain with inputs.

Injuries and Illnesses versus Fatalities

A comparison of the ratios of indirect to direct safety impacts reveals significant differences between the lost workday and fatality results. As shown in Tables 15-1 and 15-2, the ratios of indirect to direct lost workdays are numerically

TABLE 15-2. Fatality Risk per $100 Million of Output

SIC	Industry	Direct fatality rate per 1,000 workers	Direct fatalities per $100M output	Indirect fatalities per $100M output	Ratio: indirect to direct	Total fatalities per $100M output
1, 2, 7-9	Agriculture, forestry, and fishery	0.68	0.348	0.160	0.459	0.508
10	Metal mining	0.25	0.125	0.086	0.689	0.211
12	Coal mining	0.32	0.151	0.060	0.396	0.211
13	Oil and gas extraction	0.24	0.081	0.052	0.640	0.133
14	Nonmetallic materials	0.24	0.181	0.044	0.244	0.225
15-17	Construction	0.23	0.153	0.074	0.483	0.226
20	Food and kindred products	0.05	0.019	0.216	11.176	0.235
21	Tobacco	0.05	0.006	0.056	8.975	0.062
22	Textiles	0.02	0.015	0.082	5.403	0.097
23	Apparel	0.01	0.011	0.065	5.683	0.077
24	Lumber and wood products	0.29	0.228	0.195	0.853	0.423
25	Furniture and fixtures	0.02	0.025	0.083	3.288	0.108
26	Paper and allied products	0.03	0.018	0.089	5.029	0.107
27	Printing and publishing	0.02	0.020	0.043	2.149	0.063
28	Chemicals and allied products	0.03	0.013	0.065	5.193	0.078
29	Petroleum and coal products	0.09	0.010	0.114	12.011	0.124
30	Rubber and miscellaneous products	0.03	0.023	0.063	2.780	0.086
31	Leather and leather products	0.00	0.000	0.078	NA	0.078
32	Stone, clay, and glass products	0.09	0.077	0.081	1.051	0.158
33	Primary metal industries	0.09	0.043	0.086	1.998	0.130
34	Fabricated metal industries	0.04	0.029	0.065	2.206	0.094
35	Industrial machinery and equipment	0.03	0.022	0.053	2.406	0.075
36	Electronic and electric equipment	0.01	0.008	0.048	5.960	0.056

37	Transportation equipment	0.03	0.014	0.065	4.598	0.080
38	Instruments and related products	0.01	0.006	0.037	5.645	0.043
39	Miscellaneous manufacturing	0.03	0.027	0.061	2.274	0.087
40-47	Transportation	0.23	0.213	0.068	0.321	0.281
48	Communications	0.02	0.012	0.035	3.012	0.046
49	Electric, gas, and sanitary services	0.09	0.030	0.075	2.470	0.105
50-57, 59	Wholesale and retail trade	0.04	0.073	0.025	0.341	0.097
58	Eating and drinking establishments	0.03	0.059	0.085	1.433	0.145
60-64, 67	Finance and insurance	0.01	0.008	0.025	3.181	0.033
65	Real estate	0.04	0.006	0.024	4.248	0.029
70, 72, 76	Services	0.13	0.256	0.041	0.159	0.297
73	Business services	0.04	0.042	0.023	0.561	0.065
75	Auto repair, services, and parking	0.12	0.078	0.030	0.381	0.107
79	Amusement and recreation services	0.06	0.060	0.044	0.739	0.105
80-83	Health, legal, education, and social services	0.01	0.014	0.028	2.023	0.042

much different than that for fatalities. Only 7 of the 38 sectors have ratios greater than 2 for lost workdays, but 21 have ratios greater than 2 for fatalities. This indicates that lost workdays are a result of activity within a sector, but fatalities are due to demands from sectors further up the supply chain. Also, some sectors have considerable differences between the ratios for lost workdays and fatalities. For example, Food and Kindred Products (SIC 20) has a ratio of 1.4 for lost workdays, but a ratio of 11.2 for fatalities. Only eleven sectors have higher ratios for lost workdays than for fatalities.

A New Approach to Safety Regulations

OSHA pays little attention to small retail establishments such as restaurants. In addition to their small size, facilities in these sectors have low direct injury rates, which gives OSHA reason to focus inspections elsewhere. However, our model results suggest that eating and drinking establishments should receive a much higher priority. Evaluation of these workplaces to reduce common hazards could be quite beneficial in reducing overall expenditures on injuries. By targeting industries with high rates per employee, the government may be missing opportunities to demonstrate to industry leaders how costly hazards may be. This awareness in safety costs may increase the willingness of employers to seek out compliance assistance and voluntarily promote safety in the workplace, further alleviating the need for OSHA oversight and inspection.

Regulators target their efforts on workplaces where they believe their limited resources can have the most influence. Thus, they tend to focus on large workplaces and plants with the greatest safety and health burdens. The calculation of indirect safety risk adds a new dimension in setting priorities that might be used within the framework of the Government Performance and Results Act (1993). With the analysis of safety data in the input–output framework, OSHA regulators can examine the total health costs for a product or service and the effectiveness of their interventions on this cost. A large total cost implies that somewhere in the supply chain, some employer is either being lax or is simply operating a highly dangerous process. For suppliers with large plants and extremely dangerous operations, OSHA will have already made its presence felt. This analysis may provide a new way of identifying workplaces that were not previously recognized as unsafe because they are small.

Total safety risk would add a new dimension to assessing how well an industry is managing safety in its own workplace as well. Some measures to cut costs of safety may result in fewer industry-reported incidents, but an overall increase of risk. Contractor employment is a classic example (Levine 1997). An industry can subcontract a high-risk job to an outside industry, and any safety incidents will be accounted under the subcontracting firm. Since a subcontractor employee may not be familiar with a facility and its hazards, or may be new or temporarily employed and not aware of safety hazards, the subcontractor employee may actually face higher risk than a regular, fulltime industry employee. As a result, the direct safety problems and direct costs of safety are lower than realized. Use of the economic input–output analysis in this framework helps to identify industries with high indirect, supply chain safety issues. Analysis of total safety risk across the economy would also provide regulators with a measurement of whether safety risks are being reduced overall rather than merely being shifted from one industry to another.

Conclusions

While state and federal regulators have successfully reduced occupational injury and disease, the toll remains high. After decades of federal regulation and almost a century of state regulation, trying harder or marginal increases in budgets is unlikely to have much effect. Instead, exposing the costs of hazards throughout the supply chain to both employers and consumers may make a difference. Translating the OSHA data on occupational illness, injury, and death for specific industries into the direct and indirect occupational injuries for each sector provides this information. The results reveal that many service sectors, such as restaurants, are responsible for few direct occupational injury problems but, through the goods and services they purchase, are responsible for large numbers of occupational injuries throughout the economy.

Our study does not comment on whether OSHA's regulation of the most dangerous jobs is sufficiently stringent. We have not examined the costs and benefits of more stringent regulation. However, by providing companies and consumers with information on the occupational injuries associated with their purchases, we provide them with the data needed to change the system, if they desire to do that. As businesses and consumers have become more concerned about quality and the environmental implications of their actions, they have reached up the supply chain to demand better performance. An assembler can no longer hide behind the excuse that the lack of quality or unacceptable environmental performance comes from a supplier. The assembler is responsible for ensuring the quality of the assembled product, and the environmental performance of the supply chain, not just of the assembly. We think it is possible that the assembler and customer will care about the occupational hazards associated with the final good or service, not just of the final assembly. If so, responsible companies and consumers will open a new route to improve occupational safety, one independent of state and federal regulations.

16

Development of Regional Economic Input–Output Life Cycle Assessment Models

A ll the previous chapters of this book describe an LCA model and its applications based on input–output matrices of the U.S. economy, and resource use and environmental emission factors based on resource consumption, emissions, and waste data at the national level. However, input–output models can be developed for any geographic region, enterprise, or economy. In this chapter, we present an LCA model based on regional economic input–output data and environmental emission factors.

Regional input–output models are useful to assess local impacts of particular changes. For example, a user may be interested in assessing the economic impact of constructing a new stadium or the regional air emission effects of a new industrial plant. Generally speaking, the sectoral interactions for regional models are smaller than for a national model since firms often order supplies and inputs from outside the region. In the United States, regional models have been developed for portions of a state (such as southern California), a state itself, or a collection of states.

Interest in regional input–output (IO) analysis occurred almost simultaneously with the development of national-level input–output analysis. Hewings and Jensen (1986) provide an overview of the history, research, and issues in the field of regional I-O analysis.

In principle, constructing a regional I-O table is no different from constructing the table of a small nation. However, the U.S. Department of Commerce does not preserve the location of each economic entity in gathering their economic activity data. Instead, regional models are based on survey data, nonsurvey data, or hybrid methods involving a combination of data sources. The nonsurvey method uses the national tables to derive regional tables. The hybrid approach integrates the survey and nonsurvey approaches, taking advantage of the survey data and the cheaper and faster nonsurvey approaches.

The Georgia Interindustry System was among the first hybrid systems developed (Schaffer 1976). We focus on hybrid methods that are based upon the national input–output table. If accurate survey data are available, users can develop regional tables directly.

The shortage of data has been the central limitation in developing regional I-O models. While many governments have devoted resources to constructing national I-O tables as integral parts of their national accounting systems, regional models have received few resources. With a smaller number of firms operating in any particular region, issues of data confidentiality arise more frequently for regional models. For example, only a single automobile assembly plant might be operating in a particular region, so a published description of the regional auto assembly sector would reveal much of its proprietary operating information. Lack of data and issues of confidentiality have resulted in regional models that typically show less detail of economic sectors. As a result, errors of aggregation in LCA studies at the regional level may be more of a problem (see Chapter 4).

In the 1970s the Bureau of Economic Analysis (BEA) developed a method for estimating regional I-O multipliers: the Regional Industrial Multiplier System (RIMS), later updated as RIMS II (BEA 2004a). The method assumes that national data can be used to represent the composition of inputs purchased in the state. We describe this system below.

Two commercially available economic modeling software tools are the Regional Economic Models Inc. (REMI) and Impact Analysis for Planning (IMPLAN), which include input–output as a component of their model framework (REMI 2004; Minnesota IMPLAN Group 2004). REMI is a computing, forecasting, and simulation model for a region that assesses the economic and demographic impacts that a policy, project, or new industry may cause in a local economy. IMPLAN measures the one-time impact of new projects in a specified region and includes the direct, indirect, and induced effects; it builds an I-O model at the local level based on BEA's I-O accounts and other data. These models are restricted to economic issues and do not generally include environmental impacts. To date, the focus has been on economic impacts of policies (Lieu 1991), with some work on demographic impacts (Lieu and Treyz et al. 1992; Treyz 1996).

Using Regional Economic Multipliers to Develop Regional Economic Input–Output Models

The most common basis of a regional I-O system and, correspondingly, a regional LCA model (REIO-LCA) is the development of regional multipliers, which reflect the distribution of production within particular states, between states, and between regions in the United States. The multipliers are used to modify the existing national inter-industry transaction matrix (X_{kj}) in order to create regional total requirements coefficient matrices (T_{kj}) for EIO-LCA calculations.

Example: Regional Input–Output Modeling System (RIMS II)

RIMS II is the updated version of BEA's Regional Industrial Multiplier System developed in the 1970s. The multipliers are derived mainly from two data sources: the BEA's national I-O table, which shows the inter-industry relations of 491 U.S. sectors, and BEA's location quotients (LQ), which are used to adjust the I-O table to show the industrial structure and trading patterns of any region composed of one or more counties (BEA 2004a). The trading patterns here represent the imports required by the region if a sector's regional output does not meet the regional demand. The method assumes that the national data can be used to represent the composition of inputs purchased by the enterprises within a region.

The LQ is based on six-digit North American Industry Classification System (NAICS) sectoral wages and salaries from 2001 (BEA 2004c). It is calculated for sector j in region R as

$$LQ_j^R = \frac{\left[\dfrac{(SW)_j^R}{(SW)^R}\right]}{\left[\dfrac{(SW)_j^{US}}{(SW)^{US}}\right]} \tag{16-1}$$

where
    $(SW)_j^R$ = sectoral salaries and wages for sector j in region R
    $(SW)^R$ = regional total salaries and wages in R
    $(SW)_j^{US}$ = national sectoral salaries and wages for sector j
    $(SW)^{US}$ = national total salaries and wages.

The location quotients are used to create the regional direct requirements matrix (D_{kj}^S) from the national direct requirements table (D_{kj}). The BEA prepares the regional total requirements coefficients (T_{kj}^S) by calculating the Leontief inverse from the D_{kj}^S:

$$T_{kj}^S = \left(I - D_{kj}^S\right)^{-1} \tag{16-2}$$

where I = identity matrix.

The technical coefficients provided by the BEA for Pennsylvania for 20 row and 473 column industries are used to estimate total outputs purchased by the state in order to produce different final demands (BEA 2004d):

$$X^{PA} = T_{kj}^{PA} \times F \tag{16-3}$$

TABLE 16-1. Estimated Total Sectoral Outputs Purchased by Pennsylvania to Produce $10 Million of Final Demand by Aluminum Foundries (I-O 1997 33152A)

Sector number	Sector description	Estimated total outputs ($)
5	Manufacturing	14,611,000
20	Households	6,124,000
11	Real estate and rental and leasing	1,066,000
6	Wholesale trade	986,000
10	Finance and insurance	940,000
16	Health care and social assistance	826,000
8	Transportation and warehousing	805,000
7	Retail trade	680,000
12	Professional, scientific, and technical services	649,000
13	Management of companies and enterprises	519,000
19	Other services	500,000
3	Utilities	480,000
9	Information	403,000
18	Accommodation and food services	334,000
14	Administrative and waste management services	311,000
15	Educational services	126,000
1	Agriculture, forestry, fishing, and hunting	114,000
4	Construction	80,000
2	Mining	77,000
17	Arts, entertainment, and recreation	75,000
	Total for all sectors	29,706,000

Table 16-1 shows the estimated total sectoral outputs purchased by Pennsylvania to produce $10 million of final demand by aluminum foundries from the RIMS II model system.

The sectors are rank-ordered based on their estimated outputs as a result of $10 million of production of aluminum foundries. The largest contributors are the manufacturing (49%) and households (21%) sectors. Since the manufacturing sector is aggregated, incorporating 346 input–output industries, it is difficult to compare these results to those estimated using the EIO-LCA model.

Example: Gross State Product to Estimate Regional Economic Multipliers

As we noted in the introduction, a variety of different approaches can be used to develop multipliers representing the economic transactions within a particular region. In this section, we describe a regional model based upon the publicly available gross state product (GSP) for different industries. We chose GSP instead of REMI or IMPLAN to create our model since the GSP values are publicly available. Cicas (2005) provides more detail on the model.

GSP is one of the regional economic accounts provided by the Bureau of Economic Analysis of the U.S. Department of Commerce. GSP is the value added to total gross production by property located in the state and by labor (BEA 2004c). It incorporates employee wages and salaries with their supplements, tax and nontax liabilities, and property-type income, but does not include intermediate purchases. GSP estimates are provided for 63 industries for all 50 states and the District of Columbia in millions of current dollars and in millions of chained 1996 dollars.

The value added (or GSP) for industry j occurring in state S is equal to the difference between its total output produced in S and the total costs of intermediate inputs purchased in S (as illustrated in Table 1.1):

$$GSP_j^S = V_j^S = X_j^S - I_j^S \qquad (16\text{-}4)$$

where

GSP_j^S = BEA's gross state product estimate for industry j in state S

V_j^S = value added by industry j in state S

X_j^S = total output of the industry j produced in state S

I_j^S = total costs of intermediate inputs required by sector j in state S to produce X_j^S.

The 1997 GSP estimates are used to calculate state and regional economic multipliers. Since there is no direct relationship defined between the 63 aggregated GSP sectors and the 491 input–output industries in the national table, a bridge had to be created between the two industry accounting systems. The BEA defines which Standard Industrial Classification (SIC) system sectors are included in different aggregated GSP sectors (BEA 2004c). The allocation of GSP estimates to SIC industries is based on sectoral total outputs for all states as follows:

$$GSP_{SIC_j}^S = \frac{Output_{SIC_j}}{\displaystyle\sum_{i=1}^{n} Output_{SIC_i}} \times GSP_k^S \qquad (16\text{-}5)$$

where $GSP_{SIC_j}^S$ is the GSP estimate allocated to SIC sector j for state S, $Output_{SIC_j}$ stands for the total national output of SIC sector j, and n is the number of SIC sectors that are included in GSP sector k.

The U.S. Census Bureau has created a bridge between the SIC and the NAICS (USCB 2004). The NAICS sectors were mapped one-to-one to 1997 input–output industries except for construction sectors (230xxx), inventory valuation adjustment (S00700), and owner-occupied dwellings (S00800).

Since all construction industries are included in one aggregate GSP sector, the state estimates are allocated similarly to the method introduced above. As a result, the GSP values can be calculated for 489 input–output sectors for all states, the District of Columbia, and the United States. The other two sectors have not been converted because there are no NAICS equivalents.

The GSP estimates are used to compute state-level I-O multipliers in order to calculate the distribution of sectoral production between states, assuming that the proportion of total national output of sector *j* occurring in state *S* may be approximated with the ratio of GSP for industry *j* in state *S*, and the total national GSP for sector *j*:

$$\frac{X_j^S}{X_j^{US}} \approx \frac{GSP_j^S}{GSP_j^{US}} \tag{16-6}$$

where

X_j^S = total output of industry *j* occurring in state *S*
$X_j^{US} = \sum_S X_j^S$ = total national output of industry *j*

GSP_j^S = BEA's gross state product estimate for industry *j* in state *S*
$GSP_j^{US} = \sum_S GSP_j^S$ = BEA's national gross state product estimate for industry *j*

Table 16-2 provides an example for the GSP multipliers. It includes the GSP estimates (1997 state GSP) in millions of current dollars, which were calculated for the "Pulp mills" sector (322110) for the states in the BEA's Mideast economic region. The multiplier for Pennsylvania is equal to 0.062 in Table 16-2, which means that approximately 6.2% of the total national production of pulp mills occurs in Pennsylvania. The sectoral multipliers for the United States are always 1.00.

As a numerical example, Table 16-3 shows estimated GSP multipliers for ten sectors in Pennsylvania.

Regional Environmental Impact Vectors

In addition to regional input–output models, a proper REIO-LCA should have regional vectors of environmental impacts. The national EIO-LCA represents average national emissions and resource uses. However, regions can differ in important elements such as the mix of electricity generation or emission standards. In the EIO-LCA model, the national environmental emissions or resource inputs for each sector are divided by the sector outputs. Comparable data can be used to obtain regional average emissions. Unfortunately, detailed regional environmental pollution data are not easily available for all industrial sectors.

In the absence of direct regional emissions and outputs for each sector, various indirect methods can be used. For example, the average emissions of

TABLE 16-2. Example Gross State Product (GSP) Multipliers for the Pulp Mill Sector in States of the Mideast Region and the United States

I-O 1997	Region	1997 state GSP ($ million)	GSP multiplier
322110	Delaware	56.64	0.004
322110	District of Columbia	1.231	0.0001
322110	Maryland	93.08	0.007
322110	New Jersey	315.4	0.024
322110	New York	541.2	0.041
322110	Pennsylvania	818.5	0.062
322110	United States	13,255	1.000

TABLE 16-3. Example Gross State Product (GSP) Multipliers for Different Industries in Pennsylvania

I-O 1997	Sector name	1997 GSP for PA ($ million)	1997 US GSP ($ million)	GSP multiplier for PA
212100	Coal mining	1,128	10,610	0.106
221100	Power generation and supply	8,160	147,732	0.055
322110	Pulp mills	819	13,256	0.062
331111	Iron and steel mills	1,294	14,494	0.089
331312	Primary aluminum production	114	1,280	0.089
331315	Aluminum sheet, plate, and foil manufacturing	198	2,221	0.089
481000	Air transportation	2,290	58,047	0.039
7211A0	Hotels and motels, including casino hotels	1,400	53,928	0.026
S00101	Federal electric utilities	137	3,484	0.039
S00500	General government industry	29,039	757,253	0.038

different types of electricity generation can be obtained from the overall average factors for a particular region. Table 16-4 includes the national average electricity generation mix, with estimates for Hawaii and Washington using census data (Marriott 2004).

The generation mixes of Hawaii and Washington significantly differ from each other and from the national average mix. Power plants in Hawaii use mostly fuel oil to generate electricity. It causes larger air emissions than hydroelectric power, which is the main source of electricity in Washington.

In other cases, regional emissions are available but not at the level of detail required for the regional input–output model. In this case, some type of allocation may be needed. For example, the average emissions of the aggregate industrial sector may be assumed to be representative of the underlying industrial sectors.

TABLE 16-4. National and State Electricity Generation Mixes

Average electricity generation mix in the U.S.

Fuel type	Coal	Natural gas	Oil	Hydro	Nuclear	Other
Percentage	52	16	3	7	20	3

Electricity generation mix for Hawaii

Fuel type	Coal	Natural gas	Oil	Hydro	Nuclear	Other
Percentage	14.8	0	76	1	0	8.1

Electricity generation mix for Washington

Fuel type	Coal	Natural gas	Oil	Hydro	Nuclear	Other
Percentage	8.8	6.6	0.5	75	8	1.6

Source: Marriott 2004.

TABLE 16-5. Electricity Consumption and Environmental Impacts Occurring in Pennsylvania and the U.S. Due to Building a One Kilometer-long New Asphalt Pavement, Estimated with REIO-LCA and EIO-LCA

Environmental impact	Unit	Pennsylvania impacts by REIO-LCA	Average national impacts by EIO-LCA	Ratio of PA/U.S.
Electricity	kWh million	0.085	0.096	0.88
SO_2	metric ton	0.78	0.7	1.1
NO_x	metric ton	0.41	0.66	0.62
VOC	metric ton	0.22	0.56	0.40
CO	metric ton	0.6	1.9	0.32
PM_{10}	metric ton	0.55	0.35	1.6

Application of the Regional EIO-LCA Model

Here we compare the national and state environmental impacts associated with a one kilometer-long new asphalt pavement section using our REIO-LCA model created for Pennsylvania and the existing EIO-LCA model. We use the same I-O sector (324121) and material cost ($145,500) as in chapter 10.

The required state sector outputs are calculated by multiplying the total requirements coefficient matrix (T_{kj}^{PA}) by the material cost listed above. The matrix is obtained from the national table using the GSP multipliers for Pennsylvania. Table 16-5 summarizes the estimated environmental impacts in Pennsylvania.

Electricity use and SO_2 emissions are roughly the same, PM_{10} emissions are about 60% higher, NO_x emissions are about 40% lower, VOC emissions are about 60% lower, and CO emissions are only one-third of the national results. The differences are due to a different number of sectors in the Pennsylvania and the EIO-LCA models; there are only 483 in Pennsylvania against 491 in the national model. Further differences could also be due to local factors such as different technologies, transportation distances, uses of imported materials, and emission rates in Pennsylvania that differ from the national averages used in EIO-LCA.

17

A Canadian Economic Input–Output Life Cycle Assessment Model[1]

This chapter details the development and application of a national economic input–output life cycle assessment model for the Canadian economy. We apply the model to various sectors of the Canadian economy and determine the life cycle implications of demands for different commodities, including electricity and construction materials for highway design. For additional details about the model, see Bjorn et al. (2005).

Since the initial implementation of EIO-LCA models in the United States, comparable models have been developed for Japan and various European countries (Suh et al. 2004a). While several analyses of Canadian environmental issues have incorporated input–output modeling for example, Hayami et al. 1999), researchers have not previously developed an IO-based framework for use as a general tool to assess economy-wide life cycle effects in Canada.

The Canadian EIO-LCA model is derived from input–output (I-O) data from Statistics Canada and environmental and resource use data from Environment Canada and Natural Resources Canada. The resulting model is a commodity-by-commodity model for the year 1998, covering 62 industries and 102 commodities. The environmental coefficient matrix consists of vectors for marginal resource consumption, energy use, releases of National Pollutant Release Inventory (NPRI) compounds, and emissions of greenhouse gases (GHGs).

Methodology

The national EIO-LCA model for Canada has been developed in much the same way as the U.S. model. However, because of the different data collection

---

[1]This chapter is based on a paper originally written by Andrew Bjorn, Laura Declercq-Lopez, Sabrina Spatari, and Heather L. MacLean (Bjorn et al. 2005).

methods, format, and availability, as well as differences between the two economies, there are a few divergences.

Sources of Economic Input–output Data

Statistics Canada (2003) compiles and publishes I-O matrices at three levels of aggregation:

- "Small" or "S-level," with few commodity and industry sectors,
- "Medium" or "M-level," and
- "Link" or "L-level," which has the highest number of commodity and industry sectors.

The values in recently published matrices are deflated and reported in 1997 dollars, to allow for comparison between matrices of different years.

In a study such as this, the least aggregate input–output matrix (containing the largest number of sectors) is most desirable as the basis for a model; the higher the level of disaggregation, the better, with respect to determining the economic and environmental impacts of specific sector outputs. With more aggregation it is more likely that several activities will be included in one sector, making it difficult to allocate environmental burdens to specific sector outputs. However, there are tradeoffs between disaggregation and data completeness. The publicly available I-O information that Statistics Canada publishes is not complete, particularly at the L-level. This is due in part to the small size of the Canadian economy and the sensitive nature of some of this information. At the most disaggregate levels, some of the sectors may contain just one or two facilities, and there is concern that some of the associated flows that are defined in these matrices could be used to determine the use of certain commodities by individual firms or to determine their production processes. As a result, many of the rows and columns in the matrices do not follow basic identities for these types of models, and do not sum to the totals for the commodities and industries provided by Statistics Canada. Since the largest number of gaps is present in the L-level data (the most disaggregate data), we use the M-level I-O matrices for this model, which are more complete. They provide the data necessary to construct a 102 × 102-sector EIO-LCA model incorporating 62 industries and 102 commodities (a reasonable aggregation for the analyses). Primary inputs are not examined, as households are considered to be exogenous to this model. Further details on the commodity and industry classifications can be found in reports available from Statistics Canada (Lal 1998).

The make and use matrices required to develop the EIO-LCA model are taken from Statistics Canada, in CANSIM II Table 381-0014 (Statistics Canada 2003). The make and use tables are combined to obtain the transaction matrix as described in Chapter 1. These values are reported in 1997 dollars, which allow for ease of comparison with data from different years. Surrogates for any missing values are estimated by calculating the market share and commodity requirements for missing data values from previous years and averaging available values. The data used for this particular model are from the year 1998, the most recent available at the time of model development.

Sources of Environmental Data

We have selected the most consistent quantitative, publicly available environmental data for Canada for this initial version of the model. The data include energy and resource use, greenhouse gas emissions, and NPRI data for 1998 (the year of the economic I-O matrix of the model).

Energy and resource use data. Statistics for the production and use of nonrenewable resources in Canada were collected from two sources. Fuel and energy statistics were obtained from CANSIM II tables 128-0002 and 128-0003 (Statistics Canada 2003). Mineral and metal production statistics were obtained from *1998 Canadian Minerals Yearbook* (Natural Resources Canada 1999). For the model, production figures for aluminum, iron ore, copper, and nickel were used, as well as for cement and lime production.

Greenhouse gas emissions. For the EIO-LCA model, estimates for the three primary GHG—carbon dioxide (CO_2), methane (CH_4), and nitrous oxide (N_2O)— are derived from the 1998 Environment Canada Greenhouse Gas Inventory, corresponding to the year of the I-O model (Environment Canada 1999a, 2002). The categories in the model are emissions from fuel combustion, fugitive emissions from coal mining, and cement and lime production. In the 1998 inventory, emissions from these activities resulted in approximately 510 metric ton CO_2 equivalent, or about 73% of the 670 metric ton CO_2 equivalent emitted during the year by all sectors of the Canadian economy. The model does not include fugitive emissions from oil and gas extraction, solvent use, animal sources, soil management, land cover change, or waste disposal, as these values are subject to a high margin of error, or are difficult to correlate with sectors in the model. In calculating CO_2 equivalent for the purposes of reporting total GHG emissions in this model, the 100-year global warming potentials are used, which is standard for reporting under the Kyoto Protocol.

National Pollutant Release Inventory data. The National Pollutant Release Inventory is a federally legislated, publicly accessible inventory of the releases of toxic substances by Canadian industries and other organizations. The NPRI was modeled from the U.S. Toxic Release Inventory (TRI); the reporting requirements and format are similar but the TRI requires the reporting of a larger number of substances. For a detailed description of reporting requirements, see Environment Canada (1999b). As defined in NPRI regulations, a nonexempted facility must submit an NPRI report each year to Environment Canada if it meets criteria defined in the regulations. The total quantity of any compound reported under NPRI must be itemized according to on-site releases (including air, water, land, and underground emissions, which are separately reported), and off-site transport for disposal or recycling.

In the model, two categories of releases are included: total air releases and total production of wastes. These have been included as priorities since air releases can have a wide impact on the local and global environments, and an understanding of the total production of hazardous wastes from industries can be useful information on a national scale. Additional categories may be included later.

With the economic and environmental data detailed above, we have developed a 1998 national EIO-LCA model for Canada.

Application of the Canadian EIO-LCA Model

Environmental Effects Associated with Marginal Changes in Final Demand for Commodities

In the following analyses, we examine implications of marginal changes in final demand for a set of commodities within the Canadian economy. However, a basic comparison of environmental effects such as emissions or energy use by marginal increases in the value of purchased commodities is somewhat misleading; it is, in effect, comparing dissimilar quantities. One dollar's worth of electric power, for example, cannot be exchanged for one dollar of chemicals or even one dollar of gasoline. Any conclusions about environmental impacts must be based on full assessments of the life cycle impacts.

Figure 17-1 shows the total increases in GHG emissions associated with a marginal increase of $1 million in demand for the 15 commodities in the model with the highest calculated increases. Total emissions include both the direct emissions resulting from the production of the commodity examined and the subsequent indirect emissions resulting from supporting activities (the supply chain) throughout the economy. This figure shows that marginal increase in the demand for electric power results in the greatest quantity of greenhouse gas emissions associated with commodity production: approximately 4.5 kilotons CO_2eq per $ million are emitted directly from combustion of fuels used in the creation of electric power, and an additional 0.15 kilotons CO_2eq per $ million are emitted as the result of indirect effects across the economy. Although the total value is high in comparison to the other commodities in the Canadian economy, only about 29% of the electricity generated in Canada in 1999 originated from fossil-fuel plants (Statistics Canada 2003). The balance of

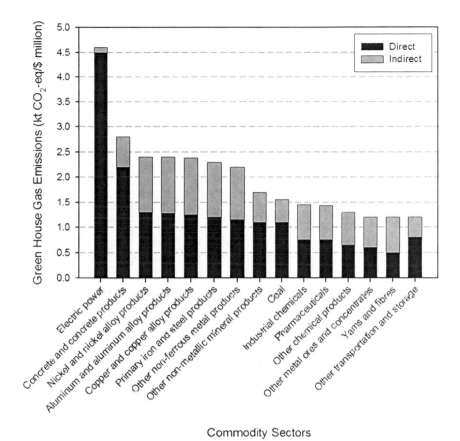

Commodity Sectors

FIGURE 17-1. Greenhouse Gas Emissions Increases from Marginal Increases in Commodity Sector Output for Top 15 Sectors

generating capacity was provided from "clean" sources that emit low levels of GHG during electricity production: hydroelectric, nuclear, and renewable energy facilities. It should be noted, though, that other portions of the life cycle of hydroelectric, nuclear, and renewable energy options can generate substantial amounts of these gases.

The 15 commodities with the highest increases in energy demand due to marginal increases in economic demand are shown in Figure 17-2. A marginal increase in the demand for electrical power results in the greatest increase in energy demands (52 TJ per $ million) over the entire economy, due primarily to direct demands for coal and natural gas for fossil fuel-fired plants. A considerable amount of direct and indirect energy demand also results from metal manufacturing, such as nickel and nickel alloy products (33 TJ per $ million), aluminum and aluminum alloy products (33 TJ per $ million), copper and copper alloy products (32 TJ per $ million), primary iron and steel products

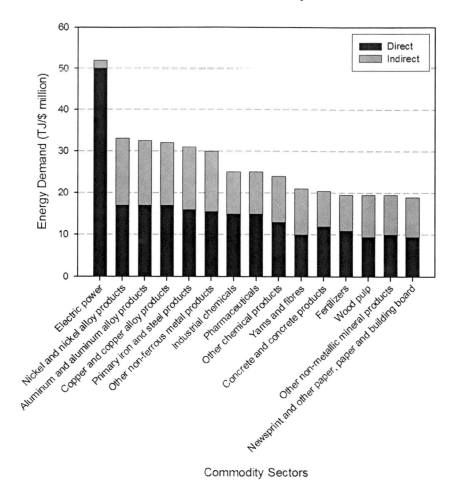

Commodity Sectors

FIGURE 17-2. Increases in Total Energy Demand From Marginal Increases in Commodity Sector Output for Top 15 Sectors

(31 TJ per $ million), and other metal products (30 TJ per $ million). Chemical and paper products, concrete and mineral commodities, and agricultural products also have high total energy demands. Because of the relationship between energy use and GHG emissions (a large proportion of the greenhouse gas emissions result from fossil fuel use), the commodities with high energy use generally also have high greenhouse gas emissions, as shown in Figures 17-1 and 17-2.

As an example of the model's ability to estimate direct and indirect production of a specific toxic compound (by sector) resulting from marginal changes in final demand, Figure 17-3 gives the direct and indirect production of benzene associated with the 15 commodities with the highest total emissions of

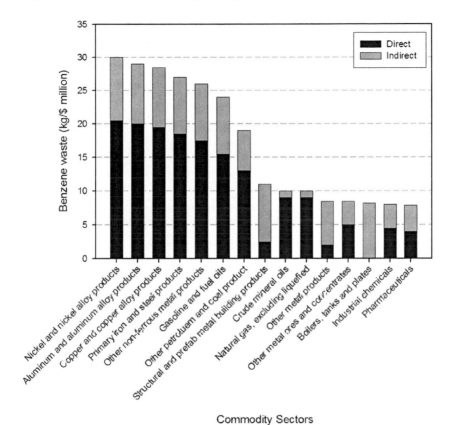

Commodity Sectors

FIGURE 17-3. Increases in Benzene Waste Production from Marginal Increases in Commodity Sector Output for Top 15 Sectors

benzene in the Canadian economy. According to these results, increases in the production of metal and metal alloy commodities, such as aluminum, copper, and iron, account for the largest increases in benzene waste production (30 kg per $ million for nickel and nickel alloy products, for example). Petroleum products, such as gasoline and fuel oil (24 kg per $ million), natural gas (10 kg per $ million), and crude mineral oils (10 kg per $ million), also result in significant emissions.

Evaluation of a Reinforced Concrete Highway using the Canadian EIO-LCA Model

Chapters 10 and 16 examine selected life cycle impacts of a steel-reinforced concrete highway using the Pennsylvania and U.S. EIO-LCA model. The quantities of concrete and steel reinforcement required for the highway are based on the design specifications. These material quantities are then multiplied by esti-

TABLE 17-1. Economic and Environmental Effects of Producing Construction Materials Required for One Kilometer of Reinforced Concrete Highway

	Direct effects	*Total effects*
Economic effects (1997 dollars)	$ 258,000	$ 383,000
Economic multiplier (total effects/final demand)		2.37
Greenhouse gas emissions	300 mt CO_2 eq	420 mt CO_2 eq
Carbon dioxide	300 mt CO_2	420 mt CO_2
Methane	30 kg CH_4	58 kg CH_4
Nitrous oxide	2.3 kg N_2O	5.3 kg N_2O
Electricity use	100 MW-hr	180 MW-hr
Energy use	2.1 TJ	3.9 TJ
Waste production		
Benzene	1.4 kg	1.7 kg
Carbon tetrachloride	8.0 g	16 g
Dichloromethane	370 g	820 g
Hydrogen fluoride	4.8 kg	5.5 kg
Methanol	3.4 kg	6.8 kg
Tetrachloroethylene	20 g	44 g
Trichloroethylene	12 g	32 g
Vinyl chloride	2.5 g	7.9 g

mates of producer prices for each of the materials, yielding the demand in dollars corresponding to the year of the model. These monetary values are the final demands into the relevant sectors of the EIO-LCA model. The relevant sectors were "primary iron and steel production" and "concrete and concrete products." We examine the same case study using the Canadian EIO-LCA model, although for a different target year and for Canadian prices.

For this example, final demands of $110,000 for "concrete and concrete products" and $51,400 for "primary iron and steel products" are input into the Canadian EIO-LCA model. These dollar amounts correspond to values calculated for 3,680 metric tons of concrete and 78 metric tons of steel.

Table 17-1 reports the results of the Canadian EIO-LCA model. This quantifies the total, direct, and indirect economic and environmental effects, throughout the Canadian economy, of the production of the two primary commodities required for a reinforced concrete highway. Many of these effects take place upstream in the supply chain; about 39% of the total greenhouse gas emissions are the result of indirect effects. Some environmental effects are not even present in the inventory of direct effects. Wastes of carbon tetrachloride, tetrachloroethylene, trichloroethylene, and vinyl chloride, for example, are not accounted for when calculating only direct effects. If a company formulated a list of substances that they desired to ban from their products, only through obtaining considerable information from their suppliers could they ensure that these compounds were not included in the components in their products.

TABLE 17-2. Energy Use, by Commodity, for Producing Construction Materials Required for One Kilometer of Reinforced Concrete Highway

Commodity	Energy demand (GJ)	Percent of total
Concrete and concrete products	1420	37
Primary iron and steel products	970	25
Electric power	440	11
Other metal ores and concentrates	123	3.2
Other transportation and storage	110	2.8
Other nonferrous metal products	95	2.4
Industrial chemicals	89	2.3
Aluminum and aluminum alloy products	82	2.1
Other nonmetallic mineral products	80	2.1
Nonmetallic minerals	73	1.9
Other chemical products	44	1.1
Wholesaling margins	29	0.8
Newsprint and other paper, paper and building board	28	0.7
Other services	25	0.6
Coated paper and paper products	22	0.6
Other commodities (85)	250	6.5
Total	390	

Effects can be itemized according to individual commodities as well. Table 17-2 details the total quantity of energy used to produce the concrete and reinforcing steel required for one kilometer of highway. As expected, the commodity sectors with the greatest energy demands reflect the direct production of the concrete and reinforcing steel: about 60% of the energy demands result from the direct production of these two commodities. Additional energy demands are also present as the result of increases in demand for electrical power, non-ferrous metal products and aluminum, chemical products, paper products, and transportation and storage.

Summary

In this chapter, we present the development and some initial applications of a national economic input–output life cycle assessment model for Canada. The model development generally follows that of the U.S. EIO-LCA model, but because of differences in data collection methods and data availability in the two countries, there are differences in the resulting models. The Canadian model is more aggregate and includes a smaller environmental matrix, but still provides useful insights related to the sectors in the Canadian economy.

18

Enterprise and Materials Flow
Input–Output Analysis

National economic input–output models have received the greatest attention, but they are not the only input–output models of interest. In this
book, we have used the 1997 U.S. national benchmark input–output model
extensively. Chapter 17 describes a comparable but smaller national model for
Canada. Similar national models exist for many countries, although few have
been developed to include a range of environmental impacts as in EIO-LCA.
Chapter 16 describes ways to estimate regional or state-wide models based
upon multipliers of the national input–output models. Small scale models and
models in physical units (rather than dollars) may also be of interest.

A small scale model could include several unit processes associated with a
plant or an enterprise. Outputs from one process can be used as inputs to other
processes. By using an input–output model formulation, the process transactions can be directly shown and any feedback loops (or circularities in flows)
properly accounted for. However, the input–output model assumes a strict proportionality of output for each unit of input. As a result, economies of scale and
diseconomies of scale are not considered, nor are effects such as worker learning curves or productivity changes.

National economic input–output models are usually based on transactions
valued in a currency, such as dollars or euros. Input–output matrix flows can
be reported in any set of consistent units. For example, one may wish to track
lead flows or total mass through different sectors in the economy. An
input–output materials flow model provides a convenient accounting scheme
for this purpose. Enterprise models can also be linked to national models
through disaggregation of a particular sector down to a company or plant level.
Appendix III describes methods for such disaggregation.

Using an input–output framework is one form of what is generally termed
"materials flow analysis" (NRC 2004). Most analyses in this area use flow dia-

grams among processes or enterprises. As described in Chapters 1 and 2, these flow diagrams can be recast as input–output matrices to facilitate quantitative analysis.

An Enterprise Input–Output Model

The input–output enterprise framework can be used to represent main products, purchased inputs, and byproducts. This is formalized in Lupis and McMichael (1999), based on the initial models of Lin and Polenske (1998) and Zuo (1985) and on data from the Aluminum Association (Weston 1998) for an integrated aluminum plant. We have simplified the numbers of inputs and outputs for this presentation.

Table 18-1 shows the direct input–output coefficient matrices for aluminum operations, with all units in metric tons. Negative values indicate use of a product by an operation. For example, alumina refining uses 2.64 metric tons of bauxite to produce one metric ton of alumina. The various operations appearing in the direct input–output model include bauxite mining, alumina refining, anode production, primary casting, secondary casting, shape casting, aluminum extrusion, hot rolling, and cold rolling.

For any particular desired final output (denoted by the vector Y), intermediate production must be sufficient to accommodate the desired production. Algebraically, this is represented as:

$$a \times X = Y \qquad (18\text{-}1)$$

where a is the direct requirements matrix, X is the vector of product outputs and Y is the vector of desired final output. The matrix a is equivalent to matrix $(I–A)$ in the national economic input–output model (Equation 1.1). Indeed, Table 18-1 includes the identity matrix (a diagonal consisting of all values of one) and subtracts the direct inputs (A). However, the units for the vectors X and Y are not dollars, but metric tons of output.

As with the national economic input–output model, we are usually interested in finding the required total production to obtain a particular final output. In this case, we can transform Equation 18-1 by using the inverse matrix a^{-1} and find:

$$X = a^{-1} \times Y \qquad (18\text{-}2)$$

where total output is the inverse of the direct requirement matrix multiplied by the vector of final demand.

We are often interested in additional items such as environmental impact. In the enterprise model, we would also like to account for purchased inputs from

TABLE 18-1. Direct Product Input-Output Coefficient Matrix for Aluminum Operations (entries in metric tons)

Main products	Bauxite mining	Alumina refining	Anode production	Al smelting	Prim. casting	Second casting	Shape casting	Al extrusion	Hot rolling	Cold rolling
Bauxite mining	1	-2.64	0	0	0	0	0	0	0	0
Alumina refining	0	1	0	-1.93	0	0	0	0	0	0
Anode production	0	0	1	-.455	0	0	0	0	0	0
Al smelt	0	0	0	1	-.990	0	0	0	0	0
Primary casting	0	0	0	0	1	0	-1.10	-1.5	-1.2	0
Second casting	0	0	0	0	0	1	-1.10	0	0	0
Shape casting	0	0	0	0	0	0	1	0	0	0
Al extrusion	0	0	0	0	0	0	0	1	0	0
Hot rolling	0	0	0	0	0	0	0	0	1	-1.2
Cold rolling	0	0	0	0	0	0	0	0	0	1

Source: Lupis and McMichael 1999.

outside the enterprise. Algebraically, these calculations would be:

$$Z^b = b \times X = b \times a^{-1}\_Y \qquad (18\text{-}3)$$
$$Z^p = p \times X = p \times a^{-1} \times Y$$

where b is the matrix of byproducts such as air emissions and p is the matrix of purchased inputs such as energy. Z^b and Z^p are the vectors of total byproducts and purchased inputs, respectively.

Table 18-2 shows a selected set of inputs for each operation. For example, production of a ton of bauxite requires 0.205 metric tons of water, 0.4 kWh of electricity, 1 kg of fuel oil, and 4 liters of diesel. Additional rows could be added to include other inputs, such as capital or labor.

Table 18-3 shows typical byproducts, with bauxite mining producing 0.136 mt of solid wastes, 0.0024 mt of particulate emissions, and 0.239 mt of water effluents for each metric ton of bauxite production. Again, additional impacts could be included by adding additional rows.

As a numerical example, suppose we wished to produce 0.738 metric tons of shape cast aluminum, 0.228 metric tons of extruded aluminum, and 0.034 metric tons of cold rolled aluminum. In this case, the vector Y would consist of all zero values except for these desired outputs.

Multiplying Y by the inverse of the a matrix (a^{-1}) reveals required process outputs as shown in Table 18-4.

The model in physical units developed above can be placed in monetary terms by multiplying by an appropriate price vector for the primary outputs, the byproducts, and the purchased inputs, P:

$$\text{Profit} = P^Y \times Y + P^b \times Z^b + P^p \times Z^p \qquad (18\text{-}4)$$

Fixed costs of production could also be added to this profit equation.

In practice, the model summarized in Table 18-1 could be altered to reflect different production strategies. In particular, the ratio of primary to secondary ingots could be readily changed. However, the ratio in the model of Table 18-1 is selected to balance prompt scrap from the different processes so that no net scrap was produced. Scrap is produced in the processes for shape casting, extrusion, hot rolling, and cold rolling. Scrap can be used in secondary casting, and the production of secondary casting in Table 18-1 is just sufficient to use the expected scrap from the other processes.

An alternative to balancing the production of prompt scrap would be to adjust production so as to maximize profit using Equation 18-4. In this case, manufactured scrap should be explicitly included as a byproduct of production with a market price.

A positive aspect of this enterprise input–output model is that it can be formulated from information routinely available within typical organizations.

TABLE 18-2. Other Inputs Coefficient Matrix for Aluminum Operations (entries in metric tons)

Main products	Bauxite mining	Alumina refining	Anode prod.	Al smelt	Primary casting	Second casting	Shape casting	Al extrusion	Hot rolling	Cold rolling
Caustic soda (mt)	0	0.074	0	0	0	0	0	0	0	0
Lime (mt)	0	0.046	0	0	0	0	0	0	0	0
Coke (mt)	0	0	0.231	0	0	0	0	0	0	0
Water (mt)	0.205	1.148	0.667	0.827	3.609	0.960	5.450	1.180	1.352	0.135
Electricity (kWh)	0.4	109	266	15,400	211	115	4	590	265	350
Fuel oil (kg)	1	93	4	0	18	0	0	0	0	0
Diesel (l)	4	0	0	0	0	0	0	0	0	0

TABLE 18-3. Byproduct Coefficient Matrix for Aluminum Operations

Main products	Bauxite mining	Alumina refining	Anode production	Al smelting	Prim. casting	Second casting	Shape casting	Al extrusion	Hot rolling	Cold rolling
Solid wastes (mt)	0.136	1.114	0.023	0.054	0.020	0.080	0.547	0.005	0.014	0.009
Particulate matter (mt)	0.0024	0.0004	0.003	0.005	0	0	0.008	0	0	0
CO_2 (C equiv. mt)	0	0	0.106	0.415	0.0002	0.018	0	0	0.0063	0.0001
Water effluents (mt)	0.239	2.126	0.671	0.827	3.609	0.922	5.450	1.180	1.347	0.138

TABLE 18-4. Some Impacts of a Case of Desired Production: 0.738 Metric Tons Shape Cast Aluminum, 0.228 Metric Tons Extruded Aluminum, and 0.034 Metric Tons Cold Rolled Aluminum

Main products	Bauxite mining	Alumina refining	Anode prod.	Al smelt	Prim. cast	Second cast	Shape cast	Al extrusion	Hot rolling	Cold rolling
Process output (mt)	6.018	2.280	0.537	1.181	1.193	0.811	0.738	0.228	0.041	0.034
CO_2 (C equiv.)	0	0	0.106	0.463	0.458	0.018	0.525	0.662	0.566	0.677
Electricity (kWh)	0	110	266	15,733	15,787	115	17,544	23,402	19,541	23,721

Source: Lupis and McMichael (1999).

TABLE 18-5. Annual Inter-sector Flows of Cadmium (metric tons)

I-O number	Sector name	212230 Copper, nickel, lead, and zinc mining	331492 Secondary processing of other nonferrous
212230	Copper, nickel, lead, and zinc mining	—	0
325180	Other basic inorganic chemical manufacturing	147	27
325211	Plastics material and resin manufacturing	49	9
331419	Primary nonferrous metal, except copper and aluminum	12	2
332812	Metal coating and nonprecious engraving	49	9
332813	Electroplating, anodizing, and coloring metal	49	9
335911	Storage battery manufacturing	918	166

The input–output model can be based on process mappings developed for environmental management systems (Matthews 2004). Price information is available from management information accounting systems. As a result, users of these models do not have to rely on aggregate statistics compiled by a national statistical office.

Materials Flow Models

The enterprise input–output model developed in the previous section can also be used as the basis for tracing material flows among different sectors of the economy. In contrast to economic input–output models, these materials flow models are commonly developed in mass units rather than currency.

As an example, Table 18-5 shows the annual flows of the metal cadmium from mining and secondary processing to various sectors using the metal. For each of these flows, costs and environmental impacts can be associated in the same fashion as Tables 18-2 and 18-3.

Once a materials flow model such as Table 18-5 has been developed, changes in production for particular products can be modeled. For example, the increase in metal flows due to changes in battery uses may be of interest. As with the enterprise model, production alternatives can also be investigated, such as increased imports or metal recycling versus primary production.

A complication of materials flow models that is not commonly addressed in economic input–output models is the effect of inventory and stocks. Metals may be stockpiled for later use. The flow of recycled materials may depend on policy decisions or economic factors. For example, recovery of reinforced steel from demolition concrete often depends upon whether the market price of steel scrap exceeds the cost of steel recovery (Horvath and Hendrickson 1998b).

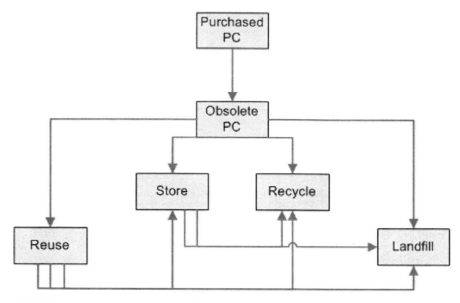

FIGURE 18-1. Personal Computer Disposal Paths

To model the effects of inventory and stocks adequately, it is often necessary to develop a dynamic model of material flows with a time dimension. Suppose we wish to model the mass flow of electronic computers into landfills or recycling facilities (Matthews et al. 1997). In this case, the sales of computers have been increasing dramatically in the period 1980-2000, with shifts from desktop machines to smaller laptops. Electronic computer recycling markets have also grown. Figure 18-1 shows a model of computer flows in different categories in which the key parameters include the overall mass of computers entering the system, the fraction of computers going to different destinations, and the residence time of computers in each destination. Table 18-6 shows the resulting flows of computers into different categories over time. In 2003 the model estimates that 44 million personal computers became obsolete, 8 million computers were recycled, the equivalent of 17 million computers were landfilled, 28 million computers were stored, and a total of 72 million computers were in storage.

Input–Output Formulation of Process LCA Models

The enterprise input–output model can also be used to represent a series of unit process models in life cycle assessment studies (Heijungs and Suh 2002; Suh 2004). The tabular, matrix formulation has the advantage of clarity and the ability to handle any feedback loops among the processes. Although most com-

TABLE 18-6. Example of Disposal Flows and Stocks for Personal Computers

Year	Obsolete PCs	Recycled	Landfilled	Stored	In storage
2003	44	8	17	28	72
2004	49	9	20	32	84
2005	45	10	23	31	92

Note: Numbers in millions of personal computers.
Source: See Matthews et al. 1997 for complete table.

mercial software retains a graphical depiction of unit processes (see Chapter 2), the equivalent matrix formulation can be adopted for computations if desired.

As with all process-based life cycle assessment studies, the critical difficulty even with the input–output formulation is the issue of process truncation or boundary definition. As discussed in Chapter 2, we advocate use of hybrid methods using national (or regional) input–output models coupled with specific process models.

Summary

In this chapter we have illustrated the use of small scale, enterprise input–output models based on physical units. These models can be estimated from enterprise-specific information, can represent different production alternatives, and can include a variety of environmental impacts. However, the models are restricted to linear, proportional production relationships. In economic terms, the input–output models represent strictly linear production functions.

We also note that the enterprise and materials flows input–output models can also be used to represent process-oriented life cycle assessment models. The tabular, matrix formulations can be helpful for establishing consistency and representing feedback loops among processes. For example, individual impact and input rows can be summed to determine the overall demand and emissions for a complete enterprise. Commercial software for life cycle assessment typically is based on graphic unit process models, as described in Chapter 2. However, the underlying computations could well be done with the enterprise input–output model representation. Of course, for either representation, the process model life cycle assessment still encounters the issue of truncation for defining an analysis boundary.

Appendix I

Sectors and Outputs in the 1997 U.S. Benchmark EIO-LCA

Sector name	IO number	Total industry output ($ Millions)
Natural Resources and Mining		
Oilseed farming	1111A0	20,250
Grain farming	1111B0	38,517
Vegetable and melon farming	111200	14,469
Tree nut farming	111335	2,200
Fruit farming	1113A0	11,251
Greenhouse and nursery production	111400	13,415
Tobacco farming	111910	3,271
Cotton farming	111920	7,181
Sugarcane and sugar beet farming	1119A0	2,230
All other crop farming	1119B0	22,128
Cattle ranching and farming	112100	60,552
Poultry and egg production	112300	24,577
Animal production, except cattle and poultry and eggs	112A00	19,944
Logging	113300	22,706
Forest nurseries, forest products, and timber tracts	113A00	4,946
Fishing	114100	3,582
Hunting and trapping	114200	2,466
Agriculture and forestry support activities	115000	12,596
Utilities and Construction		
Oil and gas extraction	211000	91,333
Coal mining	212100	23,316
Iron ore mining	212210	1,919
Copper, nickel, lead, and zinc mining	212230	4,532
Gold, silver, and other metal ore mining	2122A0	4,776
Stone mining and quarrying	212310	7,819

Sand, gravel, clay, and refractory mining	212320	5,590
Other nonmetallic mineral mining	212390	3,752
Drilling oil and gas wells	213111	9,495
Support activities for oil and gas operations	213112	13,485
Support activities for other mining	21311A	1,975
Power generation and supply	221100	212,961
Natural gas distribution	221200	53,413
Water, sewage and other systems	221300	5,904
New residential 1-unit structures, nonfarm	230110	172,439
New multifamily housing structures, nonfarm	230120	26,234
New residential additions and alterations, nonfarm	230130	57,679
New farm housing units and additions and alterations	230140	5,429
Manufacturing and industrial buildings	230210	27,487
Commercial and institutional buildings	230220	190,818
Highway, street, bridge, and tunnel construction	230230	43,401
Water, sewer, and pipeline construction	230240	17,207
Other new construction	230250	90,757
Maintenance and repair of farm and nonfarm residential structures	230310	36,384
Maintenance and repair of nonresidential buildings	230320	56,012
Maintenance and repair of highways, streets, bridges, and tunnels	230330	12,411
Other maintenance and repair construction	230340	17,833

Manufacturing

Dog and cat food manufacturing	311111	8,181
Other animal food manufacturing	311119	20,129
Flour milling	311211	7,865
Rice milling	311212	2,312
Malt manufacturing	311213	768
Wet corn milling	311221	8,202
Soybean processing	311222	13,539
Other oilseed processing	311223	1,626
Fats and oils refining and blending	311225	6,852
Breakfast cereal manufacturing	311230	8,677
Sugar manufacturing	311310	7,394
Confectionery manufacturing from cacao beans	311320	3,847
Confectionery manufacturing from purchased chocolate	311330	7,798
Nonchocolate confectionery manufacturing	311340	5,167
Frozen food manufacturing	311410	19,206
Fruit and vegetable canning and drying	311420	26,519
Fluid milk manufacturing	311511	20,155
Creamery butter manufacturing	311512	1,340
Cheese manufacturing	311513	19,661
Dry, condensed, and evaporated dairy products	311514	8,976
Ice cream and frozen dessert manufacturing	311520	5,435
Animal, except poultry, slaughtering	311611	52,915
Meat processed from carcasses	311612	24,046
Rendering and meat byproduct processing	311613	2,483

Poultry processing	311615	33,132
Seafood product preparation and packaging	311700	6,587
Frozen cakes and other pastries manufacturing	311813	2,486
Bread and bakery product, except frozen, manufacturing	31181A	28,113
Cookie and cracker manufacturing	311821	8,690
Mixes and dough made from purchased flour	311822	4,884
Dry pasta manufacturing	311823	1,759
Tortilla manufacturing	311830	1,065
Roasted nuts and peanut butter manufacturing	311911	3,988
Other snack food manufacturing	311919	9,559
Coffee and tea manufacturing	311920	7,778
Flavoring syrup and concentrate manufacturing	311930	6,431
Mayonnaise, dressing, and sauce manufacturing	311941	5,765
Spice and extract manufacturing	311942	3,820
All other food manufacturing	311990	10,984
Soft drink and ice manufacturing	312110	30,115
Breweries	312120	21,445
Wineries	312130	7,704
Distilleries	312140	6,770
Tobacco stemming and redrying	312210	3,714
Cigarette manufacturing	312221	34,763
Other tobacco product manufacturing	312229	3,212
Fiber, yarn, and thread mills	313100	12,795
Broadwoven fabric mills	313210	17,986
Narrow fabric mills and schiffli embroidery	313220	1,646
Nonwoven fabric mills	313230	4,340
Knit fabric mills	313240	5,697
Textile and fabric finishing mills	313310	13,550
Fabric coating mills	313320	2,214
Carpet and rug mills	314110	11,631
Curtain and linen mills	314120	8,821
Textile bag and canvas mills	314910	2,480
Tire cord and tire fabric mills	314992	1,191
Other miscellaneous textile product mills	31499A	6,769
Sheer hosiery mills	315111	1,547
Other hosiery and sock mills	315119	2,868
Other apparel knitting mills	315190	5,022
Cut and sew apparel manufacturing	315200	52,156
Accessories and other apparel manufacturing	315900	4,577
Leather and hide tanning and finishing	316100	3,390
Footwear manufacturing	316200	3,863
Other leather product manufacturing	316900	2,724
Sawmills	321113	24,672
Wood preservation	321114	4,478
Reconstituted wood product manufacturing	321219	5,285
Veneer and plywood manufacturing	32121A	8,579
Engineered wood member and truss manufacturing	32121B	4,812
Wood windows and door manufacturing	321911	8,497
Cut stock, resawing lumber, and planing	321912	5,787

Other millwork, including flooring	321918	4,501
Wood container and pallet manufacturing	321920	4,490
Manufactured home, mobile home, manufacturing	321991	10,183
Prefabricated wood building manufacturing	321992	2,956
Miscellaneous wood product manufacturing	321999	3,780
Pulp mills	322110	3,199
Paper and paperboard mills	3221A0	68,053
Paperboard container manufacturing	322210	38,913
Flexible packaging foil manufacturing	322225	1,545
Surface-coated paperboard manufacturing	322226	1,132
Coated and laminated paper and packaging materials	32222A	13,126
Coated and uncoated paper bag manufacturing	32222B	3,277
Die-cut paper office supplies manufacturing	322231	1,975
Envelope manufacturing	322232	3,479
Stationery and related product manufacturing	322233	1,823
Sanitary paper product manufacturing	322291	7,712
All other converted paper product manufacturing	322299	3,688
Manifold business forms printing	323116	9,225
Books printing	323117	5,539
Blankbook and looseleaf binder manufacturing	323118	2,361
Commercial printing	32311A	72,168
Tradebinding and related work	323121	1,963
Prepress services	323122	5,013
Petroleum refineries	324110	155,525
Asphalt paving mixture and block manufacturing	324121	5,843
Asphalt shingle and coating materials manufacturing	324122	4,743
Petroleum lubricating oil and grease manufacturing	324191	5,942
All other petroleum and coal products manufacturing	324199	1,665
Petrochemical manufacturing	325110	18,357
Industrial gas manufacturing	325120	5,140
Synthetic dye and pigment manufacturing	325130	6,266
Other basic inorganic chemical manufacturing	325180	24,001
Other basic organic chemical manufacturing	325190	59,318
Plastics material and resin manufacturing	325211	44,982
Synthetic rubber manufacturing	325212	6,032
Cellulosic organic fiber manufacturing	325221	1,105
Noncellulosic organic fiber manufacturing	325222	11,940
Nitrogenous fertilizer manufacturing	325311	3,789
Phosphatic fertilizer manufacturing	325312	5,724
Fertilizer, mixing only, manufacturing	325314	2,956
Pesticide and other agricultural chemical manufacturing	325320	11,259
Pharmaceutical and medicine manufacturing	325400	84,873
Paint and coating manufacturing	325510	18,076
Adhesive manufacturing	325520	7,041
Soap and other detergent manufacturing	325611	15,569
Polish and other sanitation good manufacturing	325612	7,059
Surface active agent manufacturing	325613	4,647
Toilet preparation manufacturing	325620	23,124
Printing ink manufacturing	325910	4,130

Explosives manufacturing	325920	1,272
Custom compounding of purchased resins	325991	7,542
Photographic film and chemical manufacturing	325992	12,765
Other miscellaneous chemical product manufacturing	325998	11,796
Plastics packaging materials, film and sheet	326110	24,204
Plastics pipe, fittings, and profile shapes	326120	9,137
Laminated plastics plate, sheet, and shapes	326130	3,152
Plastics bottle manufacturing	326160	6,414
Resilient floor covering manufacturing	326192	1,868
Plastics plumbing fixtures and all other plastics products	32619A	65,916
Foam product manufacturing	3261A0	11,495
Tire manufacturing	326210	15,617
Rubber and plastics hose and belting manufacturing	326220	3,946
Other rubber product manufacturing	326290	14,362
Vitreous china plumbing fixture manufacturing	327111	1,069
Vitreous china and earthenware articles manufacturing	327112	1,602
Porcelain electrical supply manufacturing	327113	1,186
Brick and structural clay tile manufacturing	327121	1,371
Ceramic wall and floor tile manufacturing	327122	830
Nonclay refractory manufacturing	327125	1,538
Clay refractory and other structural clay products	32712A	1,212
Glass container manufacturing	327213	4,153
Glass and glass products, except glass containers	32721A	18,251
Cement manufacturing	327310	6,341
Ready-mix concrete manufacturing	327320	17,809
Concrete block and brick manufacturing	327331	2,379
Concrete pipe manufacturing	327332	1,925
Other concrete product manufacturing	327390	5,803
Lime manufacturing	327410	1,139
Gypsum product manufacturing	327420	4,291
Abrasive product manufacturing	327910	4,562
Cut stone and stone product manufacturing	327991	1,222
Ground or treated minerals and earths manufacturing	327992	2,359
Mineral wool manufacturing	327993	4,299
Miscellaneous nonmetallic mineral products	327999	1,678
Iron and steel mills	331111	57,132
Ferroalloy and related product manufacturing	331112	1,201
Iron, steel pipe and tube from purchased steel	331210	7,439
Rolled steel shape manufacturing	331221	6,387
Steel wire drawing	331222	4,818
Alumina refining	331311	1,193
Primary aluminum production	331312	6,151
Secondary smelting and alloying of aluminum	331314	3,581
Aluminum sheet, plate, and foil manufacturing	331315	13,440
Aluminum extruded product manufacturing	331316	6,182
Other aluminum rolling and drawing	331319	1,647
Primary smelting and refining of copper	331411	6,361
Primary nonferrous metal, except copper and aluminum	331419	3,471
Copper rolling, drawing, and extruding	331421	7,534

Copper wire, except mechanical, drawing	331422	1,031
Secondary processing of copper	331423	1,176
Nonferrous metal, except copper and aluminum, shaping	331491	7,197
Secondary processing of other nonferrous metal	331492	3,101
Ferrous metal foundaries	331510	17,208
Aluminum foundries	33152A	7,620
Nonferrous foundries, except aluminum	33152B	3,787
Iron and steel forging	332111	4,956
Nonferrous forging	332112	1,860
Custom roll forming	332114	3,020
All other forging and stamping	33211A	14,083
Cutlery and flatware, except precious, manufacturing	332211	2,191
Hand and edge tool manufacturing	332212	6,018
Saw blade and handsaw manufacturing	332213	1,259
Kitchen utensil, pot, and pan manufacturing	332214	1,266
Prefabricated metal buildings and components	332311	3,993
Fabricated structural metal manufacturing	332312	15,140
Plate work manufacturing	332313	2,794
Metal window and door manufacturing	332321	9,823
Sheet metal work manufacturing	332322	15,725
Ornamental and architectural metal work manufacturing	332323	3,896
Power boiler and heat exchanger manufacturing	332410	3,709
Metal tank, heavy gauge, manufacturing	332420	4,669
Metal can, box, and other container manufacturing	332430	14,068
Hardware manufacturing	332500	10,474
Spring and wire product manufacturing	332600	7,984
Machine shops	332710	25,889
Turned product and screw, nut, and bolt manufacturing	332720	16,015
Metal heat treating	332811	3,495
Metal coating and nonprecious engraving	332812	8,441
Electroplating, anodizing, and coloring metal	332813	5,975
Metal valve manufacturing	332910	20,970
Ball and roller bearing manufacturing	332991	6,095
Small arms manufacturing	332994	1,327
Other ordnance and accessories manufacturing	332995	1,776
Fabricated pipe and pipe fitting manufacturing	332996	4,037
Industrial pattern manufacturing	332997	659
Enameled iron and metal sanitary ware manufacturing	332998	1,584
Miscellaneous fabricated metal product manufacturing	332999	10,375
Ammunition manufacturing	33299A	2,475
Farm machinery and equipment manufacturing	333111	15,538
Lawn and garden equipment manufacturing	333112	6,864
Construction machinery manufacturing	333120	20,388
Mining machinery and equipment manufacturing	333131	2,542
Oil and gas field machinery and equipment	333132	6,156
Sawmill and woodworking machinery	333210	1,189
Plastics and rubber industry machinery	333220	3,373
Paper industry machinery manufacturing	333291	3,233
Textile machinery manufacturing	333292	1,657

Printing machinery and equipment manufacturing	333293	3,316
Food product machinery manufacturing	333294	2,767
Semiconductor machinery manufacturing	333295	10,603
All other industrial machinery manufacturing	333298	7,986
Office machinery manufacturing	333313	2,960
Optical instrument and lens manufacturing	333314	3,133
Photographic and photocopying equipment manufacturing	333315	7,612
Other commercial and service industry machinery manufacturing	333319	8,851
Automatic vending, commercial laundry, and drycleaning machinery	33331A	1,865
Air purification equipment manufacturing	333411	2,072
Industrial and commercial fan and blower manufacturing	333412	1,838
Heating equipment, except warm air furnaces	333414	3,619
AC, refrigeration, and forced air heating	333415	21,887
Industrial mold manufacturing	333511	5,017
Metal cutting machine tool manufacturing	333512	4,975
Metal forming machine tool manufacturing	333513	2,125
Special tool, die, jig, and fixture manufacturing	333514	8,152
Cutting tool and machine tool accessory manufacturing	333515	5,112
Rolling mill and other metalworking machinery	33351A	3,967
Turbine and turbine generator set units manufacturing	333611	5,307
Other engine equipment manufacturing	333618	18,234
Speed changers and mechanical power transmission equipment	33361A	5,500
Pump and pumping equipment manufacturing	333911	6,480
Air and gas compressor manufacturing	333912	5,186
Measuring and dispensing pump manufacturing	333913	1,274
Elevator and moving stairway manufacturing	333921	1,570
Conveyor and conveying equipment manufacturing	333922	5,866
Overhead cranes, hoists, and monorail systems	333923	3,084
Industrial truck, trailer, and stacker manufacturing	333924	5,097
Power-driven handtool manufacturing	333991	3,369
Welding and soldering equipment manufacturing	333992	4,358
Packaging machinery manufacturing	333993	4,550
Industrial process furnace and oven manufacturing	333994	2,780
Fluid power cylinder and actuator manufacturing	333995	3,444
Fluid power pump and motor manufacturing	333996	2,530
Scales, balances, and miscellaneous general purpose machinery	33399A	9,156
Electronic computer manufacturing	334111	60,511
Computer storage device manufacturing	334112	13,019
Computer terminal manufacturing	334113	1,370
Other computer peripheral equipment manufacturing	334119	23,926
Telephone apparatus manufacturing	334210	37,541
Broadcast and wireless communications equipment	334220	38,861
Other communications equipment manufacturing	334290	3,982
Audio and video equipment manufacturing	334300	8,154

Electron tube manufacturing	334411	3,835
Semiconductors and related device manufacturing	334413	77,367
All other electronic component manufacturing	33441A	54,749
Electromedical apparatus manufacturing	334510	10,924
Search, detection, and navigation instruments	334511	31,990
Automatic environmental control manufacturing	334512	2,729
Industrial process variable instruments	334513	7,536
Totalizing fluid meters and counting devices	334514	3,717
Electricity and signal testing instruments	334515	13,530
Analytical laboratory instrument manufacturing	334516	6,643
Irradiation apparatus manufacturing	334517	3,657
Watch, clock, and other measuring and controlling device manufacturing	33451A	5,590
Software reproducing	334611	1,242
Audio and video media reproduction	334612	3,741
Magnetic and optical recording media manufacturing	334613	4,600
Electric lamp bulb and part manufacturing	335110	3,183
Lighting fixture manufacturing	335120	8,930
Electric housewares and household fan manufacturing	335211	3,005
Household vacuum cleaner manufacturing	335212	2,233
Household cooking appliance manufacturing	335221	3,464
Household refrigerator and home freezer manufacturing	335222	4,837
Household laundry equipment manufacturing	335224	3,557
Other major household appliance manufacturing	335228	3,259
Electric power and specialty transformer manufacturing	335311	4,650
Motor and generator manufacturing	335312	11,815
Switchgear and switchboard apparatus manufacturing	335313	7,309
Relay and industrial control manufacturing	335314	10,760
Storage battery manufacturing	335911	4,395
Primary battery manufacturing	335912	2,351
Fiber optic cable manufacturing	335921	2,741
Other communication and energy wire manufacturing	335929	12,243
Wiring device manufacturing	335930	10,079
Carbon and graphite product manufacturing	335991	2,262
Miscellaneous electrical equipment manufacturing	335999	6,714
Automobile and light truck manufacturing	336110	205,816
Heavy duty truck manufacturing	336120	14,389
Motor vehicle body manufacturing	336211	8,599
Truck trailer manufacturing	336212	5,328
Motor home manufacturing	336213	3,921
Travel trailer and camper manufacturing	336214	4,421
Motor vehicle parts manufacturing	336300	173,523
Aircraft manufacturing	336411	54,867
Aircraft engine and engine parts manufacturing	336412	22,099
Other aircraft parts and equipment	336413	20,122
Guided missile and space vehicle manufacturing	336414	15,122
Propulsion units and parts for space vehicles and guided missiles	33641A	3,976
Railroad rolling stock manufacturing	336500	8,260

Ship building and repairing	336611	10,543
Boat building	336612	5,404
Motorcycle, bicycle, and parts manufacturing	336991	3,176
Military armored vehicles and tank parts manufacturing	336992	1,023
All other transportation equipment manufacturing	336999	4,437
Wood kitchen cabinet and countertop manufacturing	337110	9,098
Upholstered household furniture manufacturing	337121	8,385
Nonupholstered wood household furniture manufacturing	337122	10,741
Metal household furniture manufacturing	337124	2,306
Institutional furniture manufacturing	337127	4,104
Other household and institutional furniture	33712A	863
Wood office furniture manufacturing	337211	3,093
Custom architectural woodwork and millwork	337212	2,256
Office furniture, except wood, manufacturing	337214	8,027
Showcases, partitions, shelving, and lockers	337215	7,750
Mattress manufacturing	337910	3,879
Blind and shade manufacturing	337920	2,213
Laboratory apparatus and furniture manufacturing	339111	2,216
Surgical and medical instrument manufacturing	339112	17,551
Surgical appliance and supplies manufacturing	339113	14,029
Dental equipment and supplies manufacturing	339114	2,400
Ophthalmic goods manufacturing	339115	3,387
Dental laboratories	339116	3,006
Jewelry and silverware manufacturing	339910	11,693
Sporting and athletic goods manufacturing	339920	10,889
Doll, toy, and game manufacturing	339930	4,362
Office supplies, except paper, manufacturing	339940	4,214
Sign manufacturing	339950	8,959
Gasket, packing, and sealing device manufacturing	339991	5,038
Musical instrument manufacturing	339992	1,321
Broom, brush, and mop manufacturing	339994	1,974
Burial casket manufacturing	339995	1,271
Buttons, pins, and all other miscellaneous manufacturing	33999A	9,493

Trade

Wholesale trade	420000	752,854
Retail trade	4A0000	729,824

Transportation and Warehousing

Air transportation	481000	119,445
Rail transportation	482000	37,967
Water transportation	483000	24,397
Truck transportation	484000	169,397
Transit and ground passenger transportation	485000	24,626
Pipeline transportation	486000	27,284
Scenic and sightseeing transportation and support activities for transportation	48A000	44,338
Postal service	491000	58,861
Couriers and messengers	492000	41,786

Warehousing and storage	493000	29,223

Information

Newspaper publishers	511110	41,043
Periodical publishers	511120	29,522
Book publishers	511130	22,306
Database, directory, and other publishers	5111A0	20,672
Software publishers	511200	61,377
Motion picture and video industries	512100	49,744
Sound recording industries	512200	11,428
Radio and television broadcasting	513100	41,272
Cable networks and program distribution	513200	45,175
Telecommunications	513300	277,605
Information services	514100	11,704
Data processing services	514200	35,812
Services/Other		
Nondepository credit intermediation and related activities	522A00	124,794
Securities, commodity contracts, investments	523000	198,075
Insurance carriers	524100	249,661
Insurance agencies, brokerages, and related	524200	90,354
Funds, trusts, and other financial vehicles	525000	64,300
Monetary authorities and depository credit intermediation	52A000	343,510
Real estate	531000	607,472
Automotive equipment rental and leasing	532100	42,162
Video tape and disc rental	532230	8,324
Machinery and equipment rental and leasing	532400	41,085
General and consumer goods rental except video tapes and discs	532A00	17,143
Lessors of nonfinancial intangible assets	533000	102,007
Legal services	541100	152,041
Accounting and bookkeeping services	541200	71,433
Architectural and engineering services	541300	131,136
Specialized design services	541400	17,739
Custom computer programming services	541511	86,327
Computer systems design services	541512	29,508
Other computer related services, including facilities management	54151A	23,429
Management consulting services	541610	69,148
Environmental and other technical consulting services	5416A0	15,915
Scientific research and development services	541700	63,340
Advertising and related services	541800	57,713
Photographic services	541920	8,874
Veterinary services	541940	10,398
All other miscellaneous professional and technical services	5419A0	41,432
Management of companies and enterprises	550000	315,497
Office administrative services	561100	29,642
Facilities support services	561200	8,044
Employment services	561300	88,653
Business support services	561400	40,562

Travel arrangement and reservation services	561500	25,097
Investigation and security services	561600	21,834
Services to buildings and dwellings	561700	61,125
Other support services	561900	28,717
Waste management and remediation services	562000	41,690
Elementary and secondary schools	611100	22,039
Colleges, universities, and junior colleges	611A00	55,821
Other educational services	611B00	23,832
Home health care services	621600	36,198
Offices of physicians, dentists, and other health practitioners	621A00	268,711
Other ambulatory health care services	621B00	75,161
Hospitals	622000	267,335
Nursing and residential care facilities	623000	93,582
Child day care services	624400	26,766
Social assistance, except child day care services	624A00	39,516
Performing arts companies	711100	8,934
Spectator sports	711200	15,696
Independent artists, writers, and performers	711500	14,264
Promoters of performing arts and sports and agents for public figures	711A00	10,511
Museums, historical sites, zoos, and parks	712000	4,514
Fitness and recreational sports centers	713940	11,068
Bowling centers	713950	2,256
Other amusement, gambling, and recreation industries	713A00	66,164
Hotels and motels, including casino hotels	7211A0	70,574
Other accommodations	721A00	8,382
Food services and drinking places	722000	344,334
Car washes	811192	7,237
Automotive repair and maintenance, except car washes	8111A0	138,414
Electronic equipment repair and maintenance	811200	36,964
Commercial machinery repair and maintenance	811300	32,976
Household goods repair and maintenance	811400	24,649
Personal care services	812100	28,756
Death care services	812200	11,408
Drycleaning and laundry services	812300	20,175
Other personal services	812900	34,924
Religious organizations	813100	40,397
Grantmaking and giving and social advocacy organizations	813A00	13,979
Civic, social, professional, and similar organizations	813B00	45,081
Private households	814000	12,035
Federal electric utilities	S00101	8,337
Other federal government enterprises	S00102	7,424
State and local government passenger transit	S00201	7,513
State and local government electric utilities	S00202	22,167
Other state and local government enterprises	S00203	94,676
General government industry	S00500	937,812
Inventory valuation adjustment	S00700	9,211
Owner-occupied dwellings	S00800	592,862

Appendix II
Some Alternative Model Forms for EIO-LCA

$\mathbf{L}$eontief (1986) has developed input–output (I-O) models to relate the pro-duction inputs of goods and services in an economy to the production outputs of other sectors, as well as to the provision of labor and other inputs. The most basic of these I-O models describes an economy only by inter-sector transactions. One of the critical assumptions in an I-O framework is that, gen-erally speaking, firms in each sector purchase some amount of input from firms within the same sector (for example, an agricultural sector where seeds are purchased to grow vegetables). In more advanced I-O models, households are included. This expansion adds a row to represent the provision of the house-hold product labor services, and a column to show the consumption of goods and services by households. Figure II-1 shows the structure of such models, including the standard nomenclature for input–output matrices. Matthews (1999) develops the derivation of the alternative model forms described here.

Other sectors, representing the gross domestic product (GDP) categories, are continually added to form more complicated models. Consumption (C), fixed investment (I), government spending (G), and net exports (NX) are examples of these additions. In any I-O model, total commodity output can be repre-sented by the sum across each row's values. Thus for each of the n commodities indexed by i, output X_i is:

$$X_i = z_{i1} + z_{i2} + ... + z_{in} + y_i \qquad \text{(II-1)}$$

However, I-O models are typically generalized by assuming inter-industry flows between sectors can instead be represented as a percentage of sectoral out-put. This flow is represented by dividing the economically-valued flow from sector i to sector j by the total output of sector j. Namely,

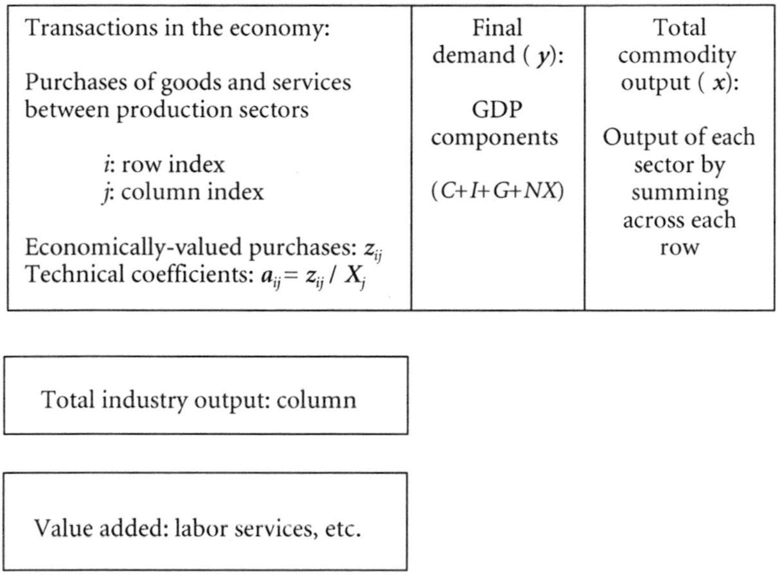

Transactions in the economy:	Final demand (*y*):	Total commodity output (*x*):
Purchases of goods and services between production sectors	GDP components	Output of each sector by summing across each row
i: row index *j*: column index	(*C+I+G+NX*)	
Economically-valued purchases: z_{ij} Technical coefficients: $a_{ij} = z_{ij} / X_j$		

Total industry output: column

Value added: labor services, etc.

FIGURE II-1. The Format of Economic Input–Output Models

$$a_{ij} = z_{ij} / X_j \qquad \text{(II-2)}$$

In such a system, the a_{ij} term is a unitless technical (or input–output) coefficient. For example, if a flow of \$250 of goods goes from sector 3 to sector 4 (z_{34}), and the total output of sector 4 (X_4) is \$5,000, then $a_{34} = 0.05$. This says that 5 cents worth of inputs from sector 3 is in every dollar's worth of output from sector 4. As a substitution, we can also see from Equation II-2 that $z_{ij} = a_{ij} X_j$. This form is more often seen since the system of linear equations corresponding to Equation II-1 is typically represented as

$$X_i = a_{i1} X_1 + a_{i2} X_2 + \dots + a_{in} X_n + y_i \qquad \text{(II-3)}$$

It is straightforward to notice that each X_i term on the left has a corresponding term on the right of Equation II-3. Thus all **X** terms are typically moved to the left side of the equation and the whole system written as

$$(1 - a_{11})X_1 - a_{12} X_2 - \dots - a_{1n} X_n = y_1$$
$$-a_{21}X_1 + (1 - a_{22})X_2 - \dots - a_{2n} X_n = y_2$$

$$-a_{i1}X_1 - a_{i2}X_2 - \dots + (1 - a_{ii})X_i - \dots - a_{in} X_n = y_i \qquad \text{(II-4)}$$

$$-a_{n1}X_1 - a_{n2}X_2 - \dots + (1 - a_{nn})X_n = y_n$$

If we let the matrix A contain all of the technical coefficient a_{ij} terms, vector x all the output X_i terms, and vector y the final demand y_i terms, then Equation II-4 can be written more compactly as

$$x - Ax = [I - A]\, x = y \qquad\qquad \text{(II-5)}$$

where I is the $n \times n$ identity matrix. This representation takes advantage of the fact that only diagonal entries in the system are $(1 - a_{ii})$ terms, and all others are $(-a_{ij})$ terms. Finally, we typically want to calculate the total output, x, of the economy for various exogenous final demands y, taken as an input to the system. We can take the inverse of $[I - A]$ and pre-multiply it to both sides of Equation II-5 to yield the familiar solution

$$x = [I - A]^{-1} y \qquad\qquad \text{(II-6)}$$

where $[I - A]^{-1}$ is the Leontief inverse matrix or, more simply, the Leontief matrix.

Classification of Results in an Input–Output System

It is important to distinguish between the various results inherent to an I-O model. The results are the total outputs generated from an exogenous final demand. The structure and components of these outputs are worth noting. Because of the inter-sector transactions shown in the A matrix, any exogenous final demand will have "ripple" effects throughout the economy expressed in an I-O model. For example, the brief numerical example shown above says that 5 cents of sector 3 product is in sector 4 output. Similarly, some amount of sector 4 product is probably required to make sector 3 output. At face value, this creates a circularity problem in determining results. However, this circularity is completely expressed in the Leontief inverse.

The Leontief inverse can also be expressed in the power-series form

$$x = Iy + Ay + A^2 y + \dots = [I + A + A^2 + A^3 + \dots]\, y \qquad\qquad \text{(II-7)}$$

The successive terms of the power-series form represent the round-by-round requirements for producing total output x that are part of the circularity problem.

For a more detailed proof and explanation of the power-series form, see Miller and Blair (1985). Because of the computational complexity of generating large inverses, this alternative form is often used since successive terms can be calculated by multiplying the previous term by A.

Equation II-7 shows that in the first round, Iy is produced (the final demand). In the second round, Ay is needed to produce the Iy of final demand. In the third round, A^2y is needed to produce the Ay from the second round, etc. The sum of these round-by-round effects, including the final demand, is x.

In this way, the input–output framework shows the total supply chain effects of producing goods and services in an economy. We can however, separate these effects between the "direct" economic effects—the effects related to the pure production of the final demands—and the "indirect" economic effects—the effects related to producing all goods and services needed to produce the final demand. In our matrix terminology, the direct effects are the $[I + A]y$ term in Equation II-7, and the indirect effects are the $[A^2 + A^3 + ...]y$ terms. In all, we call the sum of the direct and indirect effects (x) the "total" economic supply chain effect of production. The magnitude of the direct, indirect, and total effects is completely dependent on the values of the A matrix. Thus, it is possible that the indirect effects will be larger than the direct effects. When we consider the environmental effects of this production, this same result holds. Since our ultimate goal here is to create a framework for analyzing relative environmental effects of production, the concepts of direct and indirect effects are central.

Incorporation of Environmental Effects into Input–Output Models

Leontief (1970) first suggested the use of input–output models to perform environmental analysis, and it is from this point that two distinct methods of incorporating environmental impacts can be generated. The first method is Leontief's published suggestion of endogenizing environmental effects by augmenting the A matrix with pollution product rows and columns. An example of this is CO_2 pollution from each sector. The suggestion of endogenizing environmental effects within the I-O model was somewhat problematic at the time. Computational power and capacity were quite expensive, so adding even a single row and column for a particular emission created a problem in solving a larger system of equations.

This is part of the rationale behind the second method, externally augmented I-O models, and such a method is implemented in this book. Externally augmented models keep the consideration of environmental effects external to the input–output model, but use the Leontief inverse and output calculations to generate these results. The use of such alternative methods is not itself novel. Miller and Blair (1985) maintain that external methods if done correctly would yield computationally equal results, but they offer no proof of their equivalence. A theoretical exposition of each method is provided below, as well as proof of their equivalence.

Proposition: Given an $n \times n$ input–output model with transactions matrix A

and final demand vector *y*, and a function *R* of environmental impacts per dollar output of each sector, the result of endogenizing environmental impact by adding a row and column yields the same result as externally creating a unit-environmental impact function.

Proof: We begin with a sketch of the details of the externally-augmented method. In this method, the total supply chain economic output is found using the result of Equation II-6 above. Namely, the *I–A* matrix is inverted and then multiplied by the vector of final demands to find the overall economic output produced per sector. Such a method yields the "total supply chain" economic output previously discussed. Since *x* contains all output produced (direct and indirect), we can use an external per-dollar-output emissions function to find the overall environmental impact for a given amount of output produced by summing across the impacts generated by each sector's production. In particular, we propose a function of the form

$$h = e_1 X_1 + e_2 X_2 + \dots + e_n X_n = Ex = E[I - A]^{-1}y \qquad \text{(II-8)}$$

where the function *h* multiplies a vector of per-dollar emissions from each sector, e_i, by the total outputs of each sector calculated in Equation II-6. As seen above, this function effectively yields the total pollution generated. We now seek to prove that this external method of calculating emissions is equivalent to Leontief's method.

The Leontief Method of Determining Environmental Impacts

In this method, pollution is considered to be a product just like the other *n* commodities in the system. Some amount of pollution is "required" to produce each of the other *n* products. If sector 1 generates 50 pounds of pollutant, sector 2 generates 80 pounds, etc., then the pollution generated is also effectively considered as a flow resulting from production. Thus an *n*th+1 row and column are added to represent this production relationship.

First, the new row is added. To accomplish this, per-dollar-pollution generation coefficients for a single pollutant are added to the system of equations endogenously, forming an additional equation as in Equation II-1. Pollution values per-dollar-output can be found as in Equation II-2 for each sector. To differentiate the pollution coefficients from the technical coefficients already used in Equation II-3, and to compare directly with the externally-augmented method, these pollution flows for each sector are denoted as e_j. The total emissions produced could be found as

$$X_p = e_1 X_1 + e_2 X_2 + \dots + e_n X_n \qquad \text{(II-9)}$$

where X_p is total pollution produced as a function of per-dollar pollution generated and output for each sector. Note that there is also no final demand of pollution y_p, it is a negative externality and a byproduct. To stay with the format of the input–output model, this pollution equation is rearranged as

$$-e_1 X_1 - e_2 X_2 - \dots - e_n X_n + X_p = 0 \qquad \text{(II-9)}$$

Second, the nth+1 column is added representing "demand" for pollution. Again, no demand or purchase of pollution is made by any sector. The coefficient for pollution demand is zero in each equation of form II-3, as in

$$X_i = a_{i1} X_1 + a_{i2} X_2 + \dots + a_{in} X_n + 0 X_p + Y_i$$

We can visualize the resulting new system of $n+1$ equations by using partitioned matrices that follow the format of Equation II-5. The system can be represented as

$$\begin{bmatrix} (I-A) & \begin{matrix} 0 \\ 0 \end{matrix} \\ \hline -e_1 \ \dots \ -e_n & 1 \end{bmatrix} \begin{bmatrix} X_1 \\ X_2 \\ \hline X_p \end{bmatrix} = \begin{bmatrix} Y_1 \\ Y_2 \\ \hline 0 \end{bmatrix} \qquad \text{(II-10)}$$

Because of the additional row and column in the left matrix compared to the base model in Equation II-5, we call the augmented form above $(I\text{–}A^*)$. As in Equation II-6, we are looking for a solution yielding total outputs (including total pollutant releases) of the form

$$\begin{bmatrix} X_1 \\ X_2 \\ \hline X_p \end{bmatrix} = \begin{bmatrix} (I-A) & \begin{matrix} 0 \\ 0 \end{matrix} \\ \hline -e_1 \ \dots \ -e_n & 1 \end{bmatrix}^{-1} \begin{bmatrix} Y_1 \\ Y_2 \\ \hline 0 \end{bmatrix} \qquad \text{(II-11)}$$

Thus, the first step of such a solution is to find the inverse of the $(I\text{–}A^*)$ matrix. This can be done by a Gauss-Jordan reduction iterative procedure. The first step of such a procedure is to create a new partitioned matrix that contains the elements of the $(I\text{–}A^*)$ matrix on the left and the $n+1$ by $n+1$ identity matrix on the right:

$$\begin{bmatrix} (1-a_{11}) & -a_{12} & \cdots & -a_{1n} & 0 & 1 & 0 & \cdots & 0 \\ -a_{21} & (1-a_{22}) & \cdots & -a_{2n} & 0 & 0 & 1 & \cdots & 0 \\ \vdots & \vdots & \ddots & \vdots & \vdots & \vdots & \vdots & \vdots & \vdots \\ -a_{n1} & -a_{n2} & \cdots & (1-a_{nn}) & 0 & 0 & \cdots & 1 & 0 \\ -e_1 & -e_2 & \cdots & -e_n & 1 & 0 & \cdots & 0 & 1 \end{bmatrix} \qquad \text{(II-12)}$$

The Gauss-Jordan method uses linear combinations of rows to transform the matrix on the left of the partition into the inverse matrix. At the same time, this iterative procedure yields a matrix in the right partition that is actually the inverse of the original matrix on the left, that is, $(I{-}A^*)^{-1}$ is created on the right. The first step of the Gauss-Jordan method makes a pivot (the value 1) out of the element in row 1, column 1. This is done by dividing each element in row 1 by $(1{-}a_{11})$. Thus after this first step, the matrix would appear as follows:

$$
\begin{bmatrix}
1 & \frac{-a_{12}}{(1-a_{11})} & \cdots & \frac{-a_{1n}}{(1-a_{11})} & 0 & \vdots & \frac{1}{(1-a_{11})} & 0 & \cdots & 0 \\
-a_{21} & (1-a_{22}) & \cdots & -a_{2n} & 0 & \vdots & 0 & 1 & \cdots & 0 \\
\vdots & \vdots & \ddots & \vdots & \vdots & \vdots & \vdots & \vdots & \vdots & \vdots \\
-a_{n1} & -a_{n2} & \cdots & (1-a_{nn}) & 0 & \vdots & 0 & \cdots & 1 & 0 \\
-e_{p1} & -e_{p2} & \cdots & -e_{pn} & 1 & \vdots & 0 & \cdots & 0 & 1
\end{bmatrix}
\qquad \text{(II-13)}
$$

Since the goal is to have an identity matrix on the left, all off-diagonal values need to be eliminated. This is done by linear combinations of partially reduced rows. For example, we eliminate the $-a_{21}$ value from row 2 by multiplying row 1 by a_{21} and adding the result to row 2. Such a process slowly transforms diagonal entries into 1's by dividing all elements in a row by the entry in the diagonal element and creates 0's by the linear combinations mentioned. This method starts at the top left element and moves generally down and to the right. However, any subsequent row can always be transformed by using the partially transformed rows above it to create the needed inverse matrix. Without loss of generality, we consider a nearly complete step along the way in transforming Equation II-12 into the necessary form. At this point, the matrix will have the general form

$$
\begin{bmatrix}
 & & & 0 & \vdots & & & 0 \\
 & I & & \vdots & \vdots & & L & \vdots \\
 & & & 0 & \vdots & & & 0 \\
\hline
-e_1 & \cdots & -e_n & 1 & \vdots & 0 & \cdots & 0 & 1
\end{bmatrix}
\qquad \text{(II-14)}
$$

Effectively, this matrix has been almost completely reduced to the needed form to solve for the inverse. An $n \times n$ identity matrix has been created on the left, and the resulting partition L of the desired inverse has been prepared on the right. All that is left to do is to continue the iterative reduction method on the final row. However, the reason the Gauss-Jordan method is used to find the inverse of the $n{+}1$ by $n{+}1$ system is to simplify the procedure. The system of equations is always still available for our use. Thus, if we have found the "solution" for the first n rows, we could necessarily use it and the "unreduced form" of the nth+1 row to find the needed output for the nth+1 row. In other words, we can plug in the n values already found into the inherent nth+1 equation to find its output.

This finding reduces to a small degree the computation needed to invert the augmented matrix. More importantly it shows that, to a large extent, the inverse of the augmented matrix is nearly identical to the regular Leontief inverse used in the basic I-O model. The appended column of zeroes and the 1 in the nth+1 row will not change in value at any step of the Gauss-Jordan procedure because we are multiplying constants by zero and adding to the value in that column (0 or 1). This realization of subset matrices to the answer hint at the complete solution needed.

If we examine the values in the $n \times n$ system in II-13 above, they are equivalent to the solution needed for Equation II-6, with each row's general result being $X_i = \alpha_{i1} Y_1 + \alpha_{i2} Y_2 + \dots + \alpha_{in} Y_n$, where the α values are the elements of $(I-A)^{-1}$ and necessarily, $(I-A^*)^{-1}$.

We could continue the Gauss-Jordan method to explicitly determine the inverse of the entire $n+1$-square matrix, $(I-A^*)^{-1}$. However, we can use a much more elegant method to determine the elements of $(I-A^*)^{-1}$. Post-multiplying the original $(I-A^*)$ with the resulting $(I-A^*)^{-1}$ by matrix will yield I by rule. To be more clear, we know that this multiplication has the partitioned form

$$\begin{bmatrix} (I-A) & 0 \\ -E & 1 \end{bmatrix}\begin{bmatrix} P & Q \\ R & S \end{bmatrix} = \begin{bmatrix} I & 0 \\ 0 & I \end{bmatrix} \tag{II-15}$$

where the right side of this equation is a partitioned $n+1$-square identity matrix. The first matrix on the left side comes from our representation in Equation II-10. The $I-A$ partition is exactly equal to the original values in Equation II-4. We assume that E represents the $1 \times n$ vector of per-dollar-pollution terms from Equation II-9. Since we are multiplying a pair of $n+1$-square matrices, we know that the result will also be an $n+1$ square matrix. We assume that this inverse can also be partitioned into P, an $n \times n$ matrix, Q and R, vectors of size $n \times 1$, and S, a single value. By matrix algebra, we know the following to be true of the partitions:

$$\begin{aligned} (I-A)P + 0R &= (I-A)P = I \\ (I-A)Q + 0S &= (I-A)Q = 0 \\ -EP + R &= 0 \\ -EQ + S &= I \end{aligned} \tag{II-16}$$

Based on this series of equations, we can quickly see that $P = (I-A)^{-1}$. Similarly, since $(I-A)$ cannot equal 0, $Q = 0$. It follows that $R = EP = E(I-A)^{-1}$ and

$S = I + EQ = I$. Thus, the inverse of the augmented Leontief system, $(I–A^*)^{-1}$ has the form

$$\begin{bmatrix} (I-A)^{-1} & \vdots & 0 \\ \hline E(I-A)^{-1} & \vdots & 1 \end{bmatrix}$$

(II-17)

which is the expected result. When applied to the resulting final demands Y (that is, from Equation 2-11), the resulting total output of pollution will be $E(I–A)^{-1}Y$, or EX. This result is precisely what we showed as the result in Equation II-8 above. Thus the external calculation method yields the same result as Leontief's method.

Application of the Theory

Although computational power is now inexpensive, using an augmented Leontief matrix may not be the optimal method for dealing with environmental impact information in an I-O model. One reason is the need for environmental data over a broad range of impacts, which will greatly expand the I-O model. A model incorporating many distinct emissions could quickly become difficult to invert even with today's computational power. And inverting large matrices causes problems with numerical accuracy.

The user of an environmentally augmented I-O model may be only concerned with a single emission or a small set of all emissions. In such a case, there would be little reason to solve the larger system of equations. In particular, for Internet-based tools the ability to deliver data quickly and as needed is paramount to any computational considerations. Thus accurate data and solutions are needed without the computational burden of solving (through inversion) the augmented system.

Without loss of generality, the previous equivalence proof can be extended to show that a set of m environmental impacts could be added to the model (as an $m \times n$ matrix of per-dollar-output values) to achieve an equivalent multidimensional analytic result.

Appendix III

Disaggregation Options for Conducting Hybrid Life Cycle Assessments

As discussed in Chapter 1, the direct and indirect environmental burdens associated with an exogenous change in the demand for the output of the sector can be estimated using Equation 1-2. However, a typical product LCA involves estimation of environmental burdens associated with an exogenous increase in the demand of a specific product, which may be different from the average output of an industrial sector with respect to technical or environmental discharge coefficients, or a completely new product. A simple option is to assume that the product of interest is well approximated by its industry sector, an approximation used in Lave et al. (1995b); Cobas-Flores (1996); and Horvath (1997). Direct and indirect effects of incremental output of a particular product can then be estimated by treating it as a change in exogenous demand for the output of the sector. This approach is simple and quick, and provides useful information, especially when comparing broad industry sectors, or typical outputs of industry sectors. It is also useful as an initial screening device to prioritize further data collection efforts.

Creating a New Hypothetical Industry Sector

If information on the inputs required to produce the product and direct environmental burdens from the production process are available, then the product of interest can be represented as a new hypothetical sector in the economy (Joshi 1998). The economy-wide environmental burdens arising from a unit output of the new hypothetical industry sector can then be estimated.

Let $A = [a_{ij}]$ $i, j = \{1, 2, ...n\}$ be the current aggregate technical coefficient matrix of the existing economy with n sectors. Assume the product of interest is represented as sector $n+1$. Let $a_{i,n+1}$ be monetary value of input required from sector i {$i=1...n+1$} to produce a dollar's worth of the product. Further assume that the inputs used in its production are representative output of the sectors from which they are drawn. Let $[R_{n+1}]$ be the vector of direct environmental burdens associated with a dollar's worth output of sector $n+1$.

Define a new technical coefficient matrix A^*, where the first n row and column elements remain unchanged from A,

$$A^* = \left[\begin{array}{c|c} A & a_{i,n+1} \\ \hline 0 & a_{n+1,n+1} \end{array} \right]$$

Similarly, the new environmental burden matrix is reformulated as

$$R^* = [R, R_{n+1}]$$

The economy-wide environmental burden E associated with an output y_{n+1} of the new sector $n+1$ and hence the product can be calculated as,

$$E = R \times X = R \times [I - A^*]^{-1} \times Y \qquad \text{(III-1)}$$

where $Y^t = [0,...0, y_{n+1}]$

Modeling the Use and End-of-Life Management Phases

LCA by definition includes analyses of environmental burdens from the use and end-of-life management (EOLM) phases of a product. The above approach can be used to estimate direct and indirect resource use and environmental burdens from these two phases. They can be modeled as hypothetical industry sectors that draw inputs from the existing sectors that also have some direct environmental burdens, and the life cycle burdens associated with all the inputs can be estimated by calculating the economy-wide impacts for a given output of these hypothetical industry sectors. For example, the use phase of an automobile consumes gasoline, lubricants, coolants, maintenance and repair services, and insurance services, which are outputs of other industry sectors, and direct environmental burdens are the tailpipe and evaporative emissions during the operation of the vehicle. Hence the use phase of an automobile can be modeled as a hypothetical industry sector, as illustrated in Chapter 6. However, the underlying assumption is that the technical coefficients matrix for the economy remains unchanged during the lifetime of the product and the time discount rate for environmental burdens is zero. This may be a good approximation when products have short life spans. Even when the products have longer life spans, this approach provides a good starting point by providing comparative information under the current state of the technology.

Similarly, end-of-life management options such as reuse, remanufacturing, and recycling use inputs from existing industry sectors to process an obsolete product and produce an output that is demanded either for final consumption or as an intermediate input by other sectors. Typically, remanufactured products are used by the same industry sector as substitutes for new components, while recycled output may be consumed by completely different sectors. Hence, these options can be treated as additional hypothetical industry sectors in EIO-LCA. The net environmental impact from EOLM is the sum of life cycle burdens from inputs used in EOLM, direct impacts from the EOLM process itself, and credits for the recycled product. For example, the net environmental impact from recycling steel is the sum of life cycle environmental burdens from all the inputs used in collecting and processing the scrap steel, environmental burdens from the steel recycling processes, and the credits for the recycled steel. When a recovered product can substitute for the output of an existing industry sector, the environmental credit for the recovered product is the avoided life cycle environmental burdens from this substitution. For example, if a ton of steel scrap recycling results in the recovery of 0.6 million tons of steel mill products valued at $500, then the appropriate credit for recovered steel is the avoided economy-wide burdens from a reduction of $500 in the final demand for the output of the blast furnaces and steel mills sector. When the recovery process results in many products, or the recovered products are likely to be used by many other industry sectors, new industry sectors representing the EOLM options can be added to the input–output matrix. However, in using this approach we are once again assuming away the temporal effects of the useful life of the product. Chapter 7 provides a detailed example.

Disaggregating an Existing Industry Sector

The underlying assumption in Equation III-1 is that the original technical coefficient matrix is unaffected by the introduction of the new sector. However, often products of interest are already included in existing commodity sectors and used as intermediate inputs in other sectors. Suppose that the total environmental burden associated with exogenous changes in demand for a product, which is already included in one of the existing sectors, needs to be estimated. The sector, say sector n, which includes the product of interest can be disaggregated into two sectors, one of which is the product of interest (sector $n + 1$) and the other sector consisting of all other products within the sector. For example, for conducting LCA of cold rolled sheet steel, the sector "blast furnaces and steel mills" can be disaggregated into two sectors, "cold rolled sheet steel" and "all products in blast furnaces and steel mill sector except cold rolled sheet steel." This implies that a new $n+1$ by $n+1$ technical coefficient matrix A^*, with elements a^*_{ij} has to be derived to represent the same economy represented by $n \times$

n matrix A (with elements a_{ij}). The first $n-1$ sectors of A and A^* are identical.

Because the original sector n in A is a linear aggregation of sectors n and $n+1$ in A^*,

$$a_{in} = (1-s)\, a^*_{i,n} + sa^*_{i,n+1} \tag{III-2}$$

where s is the share of product $n+1$ in the total output of original aggregate sector n. Similarly, because the input purchase of sector j from aggregate sector n in A is the sum of purchases from disaggregated sectors n and $n+1$ in A^*,

$$a_{nj} = a^*_{n,j} + a^*_{n+1,j} \tag{III-3}$$

Also

$$a_{nn} = (1-s)(a^*_{n,n} + a^*_{n+1,n}) + s(a^*_{n,n+1} + a^*_{n+1,n+1}) \tag{III-4}$$

Equations III-2 to III-4 are the constraints on the coefficients of A^* such that aggregation of sectors n and $n+1$ in A^* yields A. A^* has a total of $4n$ unknown coefficients. However, because there are $2n-1$ constraints on these coefficients, data on only $2n+1$ coefficients is required. The share s of the product of our interest in the aggregate output of the original sector n can easily be obtained from secondary sources. The technical coefficient vector $[a^*_{i,n+1}]$ for the product of interest can be estimated from a detailed cost sheet of the product, because the element $a^*_{i,n+1}$ is dollars worth of inputs from sector i required to produce a dollar's worth of the product $n+1$. Data on the sales of product $n+1$ to different existing sectors j of the economy is required to estimate coefficients $a^*_{n+1,j}$. The firms manufacturing the product typically have information on the markets and market shares for its products.

Similarly if $R = [r_1...r_n]$, the environmental burden matrix associated with the original matrix is available. Only data on the direct environmental burden vector r_{n+1} associated with the product $n+1$ is needed to obtain the disaggregated environmental burden matrix R^*, because:

$$r_n = (1-s)\, r^*_n + sr^*_{n+1} \tag{III-5}$$

Once the disaggregated matrices A^* and R^* are developed, the total environmental burden associated with exogenous changes in the demand for the product (that is, output of sector $n+1$) can be obtained from Equation III-1.

Iterative Disaggregation

The approach outlined above can easily be extended and generalized when more detailed information on more than one stage of the upstream inputs is available, typically in the form of a conventional LCA. An expanded technical coefficient matrix A^* and environmental burden matrix R^* can be developed by iterative disaggregation of relevant sectors and creating additional industry sectors corresponding to each product or input for which we have detailed information.

To continue with the cold rolled sheet steel example, suppose a conventional LCA process model provides detailed information on the inputs and environmental burdens from the cold rolled sheet steel production process and mining of coking coal used in cold rolled sheet steel manufacture. Based on this information, the sector "blast furnaces and steel mills" can be disaggregated into "cold rolled sheet steel" and " all steel except cold rolled sheet steel" sectors, and the sector "coal mining" can be disaggregated into "coking coal mining" and "all coal mining except coking coal" sectors. The other inputs for which detailed process models are not available (and hence normally excluded in a conventional LCA), can be approximated by their corresponding industry sectors.

To present a general case, suppose A (with elements a_{ij}) is the aggregate matrix, and a disaggregated matrix A^n (with elements $a^*{}_{ij}^{kl}$), where each of the aggregate sectors has been disaggregated into k subsectors (k may vary for each sector) is needed. Let s_i^k be the share of output of the kth subsector in the total output of aggregate sector i. Similarly let r_i^k be the environmental burden vector associated with a dollar output of kth subsector of aggregate sector i.

Along the lines of constraints in Equations III-2 to III-5, following are the constraints on the elements of A^*.

$$\sum_k s_i^k = 1 \tag{III-6}$$

$$a_{ij} = \sum_k s_i^k a^*{}_{ij}^{kl} \tag{III-7}$$

$$a_{ij} = \sum_l a^*{}_{ij}^{kl} \tag{III-8}$$

$$r_i = \sum_k s_i^k r^*{}_i^k \tag{III-9}$$

The information on input requirements and direct environmental burdens from the manufacturing process of intermediate inputs available in the conventional LCA can thus be incorporated in an EIO-LCA model to derive the larger disaggregated matrix. The expanded technical coefficient matrix and environmental burden matrices can then be used to estimate the total environmental burden associated with an increase in exogenous demand for the sector of interest. In essence, this approach incorporates all the detailed information available in the conventional LCA, approximates missing information, and at the same time maintains the whole economy as the boundary of analysis.

Summary

This appendix (based on Joshi 2000) demonstrates how the EIO-LCA framework can be extended to conduct LCAs of specific products and life cycle stages, and how product specific data available in a conventional LCA can be integrated with EIO-LCA, thus overcoming problems of subjective boundary definition in conventional LCA and aggregation problems in EIO-LCA. Further, these models provide both flexibility and consistency. Depending on the data and cost constraints, LCAs of different levels of complexity and accuracy can be conducted while consistently maintaining the boundary of analysis as the whole economy with all its associated interdependencies.

Appendix IV
Uncertainty in Leontief Input–Output Equations
Some Numerical Examples

Tables of direct requirements and total requirements are often reported to six significant figures. It is said that these tables allow one to calculate to a single dollar the effect on a sector of a one million dollar demand. It should go without saying that we do not believe that we have information that permits us to do this kind of arithmetic. Little advice is given to the novice EIO analyst about how many significant figures merit attention. We have advised our colleagues and students to be careful when going beyond two significant figures, and in this book we restrict virtually all of our impact estimates to two significant digits. This appendix explores some ways to investigate systematically the uncertainty in Leontief input–output analysis.

We can judge the results of using the input–output estimates by considering the effects of errors or uncertainties in the requirements matrix on the solution of the Leontief system. The simultaneous linear equations called the Leontief equations are given by

$$[I - A] \ x = y \tag{IV-1}$$

where I is the identity matrix, A is the matrix of input coefficients called the direct requirements, x is the column vector of total outputs for each of the n sectors, and y is the column vector of final demands. The input coefficient A_{ij} is the fraction of a dollar's worth of commodity i needed to satisfy the production of one dollar's worth of commodity j.

If the coefficients of a are known, and if one assumes a demand vector y, one can determine the total outputs x, which are needed to permit consumers to consume the quantities described by the demand vector y, by solution of Equation IV-1:

$$x = [I - A]^{-1} y \qquad\qquad (\text{IV-2})$$

The matrix $[I–A]^{-1}$ is commonly called the Leontief inverse or simply the Leontief matrix. Here, we will generally assume that we know the elements of the final demand vector y without error. Uncertainty in the values of the elements of the total output vector x will result from uncertainty in the elements of the requirements matrix A. Uncertainties in x will result from the propagation of errors through the nonlinear operation of calculating the Leontief inverse matrix.

The Hawkins-Simon conditions require that all elements in the A matrix are positive and less than one, and at least one column sum in the A matrix must be less than 1. The determinant of the A matrix must be greater than zero for a solution to exist. For empirical requirements matrices, such as are reported by the Bureau of Economic Analysis (BEA) for the United States, values of the determinants of A are very small (on the order of 10^{-12}). Values of the determinant of the associated Leontief matrices are greater than 1.

We will use the U.S. 1998 BEA 9×9 tables for the direct requirements matrix A and the calculated Leontief inverse matrix to illustrate the meaning of the sector elements (see Table IV-1). The two tables are given below. Of the 81 terms in A, five are zero. The numbers in any column of the A matrix represent the amount, or direct requirement, that is purchased in cents from the sector-named rows to produce one dollar of output from the sector-named column. For example, for a one dollar output from the construction sector, 29.8 cents of input is required from the manufacturing sector. The column sum for the construction sector is 53.8 cents for all nine input sectors; this says that $1.00 - 53.8 = 46.2$ cents is the value added by the construction sector for one dollar of output. The values in the $[I-A]^{-1}$ matrix are the total requirements or the sum of the direct and the indirect requirements. Hence, from $[I-A]^{-1}$ we see that a one dollar direct demand from the construction sector requires a total of 52.4 cents to be purchased from the manufacturing sector to cover both the direct and indirect requirements. The sum of the A values in the construction column shows that one dollar demand for construction results in \$2.09 of economic transactions for the whole economy.

Deterministic Changes in the $[I–A]$ and $[I-A]^{-1}$ Matrices

Sherman and Morrison (1950) provide a simple algebraic method for calculating the adjustment of the inverse matrix corresponding to a change in one element in a given matrix. Their method shows how the change in a single element in A will result in the change for all the elements of the Leontief inverse, and that there is a limit to changing an element in $[A]$ that requires that the change does not lead to A becoming singular. We use the 1998 9×9 A and

TABLE IV-1. Nine Sector Input–Output Tables for the United States, 1998

	Agriculture	Minerals	Construction	Manufacturing	Transportation	Trade	Finance	Services	Other
A matrix									
Agriculture	0.242	0.001	0.006	0.037	0.000	0.001	0.005	0.004	0.000
Minerals	0.001	0.213	0.007	0.021	0.042	0.000	0.000	0.000	0.003
Construction	0.012	0.032	0.001	0.007	0.038	0.008	0.026	0.008	0.021
Manufacturing	0.174	0.098	0.298	0.349	0.056	0.044	0.008	0.098	0.015
Transportation	0.045	0.086	0.025	0.046	0.161	0.044	0.021	0.035	0.019
Trade	0.049	0.024	0.081	0.058	0.012	0.021	0.002	0.020	0.002
Finance	0.073	0.225	0.016	0.018	0.032	0.070	0.175	0.070	0.007
Services	0.032	0.040	0.103	0.061	0.116	0.141	0.075	0.153	0.011
Other	0.001	0.013	0.001	0.009	0.020	0.012	0.014	0.009	0.003
I–A inverse									
Agriculture	1.342	0.019	0.035	0.081	0.011	0.009	0.012	0.018	0.003
Minerals	0.019	1.288	0.027	0.050	0.071	0.007	0.004	0.010	0.007
Construction	0.030	0.062	1.014	0.023	0.055	0.017	0.036	0.018	0.023
Manufacturing	0.414	0.275	0.524	1.619	0.180	0.121	0.059	0.210	0.043
Transportation	0.112	0.170	0.081	0.114	1.225	0.075	0.043	0.071	0.028
Trade	0.099	0.060	0.123	0.108	0.037	1.036	0.013	0.041	0.008
Finance	0.157	0.385	0.072	0.084	0.094	0.114	1.230	0.120	0.016
Services	0.131	0.157	0.202	0.166	0.206	0.205	0.126	1.226	0.026
Other	0.012	0.030	0.012	0.022	0.031	0.019	0.020	0.017	1.005

Leontief inverse matrices to demonstrate the numerical effect of changing the value in *A* on the Leontief inverse matrix. We do not use the Sherman-Morrison equation for our calculation, but instead use the functional term for calculating the inverse matrix in the spreadsheet program Excel.

Example 1. The effect of changing one element in the *A* matrix on the elements in the Leontief matrix.

If element $A_{4,3}$ is increased by 25%, we want to know the magnitude of the changes in the Leontief inverse matrix. The original $A_{4,3} = 0.298$ in the 1998 table and the increased value is $A_{4,3} = 1.25 \times 0.298 = 0.3725$. All other elements in *A* are unchanged. All calculated elements in the new Leontief matrix show some change, but the amount of change varies. For an increase of 25% in $A_{4,3}$, the inverse element $[I - A]^{-1}_{4,3}$ increases by nearly the same amount. The manufacturing column and the construction row elements all change by the same percentage. In the Leontief matrix system, the sum of the column is called the backward linkage and the sum of the row is called the forward linkage. As a result of the 25% increase in the direct requirement of the manufacturing sector on the construction sector, each backward element in the construction sector increases by 0.17%. There is a similar increase in each element in the forward linkage of the manufacturing sector. Other sectors change by different amounts. In percentage terms, the changes for the new Leontief matrix compared to the original 1998 matrix are shown in Table IV-2.

Example 2. The effect of a small change in a single cell of *A* on the Leontief matrix.

The value of $A_{4,3}$ is rounded from three decimal places to two, from 0.298 to 0.30. The relative change in the new Leontief matrix is small for all cells, and no cell has a positive change (see Table IV-3). The largest change is in $[I\text{-}A]^{-1}_{4,3}$ of −0.6%.

Example 3. The effect of rounding all cells of *A* from three decimal places to two.

The changes in the new Leontief matrix are both positive and negative, and are larger than for the single cell rounding change illustrated in the previous example (see Table IV-4). $[I\text{-}A]^{-1}_{4,3}$ changes by −1.7% when all cells in A are rounded down. Rounding all the cells in *A* to two decimal places results in large changes in many cells of the Leontief matrix. The largest negative change is −71.1% in $[I\text{-}A]^{-1}_{1,7}$, and the largest positive change is 54.1% in $[I\text{-}A]^{-1}_{2,9}$.

Modeling Changes in the [*I–A*] and Leontief Matrices with Probabilistic Methods

The literature dealing with uncertainty in the Leontief equations is not extensive. The earliest work that we have found that deals with probabilistic errors was from the Ph.D thesis of R.E. Quandt (1956). Quandt's (1958, 1959) analy-

TABLE IV-2. Percentage Changes in the Leontief Matrix from Changing a Single Requirements Coefficient

	Agriculture	Minerals	Construction	Manufacturing	Transportation	Trade	Finance	Services	Other
Agriculture	0.01%	1.97%	17.30%	0.17%	3.02%	1.13%	1.81%	0.62%	5.59%
Minerals	0.59%	0.02%	13.72%	0.17%	0.29%	0.86%	3.12%	0.71%	1.30%
Construction	0.17%	0.17%	0.17%	0.17%	0.17%	0.17%	0.17%	0.17%	0.17%
Manufacturing	0.88%	2.74%	23.36%	0.17%	3.72%	1.74%	7.30%	1.05%	6.64%
Transportation	0.23%	0.31%	10.71%	0.17%	0.04%	0.20%	0.72%	0.22%	0.70%
Trade	0.25%	0.84%	6.67%	0.17%	1.21%	0.01%	2.25%	0.36%	2.45%
Finance	0.12%	0.10%	8.81%	0.17%	0.37%	0.10%	0.02%	0.10%	0.93%
Services	0.28%	0.49%	6.23%	0.17%	0.33%	0.11%	0.35%	0.02%	1.12%
Other	0.40%	0.33%	13.56%	0.17%	0.29%	0.15%	0.29%	0.18%	0.00%

TABLE IV-3 Percentage Changes in the Leontief Matrix from Rounding a Single Coefficient

[I - A] inverse	Agriculture	Minerals	Construction	Manufacturing	Transportation	Trade	Finance	Services	Other
Agriculture	0.0%	-0.1%	-0.5%	0.0%	-0.1%	0.0%	0.0%	0.0%	-0.1%
Minerals	0.0%	0.0%	-0.4%	0.0%	0.0%	0.0%	-0.1%	0.0%	0.0%
Construction	0.0%	0.0%	0.0%	0.0%	0.0%	0.0%	0.0%	0.0%	0.0%
Manufacturing	0.0%	-0.1%	-0.6%	0.0%	-0.1%	0.0%	-0.2%	0.0%	-0.2%
Transportation	0.0%	0.0%	-0.3%	0.0%	0.0%	0.0%	0.0%	0.0%	0.0%
Trade	0.0%	0.0%	-0.2%	0.0%	0.0%	0.0%	0.0%	0.0%	-0.1%
Finance	0.0%	0.0%	-0.2%	0.0%	0.0%	0.0%	0.0%	0.0%	0.0%
Services	0.0%	0.0%	-0.2%	0.0%	0.0%	0.0%	0.0%	0.0%	0.0%
Other	0.0%	0.0%	-0.4%	0.0%	0.0%	0.0%	0.0%	0.0%	0.0%

TABLE IV-4. Percentage Changes in the Leontief Matrix from Rounding All Coefficients

[I - A] inverse	Agriculture	Minerals	Construction	Manufacturing	Transportation	Trade	Finance	Services	Other
Agriculture	0.1%	-9.8%	-20.3%	-7.9%	-9.1%	14.6%	-71.7%	25.2%	-25.6%
Minerals	11.6%	0.4%	-13.2%	3.6%	4.4%	8.7%	-6.9%	-1.4%	54.1%
Construction	0.5%	-1.4%	-0.2%	-27.9%	-6.7%	-17.8%	-16.6%	-22.4%	3.0%
Manufacturing	1.7%	-3.0%	-1.7%	-0.6%	-6.4%	3.7%	-19.0%	-2.9%	-17.1%
Transportation	-8.2%	-4.8%	-13.6%	-9.0%	-0.1%	4.9%	-4.1%	-11.9%	-5.6%
Trade	-0.9%	8.8%	-0.7%	-3.8%	4.4%	0.1%	5.7%	-1.1%	22.8%
Finance	2.3%	-2.6%	-12.3%	-6.8%	1.2%	-0.2%	-0.8%	-1.1%	-18.6%
Services	1.9%	-2.2%	0.2%	-1.4%	-3.0%	1.0%	-7.5%	0.1%	2.8%
Other	14.0%	16.5%	4.4%	-6.1%	0.9%	13.2%	22.7%	-5.9%	0.3%

sis of probabilistic errors in the Leontief system was limited by the computing facilities of the late 1950s. His numerical experiments were confined to small (3×3) matrices. He developed equations to calculate expected values for means and variances of the Leontief matrix based on estimates of these parameters for the [A] matrix.

Quandt investigated changes in the Leontief equations by examining them in this form:

$$[I - A - E]^{-1} \, y = x \qquad \text{(IV-3)}$$

Quandt specified conditions on his errors E that each element $[A_{ij} + E_{ij}] \geq 0$ and that column j, sum of all elements $[A_{ij} + E_{ij}]$, must be less than 1, that is, the uncertain A elements satisfied the Hawkins-Simon conditions. His work examined ten discrete distributions for E, (eight were centered at the origin and two were skewed about the origin.) The probabilities of these errors were also modeled discretely with choices of uniform, symmetric, and asymmetric distributions.

For each distribution Quandt selected a sample of 100 3x3 matrices. Each sample set represented about 0.5% of the total population of $3^9 = 19,683$ matrices. From this set of experiments he calculated the variance and the third and fourth moments of the error distributions and the resulting vector x. Quandt used a constant demand vector y for all his experiments. The mean values of x were little changed from the deterministic values and the variance of A had little effect on the mean values of x.

Quandt concluded the following:

1. the skewness of the errors in A are transmitted to the skewness of the errors in the x vector.
2. The lognormal distribution provides a fairly adequate description of the distribution of the x vector elements irrespective of the distribution of the errors in A.
3. One can use the approximate lognormal distribution to establish confidence limits for the elements in the solution x.

West (1986) has performed a stochastic analysis of the Leontief equations with the assumption that elements in A could be represented by continuous normal distributions. He presents equations for calculating the moments of the elements in A. West's work is critically examined by Raa and Steel (1994) who point out shortcomings in his choice of normality for the A elements—mainly that elements in A cannot be less than zero—and suggest using a beta distribution limited to the interval for A elements between 0 and 1 to keep elements in A positive.

Some Numerical Experiments with Stochastic Input *A* + *E* Matrices

The examples presented in this section are constructed using Excel spreadsheets and @Risk software. They illustrate the ease by which we can study the effects of changes in the form of elements of *A* on the Leontief matrix and some of the multipliers and linkages commonly used in Leontief analysis. Numerical simulation is easy, and results from more than a thousand iterations are obtained quickly. Still, the critical issues are the formulation of good questions and the interpretation of the results of numerical experiments. As we have pointed out before, the lack of a detailed empirical database to support our assumptions about the statistical properties of the elements in the direct requirements A matrix is the most important limitation of this analysis.

For each of our numerical experiments, we compare the properties of the input A + E direct requirements matrix and the output $[I - A - E]^{-1}$ total requirements matrix, where E is an introduced perturbation. The results of stochastic simulations for the $[I - A - E]$ inverses are compared to the deterministic calculation of $[I - A]$ inverse. We report some representative results for four scenarios.

1. In each scenario, the means of *A* are the 1998 values reported to three decimal places.
2. Four types of input distributions are examined: a uniform distribution and two triangular distributions with both positive and negative skewness, and a symmetric triangular distribution.

An Excel spreadsheet is constructed with the 1998 9×9 matrix A, and used to calculate the Leontief inverse. @Risk uses the Excel spreadsheet as a basis for defining input and output cells. The chosen probabilistic distribution functions can be selected from a menu in @Risk; the number of iterations can be set, or one may let the program automatically choose the number of iterations to reach closure. We expect changes from the results of the deterministic calculation of the Leontief matrix from *A*; Simonovits (1975) showed that

$$Exp\,(I - A)^{-1} \geq (I - Exp\,(A))^{-1} \qquad\qquad \text{(IV-4)}$$

where *Exp* is the expected value operator. We use the software to numerically simulate the values of the Leontief matrix given an assumed distribution for *A*.

Table IV-5 shows the results of our simulations for the manufacturing:construction element in *A*, namely $A_{4,3}$. Each of the 81 values in *A* is iterated over 1,000 times for each simulation. Here only the distribution of values for one cell, the manufacturing:construction intersection, is reported.

The numerical simulations show that the mean value for $[I-A]^{-1}_{4,3}$ for the symmetric uniform distribution is identical to the deterministic value for this

TABLE IV-5. Numerical Monte Carlo Simulation on a Leontief Coefficient

Scenario	Iterations	Input [A_{43}] mean, mfrg:constr.	Input [A_{43}] std dev, mfrg:constr.	Input [A_{43}] skewness, mfrg:constr.	Input [A_{43}] COV
Deterministic	NA	0.298	NA	NA	NA
Uniform	1,200	0.298	0.0017	−0.0077	0.006
Triangular, skew low	2,300	0.295	0.210	0.576	0.711
Triangular, skew high	1,400	0.297	0.106	−0.558	0.357
Triangular, symmetric	1,200	0.298	0.117	−0.0080	0.393

Scenario	Iterations	Output $[I-A]^{-1}_{43}$ mean, mfrg: constr.	Output $[I-A]^{-1}_{43}$ std dev, mfrg:constr.	Output $[I-A]^{-1}_{43}$ skewness, mfrg:constr	Output $[I-A]^{-1}_{43}$ COV
Deterministic	NA	0.524	NA	NA	NA
Uniform	1,200	0.524	0.015	0.0017	0.029
Triangular, skew low	2,300	0.462	0.190	0.012	0.411
Triangular, skew high	1,400	0.506	0.107	−0.651	0.211
Triangular, symmetric	1,200	0.503	0.117	−0.356	0.233

sector pair of manufacturing:construction. The mean values for $[I-A]^{-1}_{4,3}$ for the two skewed distributions are both lower than the deterministic value for $[I-A]^{-1}_{4,3}$, and so is the mean value for $[A_{4,3}]$ for the symmetrical triangular distribution. The coefficient of variation (COV: the ratio of the standard deviation to the mean) of $[I-A]^{-1}_{4,3}$ is smaller than the COV for $[A_{4,3}]$ for all simulations except for the uniform input distribution. Consistent with Quandt's conjecture, the skewness for every $[I-A]^{-1}_{4,3}$ increases except for the uniform distribution input. Additional work remains to show the patterns for the entire distribution of cells in $[A]$.

Energy Analysis with Stochastic Leontief Equations

Table IV-6 is representative of the 9×9 U.S. economy with nearly $15 trillion of total transactions and the total value added, or gross domestic product (GDP), of more than $8 trillion. We have included a column called the percentage value added for this economy. If we think in terms of $100 million of value added, or final demand, for the U.S. economy, we can also think of this demand in terms of disaggregated sector demands of nearly $18 million for manufactured products, more than $5 million for construction, etc.

For this energy analysis, we show three columns of energy data in mixed units, energy per $ million of total sector output. Hence, the manufactured products sector uses nearly 3.5 TJ of total energy per $ million of output, 0.24 million kWh of electricity per $ million of output, and 0.44 TJ of coal per $ million of output.

The total energy use and the direct energy use for each sector are given by:

$$r = [R \text{ } diagonal] \quad x = [r \text{ } diagonal] \text{ } [I - A]^{-1} \text{ } y \qquad \text{(IV-5)}$$

and

$$r \text{ } direct = [R \text{ } diagonal] \text{ } [I + A] \text{ } y \qquad \text{(IV-6)}$$

where *r* is a vector of energy use by sector, [*R diagonal*] is a matrix with diagonal cells equal to the energy use per dollar of sector output and off-diagonal terms equal to zero, and *A* is the requirements matrix.

Example 1. For this example, we use Excel and @Risk to build a model to calculate the uncertainty in the physical units of both the direct and the total energy use for $100 million of final demand for the U.S. economy. The demand is distributed among the nine sectors proportionally to the distributions of value added for the economy. We assume we know the demand vector with certainty, and that we know the physical energy use with certainty. All uncertainty for this example is in *A*.

Assume that the entries in *A* may be represented by a symmetric triangular distribution with a low limit of zero, a mode equal to the three decimal place value reported by BEA, and a high limit of two times the mode. The mean of this distribution is equal to the mode. This is equivalent to saying that the coefficient of variation is constant for all entries with a value of 0.41. Previously, we presented the results of simulations for this triangular distribution on the Leontief matrix In this example, we examine the distribution of the *r direct* and the total *r*.

@Risk performed 5,000 iterations to calculate the mean value and the standard deviation of the energy use for each of the nine sectors for a $100 million increment of GDP proportionally distributed across the economy (Table IV-7). The uncertainty in the energy output for each sector is shown by the standard deviation and the COV. The sum of the total energy use for the whole economy is 730 TJ and the direct energy use is 563 TJ. The sector values for *r direct* are smaller than the total *r* values, and the *r* values have more uncertainty than the *r direct* values as shown by the COVs. The COVs for all sectors are smaller than the constant COV of 0.41 assumed for *A*. Direct energy use is lowest as a percentage of the total energy use for the agricultural products and minerals sectors. For all other sectors, the direct energy use is more than 70% of the total energy use.

TABLE IV-6. Sector Output, Value Added, and Energy Use for the U.S. Economy, 1998

Sector	Total sector output ($ million)	% total output	Value added ($ million)	% value added	Total energy (TJ/ $ million)	Electricity (MkWh/ $ million)	Coal (TJ/ $ million)
Agricultural products	297,890	2.0	110,194	1.3	2.9	0.18	0
Minerals	174,870	1.2	69,732	0.8	4.5	0.49	0.38
Construction	944,308	6.4	443,974	5.3	0.39	0.022	0
Manufacturing products	3,884,184	26.4	1,477,593	17.8	3.5	0.24	0.44
Transportation	1,198,305	8.1	613,228	7.4	24	0.10	14
Trade	1,495,287	10.2	996,291	12.0	1.9	0.15	0.011
Finance	2,349,857	16.0	1,605,509	19.3	0.28	0.031	0.003
Services	3,203,175	21.8	1,938,409	23.3	0.79	0.078	0.008
Other	1,156,154	7.9	1,063,511	12.8	6.8	0.39	0
Total	14,704,030	100.0	8,318,441	100.0	45	1.7	14.8

TABLE IV-7. Results of a Monte Carlo Simulation on Energy Use

Sector 5,000 iterations	Final demand $ million	Direct energy [r] direct Mean in TJ	Direct energy [r] direct std dev in TJ	Direct energy [r] direct coef. of var.
Agricultural products	1.3	7.6	1.0	0.14
Minerals	0.8	8.2	1.1	0.14
Construction	5.3	2.7	0.1	0.05
Manufacturing products	17.8	100.9	6.0	0.06
Transportation	7.4	289.1	18.6	0.06
Trade	12.0	27.8	1.1	0.04
Finance	19.3	7.2	0.3	0.04
Services	23.3	25.6	1.2	0.05
Other	12.8	94.0	1.6	0.02
Total	100.0	563.1		

Sector 5,000 iterations	Final demand $ million	Total energy [r] mean in TJ	Total energy[r] std dev in TJ	Total energy [r] coef. of var.
Agricultural products	1.3	12.8	2.9	0.23
Minerals	0.8	14.5	3.2	0.22
Construction	5.3	3.1	0.2	0.07
Manufacturing products	17.8	142.5	16.8	0.12
Transportation	7.4	385.9	40.5	0.10
Trade	12.0	32.3	2.2	0.07
Finance	19.3	8.6	0.6	0.07
Services	23.3	31.1	2.2	0.07
Other	12.8	99.5	2.7	0.03
Total	100.0	730.3		

Sector 5,000 iterations	Ratio of [r] direct / [r]
Agricultural products	59%
Minerals	56%
Construction	86%
Manufacturing products	71%
Transportation	75%
Trade	86%
Finance	84%
Services	83%
Other	94%
Total	77%

Summary

Uncertain values in the cells of the requirements matrix generate uncertain values in the cells of the total requirements or Leontief matrix. Three cases have been studied. Two deterministic cases are presented; in one case only a single value in A is modified, and in the second case all the values in A are changed. For a set of probabilistic examples we used Excel and @Risk to calculate the Leontief matrix for a uniform and three triangular distributions of A as input. The simulations show small effects on the mean values of the Leontief matrix and larger changes in the second and third moments.

An example of an energy analysis for a 9×9 sector model of the U.S. economy shows the effect of uncertainty from A on the total energy use r and the direct energy use r *direct* for each sector.

Appendix V

Compliance of an LCA Study Conducted Using the EIO-LCA Model with the Requirements of ISO 14040, 14041, 14042, and 14043 Standards

This appendix describes how EIO-LCA may be used in life cycle assessment (LCA) studies conducted in accordance with the ISO 14040 (ISO 1997), 14041 (ISO 1998), 14042 (ISO 2000a), and 14043 (ISO 2000b) standards. These standards primarily pertain to process requirements such as necessary documentation rather than model requirements. As a result, life cycle assessment studies intended to comply with ISO standards should review these requirements carefully.

ANSI/ISO 14040:1997 Environmental Management—Life Cycle Assessment—Principles and Framework

The ANSI/ISO 14040:1997 standard provides the basic definitions, general description, and some methodological framework for conducting LCA studies (ISO 1997). In general, the definition of goal, scope, system boundaries, types, and formats of reports and critical review are independent from the type of methodology used to conduct the LCA study.

The standard defines the two basic terms of *functional unit* and *unit process*. A functional unit is "Quantified performance of a product system for use as a reference unit in a life cycle assessment study." ("Product" denotes product systems and can also include service systems in the standard.) When using the

EIO-LCA model, the level of economic activity, or a demand for the goods and services of a selected sector given in U.S. dollars, may be considered as a functional unit.

A unit process is defined as the "smallest portion of a product system for which data are collected when performing a life cycle assessment." Data used by the EIO-LCA model are collected for production of $1 of output of a sector.

The next section discusses the applicable requirements of the standard and provides recommendations where necessary. Table V-1 presents the requirements of the ANSI/ISO 14040:1997 standard. The following abbreviations are used in the tables:

- y: the requirement is fulfilled.
- p: the requirement is partially fulfilled.
- n: the requirement is not fulfilled.
- na: the requirement is not applicable.
- y/na: the LCA study conducted using the EIO-LCA model may be in compliance with the requirement but it does not depend on the type of LCA method.

ISO 14041:1998 Environmental Management—Life Cycle Assessment—Goal and Scope Definition and Inventory Analysis

The ISO 14041:1998 standard presents specific requirements and procedures essential for definition of goal and scope for LCA, and for conducting, interpreting, and reporting an LCI (ISO 1998). It provides more detailed information in addition to the general descriptions given in the ISO 14040:1997 standard. Table V-2 presents the relevant and additional requirements of the standard.

ISO 14042:2000 Environmental Management—Life Cycle Assessment—Life Cycle Impact Assessment

The ISO 14042:2000 standard provides the general description of the life cycle impact assessment (LCIA) phase of LCA, introduces its mandatory and optional elements, and discusses the limitations of LCIA (ISO 2000a).

The use of the 1997 U.S. industry benchmark-based EIO-LCA model results in an inventory of the following environmental effects:

- Releases of "conventional" pollutants.
- Toxic releases (from the EPA's Toxics Release Inventory, or TRI).
- RCRA hazardous waste generation.
- Electricity and fuel use.

The requirements of the 14042:2000 standard are applicable to the emission of greenhouse gases estimated in metric tons of carbon dioxide using the global warming potential as a weighting factor, and toxic releases weighted by the CMU-ET method (see Table V-3).

ISO 14043:2000 Environmental Management—Life Cycle Assessment—Life Cycle Interpretation

The ISO 14043:2000 standard provides a general description of life cycle interpretation, guidelines for identification of significant issues, evaluation of results, drawing conclusions, and making recommendations based on the LCA or LCI study (ISO 2000b). Compliance with requirements of the standard does not depend on the type of LCA method used to conduct the study.

TABLE V-1. Requirements of the ANSI/ISO 14040:1997 Standard

ISO requirement	Compliance: y/p/n/na/y/na	Note/recommendation for EIO-LCA
Adequate and systematic assessment of the environmental aspects of product system throughout its life cycle.	y	EIO-LCA can address this adequately.
Ability to include new scientific findings and improved technology.	y	The regular update of the EIO-LCA model ensures compliance. It would be beneficial to do the update more frequently than 5 years (when the BEA benchmark I-O tables are published) using annual tables.
LCA studies should define goal and scope, include inventory analysis, impact assessment, and interpretation of results.	y/na	EIO-LCA provides an inventory of economic and environmental effects, and an assessment of impacts such as weighted toxic releases and global warming potential.
LCI studies should define goal and scope, include inventory analysis, and interpretation of results.	y/na	Definition of the goal and scope of LCI study does not depend on the type of LCA method used to conduct it. The use of EIO-LCA results in an inventory of economic and environmental effects. The interpretation of results is up to the user.
The goal of LCA study should define the reasons for conducting the study and the intended audience.	y/na	Compliance with this requirement does not depend on the type of LCA method.
The scope of LCA study shall include the following: • Functions of the product system • Functional unit • Product system to be analyzed • System boundaries • Allocation methods • Methodology of impact assessment • Types of impacts to be assessed • Data requirements • Assumptions	y/na	• EIO-LCA is compliant with the listed factors, except that the requirement for inclusion of allocation method is not applicable to the EIO-LCA model. • The description of methodology of impact assessment is provided by referencing the EIO-LCA model documentation (www.eiolca.net). • The types of impacts to be assessed are limited to GWP

TABLE V-1. (Continued) Requirements of the ANSI/ISO 14040:1997 Standard

ISO requirement	Compliance: y/p/n/na/y/na	Note/recommendation for EIO-LCA
• Limitations • Critical review • Type and format of report for study		and CMU-ET in the EIO-LCA model. The user may apply other methods to estimate impacts using the model's inventory results.
Functional unit should be defined, measurable, and amenable to ensure comparability of results.	y	The functional unit is expressed as the level of economic activity/demand in a selected sector, given in U.S. dollars.
System boundaries and criteria used to define them should be identified and justified.	y/na	The EIO-LCA documentation addresses this point.
Data quality requirements addressing the following characteristics should be defined: • Time related and geographical coverage • Technology coverage • Precision, completeness, and representativeness • Consistency and reproducibility • Sources of data • Uncertainty	y	• The EIO-LCA model uses national average data incorporating different technologies for the same products. • The description of sources and age of data is by referencing the EIO-LCA model documentation (www.eiolca.net).
Equivalence of systems and same methodology should be ensured in comparative studies.	y/na	Compliance with this requirement does not depend on the type of LCA method.
Quantification of relevant inputs and outputs.	y	EIO-LCA addresses this adequately.
Qualitative and quantitative data should be collected for all unit processes included within the boundaries.	y	Since the unit process for the model is defined as producing $1 sectoral output, this requirement is fulfilled when the economic and environmental vectors were estimated.
Allocation processes should be defined, documented, and justified.	na	Since the model uses a consistent, well-documented model (I-O tables), this is not applicable.

TABLE V-1. (Continued) Requirements of the ANSI/ISO 14040:1997 Standard

ISO requirement	Compliance: y/p/n/na/y/na	Note/Recommendation for EIO-LCA
Estimation of energy flow should include the different fuels and electricity.	y	EIO-LCA addresses this adequately.
The classification and characterization of impact categories and weighting methods should be transparent and documented.	y	The classification and characterization of impact categories and weighting methods may be provided by referencing the EIO-LCA model documentation (www.eiolca.net).
The interpretation of results should reflect the outcomes of sensitivity analysis that was conducted.	y/na	Compliance with this requirement does not depend on the type of LCA method.
Type and format of the report should be defined in the scope phase.	y/na	Compliance with this requirement does not depend on the type of LCA method.
The results should be communicated to a third party in a different format.	y/na	Compliance with this requirement does not depend on the type of LCA method.
If critical review is undertaken, the following criteria have to be defined during the goal and scope definition phase: • Reason for critical review • Area that will be covered • Level of detail • Who needs to be involved in the process	y/na	Compliance with this requirement does not depend on the type of LCA method.
Critical review statement should be included in the LCA study report.	y/na	Compliance with this requirement does not depend on the type of LCA method.

TABLE V-2. Requirements of the ISO 14041:1998 Standard

ISO requirement	Compliance; y/p/n/na/y/na	Note/recommendation
Data should be collected to quantify the inputs and outputs of a unit process: • Energy, raw material, and other physical inputs • Products • Emissions to air, water, land, and other environmental aspects	y	EIO-LCA addresses this adequately.
Models describing the product system should be documented.	y	The description of the model is provided by referencing the EIO-LCA model documentation (www.eiolca.net).
Functions of the product should be defined.	y	EIO-LCA addresses this adequately.
Functional unit should be defined.	y	EIO-LCA addresses this adequately.
The amount of product necessary to fulfill the function (reference flow) should be quantified.	y	EIO-LCA addresses this adequately.
Any omission of life cycle stages, processes, or inputs/outputs should be documented and justified.	y	The EIO-LCA model is consistent from one study to the next, thus no omissions are possible, unless executed by the user off-line.
The following life cycle stages, unit processes, and flows should be included in the system: • Inputs and outputs in the main manufacturing/processing sequence • Distribution and transportation • Production and use of fuels, electricity, and heat • Use and maintenance of products • Disposal of process waste and products • Recovery of used products • Manufacture of ancillary materials • Manufacture, maintenance, and decommissioning of capital equipment	p	Depends on type of product: • Use of product • Maintenance of product • Disposal of product • Maintenance and decommissioning of capital equipment

TABLE V-2. (continued) Requirements of the ISO 14041:1998 Standard

ISO requirement	Compliance: y/p/n/na/y/na	Note/recommendation
• Additional operations, e.g., lighting and heating • Other considerations related to impact assessment		
Significant fugitive emissions should be included in addition to the discharges from point or diffuse sources.	p	The EIO-LCA uses EPA AIRS emissions which includes fugitive emissions for some but not all sources.
Energy inputs and outputs should be quantified in energy units and if applicable the mass or volume of fuel should be documented.	y	The mass or volume of fuel may be estimated using the conversion factors provided in the model documentation.
The source of data that are collected from published literature should be referenced.	y	The description of source of data is provided by referencing the EIO-LCA model documentation (www.eiolca.net).
Data should be validated during collection processes.	y	Validation is conducted during estimation of economic and environmental vectors.
Missing data should be treated as follows: • Estimate non-zero data and justify it • Give zero data value and justify it • Estimate value from similar technology	p	This requirement is only partially fulfilled as justification of non-zero/zero data values is not documented.
An appropriate reference flow should be determined for all unit processes.	y	Production of $1 of sectoral output is considered a reference flow.
The interpretation of LCI should include the following: • Data quality assessment • Sensitivity analyses on significant inputs, outputs, and methodological choices	p	This requirement is only partially fulfilled as data quality assessment is missing in EIO-LCA.

TABLE V-3. Requirements of the ISO 14042:2000 Standard

ISO requirement	*Compliance:* *y/p/n/nn/yna*	*Note/recommendation*
Mandatory elements of LCIA: • Concept of category indicators – Identification of the following components for each impact cat- egory:		
– Impact category	y	• For GHG emission: climate change • For CMU-ET: toxicity
– Characterization model	y	• For GHG emission: IPCC model • For CMU-ET: the Threshold Limit Values of the American Conference of Governmental Industrial Hygienists
– Environmentally relevant cat- egory indicator	y	• For GHG emission: infrared radiative forcing • For CMU-ET: occupational health (adverse health effects)
– Characterization factor	y	• For GHG emission: global warming potential • For CMU-ET: Threshold Limit Values
– Indicator result	y	• For GHG emission: metric tons of CO_2-equivalents • For CMU-ET: metric tons of sul- furic acid equivalent
– Category endpoints	n	• For CMU-ET: occupational health (adverse health effects)
– Environmental mechanism	n	• EIO-LCA does not include fate and transport models.
• The selection of impact cate- gories shall be appropriate to address environmental issues associated with the product sys- tem being studied.	y	EIO-LCA addresses this adequately.
• Sources of impact categories, category indicators and	y y	EIO-LCA addresses this adequately.

TABLE V-3 (continued) Requirements of the ISO 14042:2000 Standard

ISO requirement	*Compliance: y/p/n/na/y/na*	*Note/recommendation*
characterization models shall be referenced.		
• Selection of impact categories, category indicators, and characterization models shall be justified.	y	EIO-LCA addresses this adequately.
• Accurate and descriptive names shall be provided for impact categories and category indicators.	y	EIO-LCA addresses this adequately.
• Characterization model and its appropriateness shall be described.	y	EIO-LCA addresses this adequately.
• The impact categories, category indicators, and characterization models should be internationally accepted.	y	• For GHG emission: EIO-LCA addresses this adequately • For CMU-ET: it has been used, but does not yet have wide international acceptance
• The impact categories should represent the aggregated emissions of the product system being studied on the category endpoint through the category indicators.	y	EIO-LCA addresses this adequately.
• Assumptions and value-choices should be minimized.	y	EIO-LCA addresses this adequately.
• Double counting should be avoided.	y	EIO-LCA addresses this adequately.
• The characterization model should be technically and scientifically valid, and based on a distinct identifiable environmental mechanism and/or reproducible empirical observation.	y	EIO-LCA addresses this adequately.

TABLE V-3. (continued) Requirements of the ISO 14042:2000 Standard

ISO requirement	Compliance: y/p/n/na/y/na	Note/recommendation
• Spatial and temporal differentiation of the characterization model should be considered.	y	• For GHG emission: EIO-LCA addresses this adequately • For CMU-ET: the TLVs are updated regularly. But there is no spatial differentiation.
• Inventory results, other than mass and energy flow data, shall be identified and their relationship to corresponding category indicators shall be determined.	p	EIO-LCA has some impact categories calculated from inventory data; users can define and calculate others.
• Environmental relevance of the category indicator or characterization model should be clearly determined.	y	EIO-LCA addresses this adequately.
• Technique of calculating indicator results shall be determined and documented.	y	The description of calculations is provided by referencing the EIO-LCA model documentation (www.eiolca.net).
Optional elements of LCIA: • Normalization – The consistency of the spatial and temporal scales of the environmental mechanism and the reference value should be considered during the selection of reference system.	y/na	Compliance with this requirement does not depend on the type of LCA method.
• Grouping – The grouping method shall be entirely transparent and consistent with the goal and scope of LCA study.	y/na	Compliance with this requirement does not depend on the type of LCA method.
• Weighting – The weighting method shall be entirely transparent and consistent with the goal and scope of LCA study.	y/na	Compliance with this requirement does not depend on the type of LCA method.
– The weighting method shall be documented.	y/na	Compliance with this requirement does not depend on the type of LCA method.

TABLE V-3. (continued) Requirements of the ISO 14042:2000 Standard

ISO requirement	Compliance: y/p/n/na/y/na	Note/recommendation
Data quality analysis may be needed:		
• Gravity analysis	y/na	Compliance with this requirement does not depend on the type of LCA method.
• Uncertainty analysis	y/na	Compliance with this requirement does not depend on the type of LCA method.
• Sensitivity analysis	y/na	Compliance with this requirement does not depend on the type of LCA method.
Reporting and critical review of LCIA results	y/na	Compliance with this requirement does not depend on the type of LCA method.

References

AASHTO (American Association of State Highway and Transportation Officials). 1972. *Interim Guide for Design of Pavement Structures.* Washington, DC: AASHTO.

ABA (American Booksellers Association). 2000. *"In Fact" Industry Newsroom.* September 28, 1998. http://www.bookweb.org (accessed July 14, 2000).

Abraham, K.G., W.L. Weber, and M.E. Personick. 1996. Improvements in the BLS Safety and Health Statistical System. *Monthly Labor Review* 119(4): 3–12.

Alsema, E.A., and E. Nieuwlaar. 2000. Energy Viability of Photovoltaic Systems. *Energy Policy* 28: 999–1010.

Amatayakul, W. 1999. Life Cycle Assessment of a Catalytic Converter for Passenger Cars. Master's thesis, Goteborg, Sweden: Chalmers University of Technology.

Amphlett, J.C., M.K. Mann, B.A. Peppley, and I.H. Knoepfel. 1996. A Framework for Environmental Impact Assessment of Long-Distance Energy Transport Systems. *Energy* (21) 7–8: 693–702.

Barlow, A., D. Contos, M. Holdren, P. Garrison, L. Harris, and B. Janke. 1996. Development of Emission Factors for Polyethylene Processing. *Journal of the Air and Waste Management Association* 46: 569–580.

BEA (Bureau of Economic Analysis). 2004a. *Regional Multipliers—A User Handbook for the Regional Input–Output Modeling System (RIMS II),* 3rd ed. Washington, DC: BEA.

———. 2004b. *Input–Output Accounts Data.* http://www.bea.gov/bea/dn2/i-o_benchmark.htm (accessed June 29, 2004).

———. 2004c. *Gross State Product.* http://www.bea.gov/bea/regional/gsp.htm (accessed June 29, 2004).

———. 2004d. *Technical Documentation of RIMS-II Multipliers, Description of Files.* Washington, DC: BEA.

Bergerson, J.A., and L.B. Lave. 2005. Should We Transport Coal, Gas, or Electricity: Cost, Efficiency, and Environmental Implications. *Environmental Science and Technology* 39(16): 5905-5910.

Bjorn, A., L. Declercq-Lopez, S. Spatari, and H.L. MacLean. 2005. Decision Support for Sustainable Development Using a Canadian Economic Input–Output Life Cycle Assessment Model. *Canadian Journal of Civil Engineering* 32:16-29.

Blanchard, S., and P. Reppe. 1998. Life Cycle Analysis of a Residential Home in Michigan. Master's thesis, University of Michigan.

BLM (Wyoming Bureau of Land Management). 2000. *Percent of Total U.S. Coal Production Mined From the Powder River Basin.* http://www.wy.blm.gov/minerals/coal/coalgraphics/prbproduction.gif (accessed August 2004).

Bloomquist, D., G. Diamond, M. Oden, B. Ruth, and M. Tia. 1993. Engineering and Environmental Aspects of Recycled Materials for Highway Construction—Final Report. Report No. FHWA-RD-93-088. Washington, DC: U.S. Department of Transportation, Federal Highway Administration, and U.S. Environmental Protection Agency.

BLS (Bureau of Labor Statistics). 1994. *Survey of Occupational Injuries and Illnesses 1992.* Washington, DC: U.S. Department of Labor.

———. 1997. *Industry Illness and Injury Data 1997.* Washington, DC: U.S. Department of Labor. http://www.bls.gov/iif/oshsum.htm (Accessed November 10, 2005).

———. 2000. *Census of Fatal Occupational Injuries, 1992–1998.* Washington, DC: U.S. Department of Labor.

Bonstedt, H.O. 1998. A Marketing Approach to Bridge Longevity. *Concrete International,* October: 65–68.

Boon, J.E., J.A. Isaacs, and S.M. Gupta. 2000. Economic Impact of Aluminum-Intensive Vehicles on the U.S. Automotive Recycling Infrastructure. *Journal of Industrial Ecology* 4(2): 117–134.

Brouwer, G. 2002. Adaptive Management Group Finds Common Ground at Glen Canyon. *Civil Engineering* 72(8): 24–25.

BTS (Bureau of Transportation Statistics). 2004. National Transportation Statistics. http://www.bts.gov/publications/national_transportation_statistics/ (Accessed November 10, 2005).

Cano-Ruiz, A.J. 2000. Decision Support Tools for Environmentally Conscious Chemical Process Design. PhD diss., MIT.

Carter, A.P. 1970. *Structural Change in the American Economy.* Cambridge: Harvard University Press.

Chapman, P.F. 1975. Energy Analysis of Nuclear-Power Stations. *Energy Policy* 3(4): 285–289.

Chapman, P.F., G. Leach, and M. Slesser. 1974. Energy Budgets 2: Energy Cost of Fuels. *Energy Policy* 2(3): 231–243.

Cicas, G. 2005. Regional Economic Input–Output Life Cycle Assessment Models. PhD diss., Carnegie Mellon University.

CMP (Center for Metals Production). 1987. Technoeconomic Assessment of Electric Steelmaking through the Year 2000. Report EPRI EM-5445. Pittsburgh, PA: Carnegie Mellon University.

Cobas-Flores, E. 1996. Life Cycle Assessment Using Input–Output Analysis. PhD diss., Carnegie Mellon University.

Constable, G., and B. Somerville. 2003. *A Century of Innovation: Twenty Engineering Achievements that Transformed Our Lives.* Washington, DC: Joseph Henry Press.

Conway, H., and J. Svenson. 1998. Occupational Injury and Illness Rates, 1992–1996: Why They Fell. *Monthly Labor Review* 121(11): 36–58.

Cross, S.A., and R.L. Parsons. 2002. Evaluation of Expenditures on Rural Interstate Pavements in Kansas. *Transportation Research Board 81ˢᵗ Annual Meeting*. Transportation Research Board, National Research Council: Washington, DC.

Curran, M.A. 1996. *Life Cycle Analysis*. New York: McGraw-Hill.

Davis, S.C., and S.W. Diegel. 2002. Transportation Energy Data Book: Edition 22. Oak Ridge, TN: Oak Ridge National Laboratory.

DeCicco, J.M., S.S. Bernow, and J. Beyea. 1992. Environmental Concerns Regarding Electric Power Transmission in North America. *Energy Policy*. January: 30–52.

Dorfman, R., P. Samuelson, and R. Solow. 1958. *Linear Programming and Economic Analysis*. New York: McGraw-Hill Book Company.

Economist. 1990. *The Economist Book of Vital World Statistics*. New York: Random House.

EIA (Energy Information Administration). 1999. Cost and Quality of Fuels for Electric Utility Plants 1999. p. 12. U.S. Department of Energy: Oak Ridge, TN.

———. 2000. Table 31: U.S. Demonstrated Reserve Base of Coal by Potential Mining Method and Ranked by State. http://www.eia.doe.gov/cneaf/coal/cia/html/t33p01p1.html (accessed December 15, 2005).

———. 2001a. Natural Gas Consumption in the United States, 1995–2001. www.eia.doe.gov/oil_gas/natural gas/info_glance/consumption.html. (accessed June 10, 2001).

———. 2001b. Quantity and Average Price of Natural Gas Production in the United States, 1930–1999. http://www.eia.doe.gov/oil_gas/natural_gas/data_publications/historical_natural_gas_annual/hnga.html (accessed June 10, 2001).

———. 2003. *Electric Power Annual*. http://www.eia.doe.gov/cneaf/electricity/epa/epa.pdf (accessed May 2003).

———. 2003a. Coal Production and Number of Mines by State and Mine Type, 2003–2002. http://www.eia.doe.gov/cneaf/coal/page/acr/table1.html (accessed June 2004)

———. 2003b. Figure E2. U.S. Net Generation by Energy Source, 2003. http://www.eia.doe.gov/cneaf/electricity/epa/figes2.html (accessed December 2004).

———. 2003c. Table 28. Average Open Market Sales Price of Coal by State and Mine Type, 2003, 2002. http://www.eia.doe.gov/cneaf/coal/page/acr/table28.html (accessed December 15, 2005).

———. 2004. A Primer on Gasoline Prices. Available at: http://www.eia.doe.gov/neic/brochure/oil_gas/primer/primer.html (accessed June 19, 2004).

Environment Canada. 1999a. *Canada's Greenhouse Gas Inventory: 1997 Emissions and Removals with Trends*. Ottawa: Environment Canada.

———. 1999b. *1998 NPRI Summary Report*. Ottawa: Queen's Printer of Canada.

———. 2002. *Canada's Greenhouse Gas Inventory: 1990–2000*. Ottawa: Environment Canada.

Florin, H., and A. Horvath. 2004. Hybrid LCA. Technical Report. Berkeley: PE Europe and University of California, Berkeley.

Ford Motor Company. 2003. Available at: www.fordvehicles.com/cars/taurus/index.asp?mode=true (accessed June 3, 2003).

GaBi. 2004. GaBi Software Product Family. http://www.gabi-software.com (accessed February 24, 2004).

Gagnon, L., and A. Chamberland. 1993. Emissions from Hydroelectric Reservoirs and Comparison of Hydroelectricity, Natural-Gas, and Oil. *Ambio* 22(8): 568–569.

Gagnon, L., C. Bélanger, and Y. Uchiyama. 2002. Life Cycle Assessment of Electricity Generation Options: The Status of Research in Year 2001. *Energy Policy* 30(14): 1267–1278.

Gandhi, H.S., G.W. Graham, and R.W. McCabe. 2003. Automotive Exhaust Catalysis. *Journal of Catalysis* 216 (1-2): 433–442.

GBC (Green Buildings Council). 2001. Leadership in Energy and Environmental Design (LEED™). http:www.usgbc.org/programs/leed.htm (accessed March 2, 2001).

Haack, B.N. 1981. Net Energy Analysis of Small Wind Energy-Conversion Systems. *Applied Energy* 9(3): 193–200.

Hauth, R.L., P.J. Tatro, R.D. Railing, B.K. Johnson, J.R. Stewart, and J.L. Fink. 1997. HVDC Power Transmission Technology Assessment. ORNL/Sub/95-SR893/1. Prepared by New England Power Service Company for Oak Ridge National Laboratory, Oak Ridge, TN.

Hayami, H., M. Nakamura, K. Asakura, and K. Yoshioka. 1999. The Emissions of Global Warming Gases: Trade between Canada and Japan. Canadian Economic Association Annual Meeting, University of Toronto, May 1999.

Hayhoe, K., H.S. Kheshgi, A.K. Jain, and D.J. Wuebbles. 2002. Substitution of Natural Gas for Coal: Climatic Effects of Utility Sector Emissions. *Climatic Change* 54(1–2): 107–139.

Heijungs, R., and S. Suh. 2002. *The Computational Structure of Life Cycle Assessment.* Berlin: Kluwer Academic Publishers.

Hendrickson, C., and A. Horvath. 2000. Resource Use and Environmental Emissions for U.S. Construction Sectors. *ASCE Journal of Construction Engineering and Management* 126(1): 38–44.

Hendrickson, C., A. Horvath, S. Joshi, and L.B. Lave. 1998. Economic Input–Output Models for Environmental Life Cycle Assessment. *Environmental Science & Technology* 32(7): 184A–191A.

Herendeen, R.A., and R.I. Plant. 1981. Energy Analysis of Four Geothermal Technologies. *Energy* 6(1): 73–82.

Hewings, G.J.D., and R. C. Jensen. 1986. Regional, Interregional, and Multiregional Input–Output Analysis. In *Handbook of Regional and Urban Economics*, vol. 1, edited by P. Nijkamp. Amsterdam: North-Holland, 295–355.

Hirst, E., and B. Kirby. 2001. Key Transmission Planning Issues. *The Electricity Journal.* October: 59–70.

Hocking, M.B. 1991. Paper vs. Polystyrene. *Science* (251): 504–505.

Horvath, A. 1997. Estimation of Environmental Implications of Construction Materials and Designs Using Life-Cycle Assessment Techniques, PhD Diss., Carnegie Mellon University.

———. 2004. Construction Materials and the Environment. *Annual Review of Environment and Resources* 29: 181-204.

Horvath, A., and C.T. Hendrickson. 1998a. Steel vs. Steel-Reinforced Concrete Bridges: Environmental Assessment. *ASCE Journal of Infrastructure Systems.* September: 111–117.

————. 1998b. A Comparison of the Environmental Implications of Asphalt and Steel-Reinforced Concrete Pavements. *Transportation Research Record* 1626: 105–113.

Horvath, A., C. Hendrickson, L. Lave, F. McMichael, and T-S. Wu. 1995. Toxic Emission Indices for Green Design and Inventory. *Environmental Science and Technology* 29(2): 86A-90A.

Houghton, J.T., Y. Ding, D.J. Griggs, M. Noguer, P.J. van der Linden, X. Dai, K. Maskell, and C.A. Johnson. 2001. *Climate Change 2001: The Scientific Basis.* Cambridge: Cambridge University Press.

IECM (Integrated Environmental Control Model). 2001. User Documentation. http://www.iecm-online.com (accessed September 29, 2005).

IPCC (Intergovernmental Panel on Climate Change). 2001. Climate Change 2001. http://www.ipcc.ch/ (accessed June 2, 2004).

ISO (International Organization for Standardization). 1997. Environmental management—Life Cycle Assessment—Principles and Framework. ISO 14040:1997. Geneva: ISO.

————. 1998. Environmental Management—Life Cycle Assessment—Goal and Scope Definition and Inventory Analysis. ISO 14041:1998. Geneva: ISO.

————. 2000a. Environmental Management—Life Cycle Assessment—Life Cycle Impact Assessment. ISO/FDIS 14042:2000. Geneva: ISO.

————. 2000b. Environmental Management—Life Cycle Assessment—Life Cycle Interpretation. ISO 14043:2000. Geneva: ISO.

Johnson, J. 2003. Blowing Green. *Chemical & Engineering News* 81(8): 27–30.

Johnson Matthey. 2004a. Platinum Today: Data Tables. http://www.platinum.matthey.com/market_data/1046092226.html (accessed March 3, 2004).

————. 2004b. Platinum Today: Price Charts. http://www.platinum.matthey.com/prices/price_charts.html (accessed March 2, 2004).

Joshi, S.V. 1998. Comprehensive Product Life Cycle Analysis Using Input–Output Techniques. PhD diss., Carnegie Mellon University.

————. 2000. Product Environmental Life Cycle Assessment Using Input–Output Techniques. *Journal of Industrial Ecology* (3) 2-3: 95-120.

Kahn, J. 2001. Federal Reports on Energy at Odds with a Bush Plan. *New York Times,* May 6.

Kalkani, E.C., and L.G. Boussiakou. 1996. Environmental Concerns for High-Voltage Transmission Lines in UNIPEDE Countries. *Journal of Environmental Engineering,* November: 1042–1045.

Kellogg. 1998. *Amazon.com: Winning the Online Book Wars.* J.L. Kellogg Graduate School of Management, January 29, 1998.

Keoleian, G.A., and D. Menerey. 1993. *Life Cycle Design Guidance Manual.* 600/R-92/226. Washington, DC: EPA.

Keoleian, G.A., S. Blanchard, and P. Reppe. 2001. Life Cycle Energy, Costs, and Strategies for Improving a Single-Family House. *Journal of Industrial Ecology* 4(2): 135–157.

Keoleian, G.A., S. Spatari, and R. Beal. 1997. *Life Cycle Design of a Fuel Tank System.* Ann Arbor: University of Michigan.

Knoepfel, I.H. 1996. A Framework for Environmental Impact Assessment of Long-Distance Energy Transport Systems. *Energy* (21)7–8: 693–702.

Koch, F.H. 2002. Hydropower—the Politics of Water and Energy: Introduction and Overview. *Energy Policy* 30: 1207–1213.

Krohn, S. 1997. The Energy Balance of Modern Wind Turbines. *Windpower Note* December 16: 1-16.

Kuemmel, B., S.K. Nielsen, and B. Sorensen. 1997. *Life Cycle Analysis of Energy Systems.* Gilling, Denmark: Roskilde University Press, Narayana Press.

Kung, H.H. 2003. Heterogeneous Catalysis: What Lies Ahead in Nanotechnology. *Applied Catalysis A* 246(2): 193–196.

Lal, K. 1998. The 1997 Historical Revision of the Canadian System of National Accounts: Industry, Final Demand and Commodity Classification Systems. Publication No. 13F0031MIE2000006. Ottawa: Statistics Canada.

Lave, L.B., C.T. Hendrickson, and F.C. McMichael. 1995a. Environmental Implications of Electric Vehicles. *Science.* May 19: 993–995.

Lave, L.B., E. Cobas-Flores, C.T. Hendrickson, and F.C. McMichael. 1995b. Generalizing Life Cycle Analysis: Using Input–Output Analysis to Estimate Economy-Wide Discharges. *Environmental Science and Technology* 29(9): 420A–426A.

Lave, L.B., A.G. Russell, C.T. Hendrickson, and F.C. McMichael. 1996. Battery-Powered Vehicles: Ozone Reduction versus Lead Discharges. *Environmental Science and Technology* 30(9): 402A–407A.

Lave, L.B., C.T. Hendrickson, N. Conway-Schempf, and F.C. McMichael. 1999. Municipal Solid Waste Recycling Issues. *ASCE Journal of Environmental Engineering* 125(10): 944–949.

Lave, L.B., H. MacLean, C. Hendrickson, and R. Lankey. 2000. Life Cycle Analysis of Alternative Automobile Fuel/Propulsion Technologies. *Environmental Science and Technology* 34(17): 3598–3605.

Lawson, A., K.S. Bersani, M. Fahim-Nader, and J. Guo. 2002. Benchmark Input–Output Accounts of the United States 1997. http://www.bea.gov/bea/ARTICLES/2002/12December/1202I-OAccounts2.pdf (accessed July 2, 2004).

Leach, G. 1975. Net Energy Analysis—Is It Any Use? *Energy Policy* 3(4): 332–344.

Lenzen, M. 2000. Errors in Conventional and Input–Output-based Life Cycle Inventories. *Journal of Industrial Ecology* 4(4): 127–148.

Lenzen, M., and J. Munksgaard. 2002. Energy and CO_2 Life Cycle Analyses of Wind Turbines Review and Applications. *Renewable Energy* 26: 339–362.

Leontief, W. 1970. Environmental Repercussions and the Economic Structure: An Input–Output Approach. *Review of Economics and Statistics* (LII)3: 262-271.

———. 1986. *Input–Output Economics.* New York: Oxford University Press.

Levine, D. 1997. They Should Solve Their Own Problems: Reinventing Workplace Regulation. In *Government Regulation of the Employment Relationship,* edited by B. E. Kaufman. Madison, WI: Industrial Relations Research Association.

Lieu, S. 1991. Regional Impacts of Air Quality Regulation: Applying an Economic Model. *Contemporary Policy Issues* 9: 24–34.

Lieu, S., and G.I. Treyz. 1992. Estimating the Economic and Demographic Effects of an Air Quality Management Plan: the Case of Southern California. *Environment and Planning A* 24: 1799–1811.

Lin, X., and K.R. Polenske. 1998. Input–Output Modeling of Production Processes for Business Management. *Structural Change and Economic Dynamics* 9: 205–226.

Linke, S., and R.E. Schuler. 1988. Electrical –Energy-Transmission Technology: The Key To Bulk-Power-Supply Policies. *Annual Review of Energy* 13: 23–45.

Lippiatt, B. 2000. BEES 2.0 *Building for Environmental and Economic Sustainability Technical Manual and User Guide*. Washington, DC: National Institute of Standards and Technology.

Lloyd, S.M., L.B. Lave, and H.S. Matthews. 2005. Life Cycle Benefits of Using Nanotechnology to Stabilize PGM Particles in Automotive Catalysts. *Environmental Science and Technology* 39(5): 1384-1392.

Lombardi, L. 2003. Life Cycle Assessment Comparison of Technical Solutions for CO_2 Emissions Reduction in Power Generation. *Energy Conversion and Management* 44: 93–108.

Longwell, J.P., and E.S Rubin. 1995. Coal: Energy for the Future. U.S. National Research Council, Committee on the Strategic Assessment of the U.S. Department of Energy's Coal Program. Washington, DC: National Academy Press.

Lupis, C.H.P., and F.C. McMichael. 1999. Input–Output Microeconomic Model for Process and Environmental Analysis. Global Symposium on Recycling, Waste Treatment, and Clean Technology. San Sebastian, Spain, September 5–9.

MacLean, H.L., and L.B. Lave. 1998. Life Cycle Model of an Automobile. *Environmental Science and Technology* 32: 322A-333A.

———. 2003. Evaluating Automobile Fuel/Propulsion System Technologies. *Journal of Progress in Energy and Combustion Science* 29: 1-69.

Marland, G., and A.M. Weinberg. 1988. Longevity of Infrastructure. In *Cities and Their Vital Systems*, edited by J.H. Ausubel and R. Herman. Washington, DC: National Academy Press, 312–332.

Marquis, C. 2001. Whitman Backs Clinton Rules Designed to Cut Diesel Pollution. *New York Times*, March 1.

Marriott, J. 2004. Creation of U.S. Industry Sector Consumption Mixes— Disaggregating Electricity Generation and Estimating Interstate Electricity Transfers. Technical Report, Green Design Institute. Pittsburgh: Carnegie Mellon.

Matthews, D.H., and L.B. Lave. 2001. Evaluating Occupational Safety Costs and Policy in an Input–Output Framework. In *Improving Regulation: Cases in Environment, Health, and Safety*, edited by P. Fischbeck and S. Farrow. Washington, DC: Resources for the Future.

Matthews, D.H., G.C. Christini, and C. Hendrickson. 2004. Five Elements for Organizational Decision-Making with an Environmental Management System. *Environmental Science and Technology* 39: 1927-1932.

Matthews, H.S. 1999. The External Costs of Air Pollution and the Environmental Impact of the Consumer in the U.S. Economy. PhD diss., Carnegie Mellon University.

———. 2001. The Benefits of the Clean Air Act. In *Improving Regulation: Cases in Environment, Health, and Safety*, edited by Paul Fischbeck and Scott Farrow. Washington, DC: Resources for the Future.

Matthews, H.S., and L.B. Lave. 2000. Applications of Environmental Valuation for Determining Externality Costs. *Environmental Science and Technology* 34(8): 1390–1395.

Matthews, H.S., C.T. Hendrickson, and D.L. Soh. 2001. Environmental and Economic Effects of E-Commerce: A Case Study of Book Publishing and Retail Logistics. *Transportation Research Record* 1763: 6–12.

Matthews, H.S., L.B. Lave, and H. MacLean. 2002. Life Cycle Impact Assessment: A Challenge for Risk Analysts. *Risk Analysis* 22(5): 853–859.

Matthews, H.S., C.T. Hendrickson, F.C. McMichael, and D.H. Matthews. 1997. Disposition and End-of-Life Options for Products: A Green Design Case Study. Green Design Institute, Carnegie Mellon. http://gdi.ce.cmu.edu/ (accessed September 29, 2005).

Meridian Corporation. 1989. *Energy System Emissions and Materiel Requirements.* Alexandria, VA: Meridian Corporation.

Metz, B., D. Ogunlade, R. Swart, and J. Pan. 2001. Climate Change 2001: Mitigation. Intergovernmental Panel on Climate Change. New York: Cambridge University Press.

Miller, R.E., and P.D. Blair. 1985. *Input–Output Analysis: Foundations and Extensions.* Prentice-Hall.

Minnesota IMPLAN Group. 2004. Impact Analysis for Planning. http://www.implan.com (accessed April 1, 2004).

Morgan, M.G., and M. Henrion. 1990. *Uncertainty.* Cambridge, UK: Cambridge University Press.

Natural Resources Canada. 1999. 1999 Canadian Minerals Yearbook. Ottawa: Natural Resources Canada.

Niewlaar, E., E. Alsema, and B. Van Engelenburg. 1996. Using Life Cycle Assessments for the Environmental Evaluation of Greenhouse Gas Mitigation Options. *Energy Conversion and Management* 37(6–8): 831–836.

NMFS (National Marine Fisheries Service). 2000. Employment, Craft, and Plants (Table) Processors and Wholesalers. Silver Spring, MD: National Oceanic and Atmospheric Administration.

NRC (National Research Council). 2002. *Effectiveness and Impact of Corporate Average Fuel Economy (CAFE) Standards.* Washington, DC: National Academy Press.

———. 2003. *Beyond the Molecular Frontier: Challenges for Chemistry & Chemical Engineering.* Washington, DC: National Academy Press.

———. 2004. *Materials Count: The Case for Materials Flows Analysis.* Washington, DC: National Academy Press.

Ochoa, L., C. Hendrickson, and H.S. Matthews. 2002. Economic Input–Output Life Cycle Assessment of U.S. Residential Buildings. *ASCE Journal of Infrastructure Systems* 8(4): 132–138.

Oh, S.H., E.J. Bissett, and P.A. Battiston. 1993. Mathematical Modeling of Electrically Heated Monolith Converters: Model Formulation, Numerical Methods, and Experimental Verification. *Industrial & Engineering Chemistry Research* 32(8): 1560–1567.

OSAT (Office for the Study of Automotive Transportation). 1996. *Delphi VIII: Forecast and Analysis of the North American Automotive Industry: Volume 3 Materials.* Ann Arbor, MI: Office for the Study of Automotive Transportation, University of Michigan Transportation Research Institute.

OSHA (Occupational Safety and Health Administration). 2005. Workplace Injury, Illness, and Fatality Statistics. http://www.osha.gov/oshstats/work.html (accessed September 30, 2005).

Pacca, S., and A. Horvath. 2002. Greenhouse Gas Emissions from Building and Operating Electric Power Plants in the Upper Colorado River Basin. *Environmental Science and Technology* 36: 3194–3200.

Polenske, Karen R., and Francis C. McMichael. 2002. A Chinese Cokemaking Process-Flow Model for Energy and Environmental Analyses. *Energy Policy* 30: 865–883.

Publishers Weekly. 1997. They Shall Return. http://www.publishersweekly.com/ (accessed November 10, 2005).

Quandt, R.E. 1958. Probabilistic Errors in the Leontief System. *Naval Research Logistics Quarterly* 5(2): 155–170.

———. 1959. On the Solution of Probabilistic Leontief Systems. *Naval Research Logistics Quarterly* 6(4): 295–305.

Raa, T., and M.F.J. Steel. 1994. Revised Stochastic Analysis of an Input–Output Model. *Regional Science and Urban Economics* 24: 361–371.

Reijnders, L. 1996. *Environmentally Improved Production Processes and Products: An Introduction.* Berlin: Kluwer Academic Press.

REMI (Regional Economic Models Inc.). 2004. http://www.remi.com (accessed April 1, 2004).

Rosa, L.P., and R. Schaeffer. 1994. Greenhouse-Gas Emissions From Hydroelectric Reservoirs. *Ambio* 23(2): 164–165.

Rosenblum, J., A. Horvath, and C. Hendrickson. 2000. Environmental Implications of Service Industries. *Environmental Science and Technology* 34(22): 4669–4676.

RS Means Company, Inc. 2000. RS Means Building Construction Cost Data 2001. Kingston, MA: RS Means.

Rudd, J.W.M., R. Harris, C.A. Kelly, and R.E. Hecky. 1993. Are Hydroelectric Reservoirs Significant Sources of Greenhouse Gases? *Ambio* 22(4): 246–248.

San Martin, R.L. 1989. Environmental Emissions from Energy Technology Systems: the Total Fuel Cycle. Washington, DC: U.S. Department of Energy.

Schaffer, W. 1976. On the Use of Input-output Models for Regional Planning. *Studies in Applied Regional Science* 1. Leiden.

SETAC (Society of Environmental Toxicology and Chemistry). 1993. Guidelines for Life Cycle Assessment: A Code of Practice. Pensacola, FL: SETAC.

Sherman, J., and W.J. Morrison. 1950. Adjustment of an Inverse Matrix Corresponding to a Change in One Element of a Given Matrix. *Annals of Mathematical Statistics* 21(1): 124–127.

Simon, J.L. 1996. *The Ultimate Resource 2.* Princeton, NJ: Princeton University Press.

Simonovits, A. 1975. A Note on the Underestimation and Overestimation of the Leontief Inverse. *Econometrica* 43(3): 493–498.

Snyder, L.P. 2003. Revisiting Donora, Pennsylvania's 1948 Air Pollution Disaster. In *Devastation and Renewal,* edited by J. Tarr. Pittsburgh, PA: University of Pittsburgh Press, 126-144.

Spath, P.L., and M.K. Mann. 2000. *Life Cycle Assessment of a Natural Gas Combined-Cycle Power Generation System.* Golden, CO: National Renewable Energy Laboratory.

Spath, P.L., M.K. Mann, and D.R. Kerr. 1999. *Life Cycle Assessment of Coal-fired Power Production.* Golden, CO: National Renewable Energy Laboratory.

St. Louis, V.L., C.A. Kelly, E. Duchemin, J.W.M. Rudd, and D.M. Rosenberg. 2000. Reservoir Surfaces as Sources of Greenhouse Gases to the Atmosphere: A Global Estimate. *Bioscience* 50(9): 766–775.

Statistics Canada. 2003. *Canadian Socio-Economic Information Management System (CANSIM)*. Ottawa: Statistics Canada.

Sterdis, A. 1997. *The Future of Automobile Materials Recovery*. Unpublished paper. Pittsburgh: Department of Engineering and Public Policy, Carnegie Mellon University.

Suh, S. 2004. *Materials and Energy Flows in Industry and Ecosystem Networks*. Leiden, Netherlands: Leiden University.

Suh, S., M. Lenzen, G. Treloar, H. Hondo, A. Horvath, G. Huppes, O. Jolliet, U. Klann, W. Krewitt, Y. Moriguchi, J. Munksgaard, and G. Norris. 2004. System Boundary Selection for Life Cycle Inventories. *Environmental Science and Technology* 38(3): 657–664.

TIAX LLC. 2003. Platinum Availability and Economics for PEMFC Commercialization. Report to: U.S. Department of Energy, DOE:DE-FC04-01AL67601.

Tonn, B.E., and S. Das. 2001. *An Assessment of Platinum Availability for Advanced Fuel Cell Vehicles*. Oak Ridge, TN: Oak Ridge National Laboratory.

Treyz, G.I., R. Bradley, L. Petraglia, and A.M. Rose. 1996. Predicting the Local Economic Effects of Proposed Trip-Reduction Rules: The Case of San Diego. *Environment and Planning A* 28: 1315–1327.

Uchiyama, Y. 1992. Total System Analysis of Greenhouse Effect from Power Generation Plants. Energy Forum Conference.

———. 2002. Present Efforts of Saving Energy and Future Energy Demand/Supply in Japan. *Energy Conversion and Management* 43: 1123–1131.

ULINE Shipping Supply Specialists. 2001. http://www.uline.com/ (accessed December 10, 2001).

UNEP (United Nations Environmental Program). 1996. *Cleaner Production at Pulp and Paper Mills: A Guidance Manual*. Bangkok: UNEP Regional Office for Asia and Pacific.

USCB (U.S. Census Bureau). 1995. Wrecking and Demolition Work Special Trade Contractors. 1992 Census of Construction Industries. http://www.census.gov/prod/www/abs/cciview1.html (accessed November 11, 2005).

———. 1997. 1997 Economic Census: Industry Statistics. http://www.census.gov/epcd/ec97/industry/ (accessed June 29, 2004).

———. 2001a. *Statistical Abstract of the United States: 2000*. Washington, DC: Department of Commerce.

———. 2001b. *C50—Expenditure for Residential Improvements and Repairs*. Washington, DC: Department of Commerce.

———. 2004. 1997 Economic Census: Bridge Between NAICS and SIC. http://www.census.gov/epcd/ec97brdg/ (accessed June 29, 2004).

USDA (U.S. Department of Agriculture). 1996. Agricultural Exports and the Rural Economy in the 1990s. http://www.ers.usda.gov/publications/rct71/rct71f.pdf (accessed November 11, 2005).

U.S. Department of Commerce. 1986. Water Use in Manufacturing: 1982 Census of Manufactures, Subject Series, MC82-S-6. Washington, DC: Department of Commerce.

———. 2004. Retail E-Commerce Sales in First Quarter 2004 Were $15.5 Billion, Up 28.1 Percent from First Quarter 2003, Census Bureau Reports. Press Release, May 21.

U.S. DOT (U.S. Department of Transportation). 1993. A Study of the Use of Recycled Paving Material: Report to Congress. Report FHWA-RD-93-147, EPA/600/R-93/095. Washington, DC: Federal Highway Administration.

———. 2004. Bureau of Transportation Statistics. Transportation Statistics Annual Report 2004. Available at: http://www.bts.gov/publications/transportation_statistics_annual_report.

U.S. EPA (U.S. Environmental Protection Agency). 1994a. *Automobile Emissions: An Overview.* EPA 400-F-92-007. Washington, DC: U.S. EPA.

———. 1994b. *Milestones in Auto Emissions Control.* EPA 400-F-92-014. Washington, DC: U.S. EPA.

———. 1997a. *Estimated Economic Impact of New Emission Standards for Heavy-Duty On-Highway Engines.* EPA 420-R-97-009. Washington, DC: U.S. EPA.

———. 1997b. *The Benefits and Costs of the Clean Air Act, 1970–1990.* EPA 410-R-97-002. http://www.epa.gov/oar/sect812/ (accessed November 11, 2005).

———. 1999. *Regulatory Impact Analysis—Control of Air Pollution from New Motor Vehicles: Tier 2 Motor Vehicle Emissions Standards and Gasoline Sulfur Requirements.* EPA 420-R-99-023. Washington, DC: U.S. EPA.

———. 2000a. *Regulatory Impact Analysis: Control of Emissions of Air Pollution from Highway Heavy-Duty Engines.* EPA 420-R-00-010. Washington, DC: U.S. EPA.

———. 2000b. *Regulatory Impact Analysis: Heavy-Duty Engine and Vehicle Standards and Highway Diesel Fuel Sulfur Control Requirements.* EPA 420-R-00-026. Washington, DC: U.S. EPA.

———. 2001a. *Inventory of U.S. Greenhouse Gas Emissions and Sinks: 1990–1999 (2001 draft).* EPA 236-R-01-001. http://www.epa.gov/oppeoee1/globalwarming/publications/emissions/us2001/2001-inventory.pdf (accessed April 11, 2001).

———. 2001b. *The Preliminary National Biennial RCRA Hazardous Waste Report (Based on 1999 Data).* http://www.epa.gov/epaoswer/hazwaste/data/brs99/ ntanal99.pdf (accessed May 2, 2001).

———. 2001c. *Toxics Release Inventory 1999, Executive Summary.* EPA 260-R-01-001. http://www.epa.gov/tri/tri99/pdr/execsummary.pdf (accessed May 2, 2001).

———. 2002. U.S. National Emissions, Carbon Dioxide Emissions. www.epa.gov/globalwarming/emissions/national/co2.html (accessed August 1, 2002).

———. 2003. *Draft Regulatory Impact Analysis: Control of Emissions from Nonroad Diesel Engines.* EPA 420-R-03-008. Washington, DC: U.S. EPA.

Veshosky, D., and R.L. Nickerson. 1993. Highway Bridges: Life Cycle Costs versus Life Cycle Performance. *Better Roads* May: 33–35.

Vigon, B.W., D.A. Tolle, B.W. Cornaby, H.C. Latham, C.L. Harrison, T.L. Boguski, R.G. Hunt, and J.D. Sellers. 1993. *Life Cycle Assessment: Inventory Guidelines and Principles.* EPA 600/R-92/245. Washington, DC: U.S. EPA.

Wald, M. 2001a. Bush Relaxes Clinton Rule on Central Air-Conditioners. *New York Times,* April 14, A7.

———. 2001b. Administration Keeps 2 Rules on Efficiency of Appliances. *New York Times,* April 13, A14.

Watson, R.T. (ed.). 2000. *IPCC Special Report on Land Use, Land-Use Change and Forestry: A Special Report of the Intergovernmental Panel on Climate Change.* New York: Cambridge University Press.

West, G.R. 1986. A Stochastic Analysis of an Input–Output Model. *Econometrica* 54: 363–374.

Weston, R.F. 1998. *Life Cycle Inventory Report for the North American Aluminum Industry.* Washington, DC: The Aluminum Association.

Wiese, A., and M. Kaltschmitt. 1996. Global Link of Renewable Energy Sources: Technical, Economical, and Environmental Aspects of an Intercontinental Electricity Transmission and Distribution System. *Energy Sources* 18: 841–854.

Ying, J.Y., and T. Sun. 1997. Research Needs Assessment on Nanostructured Catalysts. *Journal of Electroceramics* 1(2): 219–238.

Zuo, Y. 1985. New Type of Input–Output Model. In *Introduction to Environmental Systems Analysis.* Nanjing: Nanjing University Press, 59–89.

Index

About the Authors

Chris T. Hendrickson is the Duquesne Light Company Professor of Engineering, head of the Department of Civil and Environmental Engineering, director of the Steinbrenner Institute for Environmental Engineering and Research, and co-director of the Green Design Institute at Carnegie Mellon University. His research, teaching, and consulting are in the general area of engineering planning and management, including design for the environment, project management, transportation systems, finance and computer applications. He has co-authored two textbooks, *Project Management for Construction* and *Transportation Investment and Pricing Principles*, and two monographs, *Knowledge Based Process Planning for Construction and Manufacturing* and *Concurrent Computer Integrated Building Design*. Hendrickson has been the recipient of the 2002 American Society of Chemical Engineers Turner Lecture Award, the 2002 Fenves Systems Research Award, the 1994 Frank M. Masters Transportation Engineering Award, Outstanding Professor of the Year Award of the ASCE Pittsburgh Section (1990), the ASCE Walter L. Huber Civil Engineering Research Award (1989), the Benjamin Richard Teare Teaching Award from the Carnegie Institute of Technology (1987), and a Rhodes Scholarship (1973).

Lester B. Lave is University Professor and Harry B. and James H. Higgins Professor of Economics at Carnegie Mellon University, with appointments in the business, engineering, and public policy schools. He was elected to the Institute of Medicine of the National Academy of Sciences and is a past president of the Society for Risk Analysis. He has acted as a consultant to many government agencies and companies. He has received research support from a wide range of federal and state agencies, as well as foundations, nongovernmental organizations, and companies. With Chris Hendrickson, Lave directs the CMU university-wide Green Design Institute and, with Granger Morgan, directs the

CMU Electricity Industry Center. His research is focused on applying economics to public policy issues, including those related to energy in general and electricity in particular.

H. Scott Matthews is the research director of the Green Design Institute and a faculty member in the Departments of Civil and Environmental Engineering and Engineering and Public Policy at Carnegie Mellon University. At Carnegie Mellon, he has taught graduate and undergraduate courses in the Departments of Economics, Civil and Environmental Engineering, Engineering and Public Policy, and Computer Science. He has received four AT&T Industrial Ecology Faculty Fellowship awards for his research and educational work on the life cycle environmental implications of emerging technologies, including wired and wireless telecommunications as well as retail logistics systems.

Breinigsville, PA USA
04 March 2010
233646BV00002B/3/P